FAITH SEEKING UNDERSTANDING

FAITH SEEKING UNDERSTANDING

ESSAYS IN MEMORY OF PAUL BRAND AND RALPH D. WINTER

EDITED BY

DAVID MARSHALL

WILLIAM CAREY
LIBRARY

All scripture quotations, unless otherwise indicated, are taken from the Holy Bible, New International Version®, NIV®. Copyright ©1973, 1978, 1984, 2011 by Biblica, Inc.™ Used by permission of Zondervan. All rights reserved worldwide. www.zondervan.com The "NIV" and "New International Version" are trademarks registered in the United States Patent and Trademark Office by Biblica, Inc.™

Scripture quotations marked (NKJV) are taken from the New King James Version®. Copyright © 1982 by Thomas Nelson, Inc. Used by permission. All rights reserved.

Scripture quotations marked (NRSV) are from Revised Standard Version of the Bible, copyright © 1946, 1952, and 1971 National Council of the Churches of Christ in the United States of America. Used by permission. All rights reserved.

Scripture quotations marked (*The Message*) are taken from *The Message*. Copyright © 1993, 1994, 1995, 1996, 2000, 2001, 2002. Used by permission of NavPress Publishing Group.

Scripture quotations marked (GNT) are from the Good News Translation in Today's English Version—Second Edition Copyright © 1992 by American Bible Society. Used by Permission.

Published by William Carey Library
1605 E. Elizabeth St.
Pasadena, CA 91104 | www.missionbooks.org

Brad Koenig, copyeditor
Francesca Gacho, editor
Rose Lee-Norman, index
Hugh Pindur, graphic design

William Carey Library is a ministry of the
U.S. Center for World Mission
Pasadena, CA | www.uscwm.org

16 15 14 13 12   5 4 3 2 1 BP2000
Printed in the United States of America

Library of Congress Cataloging-in-Publication Data

Faith seeking understanding : essays in memory of Paul Brand and Ralph
Winter / [edited by] David Marshall.
    p. cm.
ISBN 978-0-87808-436-4
1. Christianity. 2. Christianity and culture. 3. Faith. 4. Brand, Paul
W. 5. Winter, Ralph D. I. Marshall, David, Rev. II. Brand, Paul W. III.
Winter, Ralph D.
BR50.F363 2012
230--dc23
                    2012015384

CONTENTS

INTRODUCTION: CLIMBING BY FAITH

DAVID MARSHALL

"Faith seeking understanding" was the motto of Saint Anselm, remembered today as a kindly reformer, philosopher, and gadfly, an eleventh-century archbishop of Canterbury who was exiled by two English kings. But long before such career advances and recessions, Anselm was a climber of mountains. What Anselm meant by "faith seeking understanding" and how this medieval relic of an idea can transform the world as we see it today was foreshadowed in his experiences growing up in the Alps of what is now northern Italy.

The city of Aosta, Anselm's hometown, rests in a narrow valley surrounded by ten-thousand-foot peaks on three sides. Anselm believed (it seems more literally than most young hikers) that heaven was to be found above the tree line. One night in a dream, he was told to climb a mountain to the court of God. On the way up, he passed women who were reaping the king's grain in a slipshod and lazy manner. Received by God and his steward at court (everyone else was out working the harvest), the steward presented him with the "whitest of bread" to eat.

Sometime after this dream, Anselm's mother died, and his religious zeal waned. He fell out with his father, renounced his patrimony, and set off across the Alps westward with a servant. On a fine day, climbing to the pass below Mount Cenis (now, fittingly, part of Gran Paradiso National Park) must indeed have seemed like entering the courts of heaven: serrated peaks rise on all sides, ibex graze the slopes, grass and wildflowers wave in the breeze, and a large alpine lake reflects valleys and clouds beyond.

But the main pass (which Constantine and Charlemagne have also ascended) was almost seven thousand feet above sea level, and Anselm tired. The travelers ran out of food; Anselm gnawed snow to assuage his hunger. His servant gave the donkey's saddlebag a final, desperate search and was surprised to uncover bread "of exceptional whiteness," like the bread in Anselm's dream. Refreshed, the travelers resumed their journey.

Anselm later wrote of God as "the highest of all beings." His famous ontological argument, still debated by philosophers, can be read as a kind of prayer in dialogue with and in search of God, "he than whom there is no greater," as if he were still looking for firm footing, ascending some alpine valley. Nor did he forget the lazy farmers in his dream. He worked in the fields of God with diligence and compassion. People who were afraid to approach the pope "hurried" to meet Anselm, including Muslim vassals of Count Roger of Sicily. He gently admonished kindness to children in the monasteries he supervised, was offended by abuse of animals, and played an early role in the antislavery movement. Doubtless it is due to Anselm's kindness that his story comes down to us: the historian Eadmer, who tells it, was one of many devoted students.

Christians believe not just in abstract dogmas, but in truth "made flesh, and dwelt among us" (John 1:14 KJV). From Anselm's life we similarly begin to see what "faith seeking understanding" might mean, not just as a sticker a medieval schoolman might have pasted to the rear bumper of his oxcart, but as a lived solution to the urgent intellectual challenges of our own time.

Two great errors confuse the modern world about faith. Many see faith as a leap off an intellectual precipice. Faith, Richard Dawkins famously informed us (although he was not the first), means believing "not only in the absence of evidence, but in the teeth of evidence."[1] Others seem to see faith as the ultimate karmic bailout: live as seedy and frivolous a life as you please, then Jesus comes with a big red checkbook and bails you out of prison.

But faith for a mountain climber is neither blind nor lazy. Calf muscles and eyes engage in the climb as you step over stones and roots and skirt puddles. Or else you trip, lose your way, maybe even wind up like Otzi the Ice Man, found after 5,300 years, encased in a glacier near another Italian border. For Anselm, faith meant applying a mind rich in curiosity, imagination, and insight, along with alert senses and reasonable trust in other people, to explore the rugged landscape of an often demanding and complex medieval world.

The two men to whom this book is dedicated also set remarkable examples of lives fully engaged in ascending the peak of God's truth and describing what they saw from different slopes of that summit.

Surgeon General C. Everett Koop once paid an extravagant compliment to the first, like himself a medical doctor (the extravagance of the remark measured in part by the stature of the man who made it). Koop confessed that he sometimes daydreamed about "who I would like to have been if I had not been born C. Everett Koop." The person who came most often to mind, he said, was Dr. Paul Brand (1914–2003).

Paul was born into a missionary family in the Kolli Hills of South India. Gaining early experience as a trauma surgeon during the Blitz in London, Paul then took his young wife, Margaret, back to India, working at the Christian Medical College and Hospital in Vellore. Over nineteen years, Brand established the New Life Centre to explore ways of helping leprosy patients rebuild hands, feet, faces and, most importantly (he recognized), lives that had been shattered as much by the disease's stigma, as by the physical disability it wrought. Meanwhile, as an optometrist, Margaret operated on thousands of people with eye infirmities, and raised six children. Paul then served another twenty years as chief of rehabilitation at the National Hansen's Disease Center at Carville, Louisiana, where he applied the methods

---

1   Richard Dawkins, *The Selfish Gene* (Oxford: Oxford University Press, 1989), 198.

and philosophy he had learned to ultimately help millions of people suffering from various pain impairments, including diabetes.

The Brands were "doctors without borders" before the phrase became popular. As a Christian doctor and scientist, Paul was also a thinker who readily crossed intellectual boundaries into ecology, trout fishing, world religions, carpentry, and biological origins. After meeting writer Phillip Yancey, Paul launched a second or third career as a best-selling author, with Yancey as his initial collaborator.

Paul and Margaret "retired" to Seattle—those who tried to follow their subsequent activities will laugh at this pathetically misleading (in) action verb. Aside from teaching at the University of Washington, and serving in many capacities at Westside Presbyterian Church—among other things, on the missions committee that supported my work in East Asia—Paul and Margaret kept up a busy schedule of speaking around the world, including frequent trips to India.

Like Anselm, Paul was beloved not just because of his insights and professional contributions, and not even because he improved the lives of so many people. He and Margaret were loved because (like their Lord) they first loved others.

I once visited the couple in their "cottage" overlooking Puget Sound. This is not a word one normally uses to describe American homes, but it was small, surrounded by trees, and a bit lonely at the end of the road, and the word seemed to fit both house and the accent of its occupants. Over tea, I noticed a bird feeder resting on a stand outside the kitchen window. The trees around their house provided cover, and Margaret had come into an amicable relationship with Northwest aviary life.

About then, a Chinese lady came to the door with a little girl in tow. She had come to clean house—the Brands needing some help by this time—but was greeted like an old friend. Her husband, they told me after she left, was crippled, living in Canton, and she was working to support the family. Did I know any work she might do? They paid her, it turned out, well above the going rate.

Such was the consistent tenor of the Brands' interactions with those around them. Not an abstract or distant charity, but the quality, so evident in the Gospels, of genuine interest in others, patient listening, and practical but respectful concern. Like Anselm, Paul Brand lived a life of "faith seeking understanding" that revealed faith as something intellectual but also the quality of a life well lived.

Ralph Winter (1924–2009) obtained his PhD in linguistics, anthropology, and statistics from Cornell. He influenced modern thinking about missions as deeply as few have. He encouraged focus on the concept of "people groups," and created numerous institutions, like the U.S. Center for World Missions and the Perspectives study program. The breadth of his thinking, and the holistic character of the understanding he sought from history, belie a simple *Four Spiritual Laws*-type approach to evangelism, as he sought to set the missions movement into the context of an integrated understanding of life. Like Brand, there seemed to be few fixed boundaries to his thinking.

In 2001, Ralph's beloved wife Roberta died of cancer. Dr. Winter was confronted with the causes of disease and its theological meaning. Somehow I wound up reading a copy of proposals he wrote on these subjects. Some of his scientific speculation seemed highly dubious to me. I raised a number of objections by email, noting in passing that Dr. Brand, who had written insightfully on pain, had just attended a seminar we had put on in Seattle about Islam. Winter asked me to pass his ideas on to Brand. But during those weeks, Brand fell and suffered the head injury that would prove fatal.[2]

The question of why God allows so much suffering has always been difficult, and I expressed doubts about Winter's proposed solutions: "I am frankly not convinced by all of Dr. Winter's argument."

I was surprised to receive a response directly from Dr. Winter in block letters: "NEITHER AM I."

Later, answering my criticisms one by one, he again admitted, "You are not convinced, neither am I. Speculation, not belief, is the right word."

Why did Winter bother answering me at all? The humility with which, near the end of a long and productive career, he engaged an obscure critic in an email conversation impressed me.

Three years later, Winter invited me to participate in the inaugural meeting of the Roberta Winter Institute. He paid for my flight from London, it seemed, just to rain on his parade. Apparently he wanted a devil's advocate—almost literally, since Winter blamed Lucifer for the unsavory parts of creation! So I vocally criticized his proposed solutions to this most pressing problem in Christian philosophy, not to mention in our lives, as Winter had recently experienced firsthand.

On the last day of the conference, Winter drew me aside, getting out of the elevator going to lunch, as I recall. "Uh-oh, here it comes," I thought. "I want to thank you for coming," he said. "I feel like you really understand what I'm getting at."

Faith is humble because it is hungry and desires the bread of truth, not caring in which donkey's saddlebag it might be found. Faith is the means by which we find truth. Understanding, or truth (which Jesus claimed to be), is the goal we seek in our journey of faith.

In these chapters, we will get to know these two men better, along with contemporary Christians who are climbing yet other faces of this great peak. Some of the men and women who share their own stories of "faith seeking understanding" in the following pages are well-known. Others may be new to most readers. The subjects they study may be classified as science, history, philosophy, or theology. But "truth is one," as the ancient Christian philosopher Clement of Alexander put it. Thinkers like Anselm, Brand, and Winter delight in exploring a diversity of insight within the unity of faith. Each contributor deals, in his or her own way, with questions that matter to us all: the nature of the physical universe, where we come from, who Jesus is, what effect he has had on our world, how to live, how to understand other religions. By telling stories about his beloved mentor, Eadmer helped show what it means to follow Jesus as a person fully engaged with life, body, soul, mind, and spirit. May the stories and arguments that follow draw readers towards the same splendid summit.

Some of the ideas in this book are, as Ralph Winter put it, speculative. In the book's concluding interview, the elder statesman of contemporary Christian philosophers, Alvin

---

2   Don Richardson spoke at the conference (see chapter 8). I was delighted to notice Don and Paul engaged in lively conservation during a break.

Plantinga, admits he is still looking for answers to heart-felt questions, as Winter was—and apparently some of the same questions. I don't expect readers to readily accept everything in this book. I don't agree with, or even like, all of them myself. But I admire the curiosity, knowledge, and intellectual courage of these fellow pilgrims, who by faith are in search of a better and heavenly country (Heb 11:16).

PART I.
TUTORS

–ONE–

A DOCTOR'S DEFENSE OF PAIN

PHILIP YANCEY

Philip Yancey has some fourteen million books in print. He writes on some of the
most difficult issues in the Christian life, in a sensitive and forthright style. Three of
his titles were collaborations with Dr. Paul Brand.

Ask any group of university students what they have against Christianity and they'll likely echo variations on the theme of suffering: "I can't believe in a God who would allow Auschwitz"; "My teenage sister died of leukemia despite all the Christians' prayers"; "One-third of the world went to bed hungry last night—how does that fit in with your Christianity?" The Christian's defense usually sounds like an apology, not in the classic theological sense of a well-reasoned defense, but in the red-faced, foot-shuffling, lowered-head sense of embarrassment. Both Ralph Winter and Dr. Paul Brand sensed the problem and offered creative ways of addressing it.

Pain is usually defined as "unpleasantness." If you pinned them against the wall, many Christians would probably concede that pain was God's mistake. The Creator should have worked harder and invented a better way of alerting us to the world's dangers. I once felt that way too, but now I am convinced that pain gets a bad press. In our embarrassment over the problem of pain, we seem to have forgotten a central fact which was repeatedly brought to my attention by Dr. Brand, the missionary surgeon who went on to head the rehabilitation branch of America's only leprosarium before his death in 2003. "If I had one gift which I could give to people with leprosy, it would be the gift of pain," Dr. Brand used to say. The gift of pain: an alien, paradoxical concept that might never have occurred to us, but that flows naturally from the experience of a surgeon who treated leprosy patients.

Doctors once believed the disease of leprosy caused the ulcers on hands and feet and face which eventually led to rotting flesh and the loss of limbs. Dr. Brand's research established that in 99 percent of the cases, leprosy only numbs the extremities. The destruction of tissue occurs solely because the warning system of pain has been silenced. After years of working with leprosy patients, Dr. Brand learned to appreciate the sensation that results from cutting a finger, turning an ankle, stepping into a too-hot bath. "Thank God for pain!" he said.

Visitors to rural villages in Africa and Asia have sometimes observed a horrifying sight: the town leper standing by the heavy iron cooking pot watching the potatoes. As the potatoes are cooked, without flinching he thrusts his arm deep into the scalding water and retrieves them. Dr. Brand found that abusive acts such as this were the chief cause of bodily deterioration in persons with leprosy. The potato-watching leprosy victim had felt no pain, but his skin blistered, and his cells were destroyed and laid open to infection. Leprosy had not destroyed the tissue; it had merely removed the warning sensors which alerted him to danger.

The daily routines of life endangered these patients' hands and feet, but without a warning system to alert them, they succumbed. If an ankle turned, tearing tendon and muscle, they would adjust to a different gait and continue walking. If a rat chewed off a finger in the night, they would not discover it until the next morning. (In fact, Brand required his patients in India to take a cat home with them to prevent this common occurrence.) Almost a third of leprosy patients went blind, simply because the tiny pain cells that force us to blink fell silent and their eyes dried out.

This discovery revolutionized medicine's approach to leprosy, as well as other numbing diseases such as diabetes. And it starkly illustrates why Paul Brand could say with utter sincerity, "Thank God for pain!" By definition pain is unpleasant, so unpleasant as to *force* us to withdraw instantly a finger from boiling water—the very quality which saves us from destruction. Unless the warning signal demands response, we might not heed it.

I had the priceless opportunity, early in my writing career, to spend years learning from Dr. Brand. In a variety of settings—a leprosy hospital in India, the Royal College of Surgeons in London, an animal laboratory in Louisiana, his retirement home in Seattle—I spent hours interviewing him and presenting to him my own questions about pain, theology, and whatever else crossed my mind. At a time when my own faith was forming, he became a wise mentor. Every question I asked, he had already thought of in depth. Like Ralph Winter, he thought "outside the box" of normal theological categories even as he held to a very high view of Scripture.

Dr. Brand achieved renown in medical circles for two major accomplishments. First, as I have mentioned, he pioneered the startling notion that the damage from leprosy was a secondary effect of painlessness and was thus preventable. The theory, radically new when Brand first proposed it as a missionary surgeon in India, went on to gain worldwide acceptance. Former Surgeon General C. Everett Koop estimates that Dr. Brand's discoveries led to medical practices that prevented hundreds of thousands of amputations in those who suffer from diseases such as leprosy and diabetes.

Second, he was hailed as a skilled and inventive hand surgeon, and most major textbooks on hand surgery contain chapters by him. Brand was the first to apply tendon transfer techniques to the specific problems of leprosy patients, whose hands often harden into rigid claw-hands. For these accomplishments, Brand was awarded the U.S. Public Health Service Gold Medallion Award and the prestigious Albert Lasker Medical Award and was made a Commander of the Order of the British Empire.

My conversations with Brand ranged over many issues regarding Christian belief—the doctrine of the atonement, the Trinity, verbal inspiration, social concern—as well as his own avocations of genetics, carpentry, and ecology. He ranked among the handful of brightest minds in evangelicalism, and yet few evangelicals had ever heard of him. I liked that about him. He had not written a book or started a radio program or named an organization after himself. A promising British surgeon, he had humbly worked among the lowest class of people in the entire world: the leprosy-afflicted "untouchables" of India.

I spent most of ten years working on books which grew out of my relationship with Dr. Brand: first *Where Is God When It Hurts?*, then *Fearfully and Wonderfully Made*, and its sequel *In His Image*, and finally *The Gift of Pain*. I have culled transcripts to pull together snatches of our many conversations, focusing specifically on the problem of pain.

The conversation that follows, focusing on physical pain, does not begin to "solve" the problem of pain. It does not address such questions as suffering that results from moral evil such as the horror of Auschwitz, or why creation contains this virus or that bacteria, or natural disasters such as droughts and earthquakes. To address such issues would require much more space—and in fact I have written several books with those very questions in mind. Largely because of the influence of Dr. Brand, however, I learned to approach such questions with the humility of Job who, faced with God's roaring defense of creation, replied simply, "Surely I spoke of things I did not understand, things too wonderful for me to know." That is how I felt as I discussed the underlying aspect of physical pain with Paul Brand.

Philip Yancey: **You once headed up a research project in which you tried to develop an alternative pain system for people who are insensitive to pain, such as leprosy patients. In a sense, you and your team of scientists and bioengineers were playing creator with the human body. What did this teach you about the creation process God went through?**

Paul Brand: Our most overwhelming response was a profound sense of awe. Our team worked specifically with the pain system of the human hand. What engineering perfection we find there! I could fill a room with volumes of surgical textbooks that describe operations devised for the injured hand: different ways to rearrange the tendons, muscles, and joints; ways to replace sections of bones and mechanical joints—thousands of procedures. But I don't know of a single operation anyone has devised that has succeeded in improving a normal hand. It's beautiful. All the techniques correct the deviants, the one hand in a hundred that is not functioning as God designed. We have found no way to improve on the hand that God gave us.

I concur with Isaac Newton, who said, "In the absence of any other proof, the thumb alone would convince me of God's existence." I think of the complex mechanical hands you see in nuclear labs for handling radioactive materials. Millions of dollars went into the circuitry and mechanical engineering to develop those hands. Yet they are so bulky and slow and limited compared to the hand of a child.

Nearly everyone would acknowledge the marvelous structure of the human body. But what of the one in a hundred abnormal hands? Why did God's creation include the potential for these exceptions that fill our hospitals?

A partial answer to that lies, I believe, in the inherent limitations of any medium that obeys physical laws. In creating the world, God chose to work with atomic particles made to operate according to physical and chemical laws, thus imposing certain limits. Those were the building blocks of creation. At the upper end of the whole process, for the highest creative achievement God chose to make a human brain that would be independent and have freedom of choice.

C. S. Lewis' example of wood illustrates the limitations on law-abiding material. To support leaves and fruit on a tree, God had to create a substance with properties of hardness and unpliability. We use wood for furniture and to build homes because of these qualities. Yet, in a free world, that characteristic invites abuse. Wood can be used as a club to bash someone's head. The nature of the substance allows the possibility of a use other than that for which it was intended.

I am glad that the world is governed by laws: that fire is hot and ice is cold, that wood is hard and cotton is soft. As a doctor and scientist, I must rely on those properties for my techniques of treatment and surgery. If I could not rely on plaster to be firm, for instance, it would be useless as a splint for a broken bone.

We eventually had to abandon our own attempts at an alternative pain system partly because of these laws. The substances we tried to use—metal and electronic components—would break down after a few hundred uses, whereas the body expects millions of uses from each of its pain cells. We were unable to come close to duplicating the complexity and flexibility built into the simplest nerve cell.

As you studied the human body, especially in its sensitivity to pain, and as you tried to think like God, did you see anything you would have designed differently?

I would not be so bold as to express it like that, but I have contemplated the choices God must have considered in creating the body. One of the beauties of the pain system in the body is the way in which each pain ending in a tissue fires off its message at a level of stress appropriate to the preservation of that particular tissue. Your foot, for example, reacts dully to pain, since it must be tough enough to face a daily rigor of pounding and stomping. Yet your eye is incredibly sensitive. I visualize the Creator pondering the pain reflex in the cornea. Here is a tissue highly specialized for transparency and thus must do without a regular blood supply (which would make it opaque). A wound there represents a real disaster, as even a small wound can cause blindness. The pain endings are so sensitive that they call for a blink reflex when a thin eyelash touches the surface—no other part of your body would react to the weight of an eyelash.

In setting the levels of sensitivity, the Designer must have recognized that if the eye were made even more sensitive it would be impossible to keep it open in a slightly dusty atmosphere, or in smoke, or perhaps when the wind is blowing. Yet as a doctor concerned primarily with disease and injury, I might have wished for that greater sensitivity.

The same is true with the lining of the trachea and larynx. We get impatient when we are forced to cough, but patients dying of lung cancer must sometimes wish that the Creator had made the mucosa of the trachea less tolerant of tobacco smoke so that their own physiology would prohibit smoking. Even omnipotence cannot please everybody.

Let's talk for a moment about your concept of omnipotence. As I understand it, you view omnipotence in terms of the potential power, not the process it describes. For example, a Russian weightlifter can be called the most powerful man in the world. Yet his task of lifting weights is no easier for him than my lifting the level of weights that challenges me; he still has to grunt and sweat and exert. Is there an analogy there to how you interpret God's omnipotence?

There may be. I don't like the word "omnipotence." The word conveys a simplistic view of the creator and sustainer of the universe, as if God merely had to wave a magic wand for it all to come into being. Our human efforts in producing the Sistine Chapel or a spacecraft required tremendous planning and forethought, and I can envision God going through a similar process of planning and experimentation in the original act of creation.

The more I delve into the natural laws—the atom, the universe, the solid elements, molecules, the sun and, even more, the interplay of all the mechanisms required to sustain life—I am astounded. The whole creation could collapse like a deck of cards if just one of those factors were removed. To build a thing like our universe had to require planning and thought, and that, I believe, is the strongest argument for the presence of God in creation.

From the chance collision of molecules you may sometimes derive a sudden, exciting pattern, but it quickly disperses. Some people really think that all the design and precision in nature came by chance, that if millions of molecules bombard each other for long enough, a nerve cell and sensory ending at exactly the right threshold will result. To those people I merely suggest that they try to make one, as I did, and see what chance is up against.

I see God as a careful, patient designer, and I don't think that the fact that I call him God makes the process of creation easy. There are billions of possible ways in which atoms could combine, and God had to discard all but a very few as being inadequate. I don't think I can fully appreciate God unless I use the word "difficult" to describe the creative process.

I like to think of God developing skills, as it were, by creating amoebae and then ants and cockroaches, developing complexity until it comes to humankind, the zenith of creation. Again, God was confronted with options at every decision. Someone who breaks her leg skiing could wish for stronger bones. Perhaps bone could have been made stronger (though scientists have not been able to find a stronger, suitable substance for implanting), but then the bones would have been thicker and heavier. If they were heavier, you probably wouldn't be able to ski because you would be too bulky and inert.

Take a model of the human skeleton and look at the size of the tiny bones in the fingers and toes. Those bones in the toes support all your weight. If they were larger and thicker, many athletic events would be impossible. If fingers were thicker, many human activities, such as playing keyboard or stringed instruments, would be impossible. The Creator had to make those difficult choices between strength and mobility and weight and volume.

And animals were given different qualities based on their needs. Some are stronger and faster than humans, and can see and hear better. Some can fly, some can echo-locate.

Right, you can only call creation perfect in relation to other options available. Even human types differ. Is an American better than a Vietnamese person? The American is bigger, but it takes more food to sustain him. If food becomes short, the Vietnamese will survive because they can get by on a bowl of rice and the Americans will die out. So physical qualities are not good or bad, but good in certain circumstances. I have tremendous admiration for how the world has come out, with evidence of thought behind it. But every stage of development—moving from the inanimate to the animate, single cell to multicell, developing the nervous system—required thought and choice. That's why I define omnipotence the way I do.

When you speak of pain, and even death, you seem to include these within God's overall design for this planet. These are generally seen as evidence of the twisted, or fallen, state of the world. How do you reconcile these elements with your belief in a wise, loving Creator?

I cannot easily imagine life on this planet without pain and death. Pain is a helpful, essential mechanism for survival. I could walk with you through the corridors of a leprosarium and show you what life is like for people who feel little pain. I see patients who have lost all their toes simply because they wore tight, ill-fitting shoes that caused pressure and cut off circulation. You or I would have stopped wearing those shoes or adjusted our way of walking. But these patients didn't have the luxury of pain to warn them when they were abusing their flesh.

Through books and Hollywood movies we're familiar with the stereotyped image of leprosy, with its loss of fingers. That abuse comes because the leprosy bacillus destroys pain cells and the victims are no longer warned when they harm their bodies through normal activity. In this world, given our material environment, I would not for a moment wish for a pain-free life. It would be miserable. I mentioned earlier that ninety-nine of a hundred hands are perfectly normal. The statistics are reversed for those people insensitive to pain: the vast majority of them have some sort of malformity or dysfunction simply because their pain system is not working properly.

As for death, when I look at the world of nature, its most impressive feature as a closed system is the lavish expenditure of life at every level. Every time a whale takes a mouthful it swallows a million plankton. Every garden pond is a scene of constant sacrifice of life for the building up of other life. Death is not some evil intruder that has upset beautiful creation; it is woven into the very fabric and essence of the beautiful creation itself. Most of the higher animals are designed so that they depend for their survival on the death of lower levels of life. Having created this food pyramid, and placed human beings at its apex, the Creator instructed us to enjoy it and use it responsibly. In modern culture we tend to see a certain ruthlessness and lack of love in nature, but I believe that viewpoint comes from a civilization whose main contact with animal life is through domestic pets and children's anthropomorphic animal stories.

Just a minute now. It is true that pain and death fit into the present system of life on earth, but theologians claim these factors were introduced as a result of man's rebellion and fall. Are you saying that the garden of Eden contained pain and death?

Well, anything I say about the garden of Eden must be conjecture, because we've been given very little data about it. I feel reasonably sure that Adam felt pain if his body was like mine. If there were sharp rocks on which he could have hurt himself, I would hope he had a pain system to warn him. The pain network is so inextricably woven into bodily functions—it tells you when to go to the bathroom and how close you may stand to the fire, and it carries feelings of pleasure as well as pain—that I could not imagine a worthwhile body in this world without it. Note also that in the curse God told Eve he would *multiply* her pain in childbirth.

I believe physical death was present before the fall also. The very nature of the chain of life requires it. You cannot have soil without the death of bacteria; you cannot have thrushes without the death of worms. The shape of a tiger's teeth is wholly inappropriate for eating plant matter—and even vegetarians thrive off the death of plants, part of the created order. A vulture would not survive apart from something dying. I don't see death as being a bad thing in itself.

But the explicit warning given Adam was, "In that day you shall surely die."[1]

The precise phrasing is important: "in that day." The whole story strongly indicates to me that God was speaking of spiritual life: the breath of God, the image of God's self reserved exclusively for human beings. I believe Adam was biologically alive before God breathed into him the breath of life; the Hebrew suggests a spiritual life, a direct link of communication and fellowship between God and man. And after Adam's rebellion immediately, "in that day," the spiritual link was broken. God had to search out Adam after his sin. I don't think the curse referred to physical death at all, and I assume Adam would have died biologically even if he had not rebelled.

It still sounds strange to hear someone vigorously defending pain. You work in a hospital populated by people insensitive to pain. Having met leprosy patients, I can easily agree to the void created in their lives by the absence of pain. But if you worked in a cancer ward, say, among people who feel constant, unrelieved pain, could you praise pain so confidently there?

I have worked in places of great suffering: the clinics treating victims of the London bombings during the war, surgical wards in Indian hospitals. The one legitimate complaint you can make against pain is that it cannot be switched off. It can rage out of control, as with a terminal cancer patient, even though its warning has been heard and there is no more that can be done to treat the cause of pain. I'm sure that less than 1 percent of pain is in this category that we might call out of control. Ninety-nine percent of all the pains that people suffer are short-term pains, correctable situations that call for medication, rest, or a change in a person's lifestyle.

In our experiments with alternative pain systems, we learned it was self-defeating to attach a cutoff switch. We had a glove that, when pressed hard, would emit an electric shock. But if the patient was turning a screwdriver too hard and the electric shock went off, he simply overruled the pain signal and switched it off. As a result, he often injured himself. To make a useful system we would have to eliminate the cutoff switch, or place it out of the patient's reach. I can see why God didn't allow a cutoff switch.

God did make allowances for pain that rages out of control. Don't forget, the best pain-relieving drug in the world is the opium seed of the poppy, which people have used throughout recorded history. There are many ways in which we can relieve the pain of a person with terminal cancer.

Have you given any thought to the resurrected world of the afterlife? The Bible gives little evidence about it, and yet you insist so strongly on the necessity of

---

1   "In that day that you eat of it you shall surely die" (Gen 2:17 NKJV).

pain in this world ... what about the next? The Bible hints that in the matter of pain heaven will be radically different.

I really don't know. Jesus could walk through a solid door in his resurrection body, so it seems clear the afterlife will be governed by a different set of physical laws. There will be some continuity. Jesus' body and those of the others on the Mount of Transfiguration were recognizable, and it's true that the resurrected Jesus even bore the scars of his pain from this world. The disciple Thomas touched them.

Heaven is a spiritual world, and it's difficult to conjecture what we will be like when our spiritual forms are fully developed. Will children still have resurrection bodies of children? I think of my mother, Granny Brand, who lived to be ninety-five. She labored as a missionary for seventy years under harsh conditions in India. Gradually the decades of poor sanitation and Indian diseases and poor nutrition caught up with her, and her body became bent and twisted. She thought herself so ugly that she would not allow a mirror in her house. Yet when she rode her donkey into a village, the people who knew her saw her as a beautiful person, a messenger of love. Perhaps we will relate in heaven so much on that basis that physical appearance will become irrelevant. I don't know how pain fits in. If the verse "tears shall be no more" [Rev 21:4] is to be taken literally, then our eyes will be very different, for in this world we quickly go blind without tears.

What about some of the psychological parallels to physical pain? I'm thinking particularly of emotions we generally view as negative, such as guilt and fear. Do you see these as contributing to health in the same way that physical pain does?

Guilt has spiritual value: it impels you toward cleansing. It serves as a pain to the conscience that something is wrong that should be dealt with. Two steps are necessary. First, the person must find the cause of the guilt, just as a person must find the cause of his pain. Much of modern counseling deals with this process of rooting out reasons for guilt.

A further step must follow: a pathway out of the guilt. Unless it is aimed at cleansing, guilt is a useless encumbrance. Guilt as such doesn't lead you anywhere, just as pain does not: they both simply point out a condition that needs attention. In this sense, guilt is certainly a good thing if it is directional, pushing you toward something. The perceived purpose of it is for you to get rid of the sense of guilt, which you don't like. Underlying that is the more significant purpose of uprooting and dealing with the cause of guilt. It's the same with pain.

In modern society we tend to approach pain as if it were the enemy. We get rid of the pain without asking why the pain came. Painkilling medicine can quiet the pain, but that can be bad if its cause is not determined. Similarly, I believe modern psychology has concentrated on guilt as an evil and attempted to suppress or excise guilt. Just stop feeling guilty, they say. Live your life as you want. But in the Christian context, guilt is very valuable. It pushes you to right the wrong that is the cause of your guilt and gives you the outlet of forgiveness to purge it.

Fear, too, is an essential element of human life, a protective instinct without which the human race would never have survived. A mother shouldn't leave a baby alone until it has grown to have a healthy fear of fire or of heights. Fear also supplies, through adrenaline, increased heart rates and other mechanisms to tap abnormal reserves of strength. The trick is to have the right amount of fear, and to control it properly.

We know that pain and struggle produce character, and that often in the realm of music and art the tensions of childhood result in creative genius. Do you think the modern therapeutic tendency to balance everyone's personality through self-help books, counseling, and medication can be unhealthy? I often wonder how a psychiatrist would have handled Beethoven, a man clearly unbalanced in some ways.

There are problems in this area. One is a trend to eliminate variety. I think variety is exciting and lovely, yet we set up norms and tend to reject people who do not match. If one does not have the proper standard of height, weight, figure, shape of nose, outgoing personality, and extroversion, the psyche is bruised and he or she loses the will to succeed. Anyone who doesn't conform to our artificial goals does badly. When a child is bookish and is clumsy with sports and doesn't shine in conversation, society tends to discard him or her. But that's the material from which research scientists come. I feel we try too much to push people into molds.

Another danger is the tendency of modern culture to remove risk and adventure from life. Most of our excitement happens to us vicariously, as we watch it on television. We shelter our kids, removing them from risky situations, and as a result stunt their growth. I have always maintained that of our six children, I would much rather have four survivors who truly lived, with adventure and self-determination in the face of risk, than end up with six fearful, timid youngsters. Fortunately, all six have survived, but they could all tell you some hair-raising tales of what they went through in finding their own independence.

This tendency to eliminate risk is compounded upon the elderly. I visited a very tidy hospital for old people, where the superintendent showed me with great pride how each person had a separate room and a clean bed. They lie there all day. I asked why they were not allowed to get up and walk about. He said, "Well, if they do, we find that they sometimes fall and break their hips. If they go outdoors they catch cold, and if they meet with each other they exchange infections. By keeping them in their separate little rooms they don't get infected, they don't break their legs, they don't catch cold." I carried away from there a memory of bodies that were alive, but of spirits that were caged.

Your emphasis on restoring the human spirit brings up an interesting line of questions. In rehabilitation you work with very few patients, lavishing thousands of dollars and man-hours a year on each one. In fact, at the leprosy hospital in Louisiana the ratio of staff to patients was almost one-to-one. Does it bother you that in India millions of people were going without the most primitive kind of medical treatment while these patients received so much?

I don't like the juxtaposition of the two cases—patients in India and in the United States. I work with quadriplegics and other disabled persons who require large expenditures of money, yes. The opportunity to work with a person and to help set his or her spirit free is one of my most inspiring challenges. No effort is too great and no expense should be spared to restore activity to such a person or to help the spirit rise above its physical limitations.

Even in India I was faced with terrible choices of priorities. After I applied hand surgery techniques to the specific case of leprosy, our staff was able to remake hands. We could turn a rigid, frozen claw-hand into a flexible, usable hand and allow a beggar to find work. Yet our time and resources were limited, so we had to make choices, just as hospitals in wealthier countries have to make choices among their transplant patients. Did we give a hospital bed to one long-term case for a year, or to twelve short-term cases for one month each, or fifty cases for one week each? Did we repair an older patient with gross deformities or a younger one who had a whole life ahead of her? The most pathetic cases—those with missing limbs and exposed bones—were often the last we would treat; we tried to focus on less advanced cases in order to prevent further abuse. These were wrenching choices. Yet in no way did that background of alternatives devalue the worth of the human spirits we eventually treated.

I have heard it said, by an Indian in fact, that Western medical advances applied to India upset the natural balance. Years ago, the birthrate was high, but only a third of the babies survived infancy. Now the birthrate remains high, but most of the babies live. He accused the West and missionaries in particular of causing India's overpopulation because of their "charitable" aid.

In a real sense, he's right. Missionaries on the whole have not been the chief offenders. They're too inefficient and localized. But the World Health Organization comes in with massive resources and wipes out killing diseases. I would have to say I would not go to India with a lifesaving mission without tying it to education for limiting population. While in India, my specific task was with crippling diseases; I helped remake human spirits, and that, I think, is wholly legitimate. The expense required by one of our operations could have saved a hundred people from cholera, but I still maintain that spirit-saving activity was worth it.

Jesus said, "Love your neighbor as yourself." Modern media has made that command infinitely more complex and burdensome. Because of television, the whole world is our neighbor. On evening news programs we watch the effect of famines, wars, and epidemics. How can we possibly respond to all of these disasters?

You can't, not in the sense in which Jesus meant it, at least. You must remember the context in which Jesus was speaking. He meant family, nearby villages, Capernaum. Jesus healed people, but in a very localized area. In his lifetime he did not affect the Celts or the Chinese or the Aztecs. And I think an intolerable burden of guilt such as you describe merely numbs us and keeps us from responding. We must have a sense of touch with those we love.

Westerners, with our opulent lifestyles, are very sensitive on this point. But I really don't believe that children born in Bangladesh amid poverty suffer all that much more than a spoiled child in a rich country. In *The Cave*, Plato pictured people being born and brought up entirely in darkness, and as a result their range of appreciation of beauty, light, and joy was very different from that of a person outside. When they come up to the light, dazzled, they learn to appreciate a new range of happiness. This, to me, is a deep perception of the human spirit. A child develops a norm, above which is happiness and below which is suffering.

Not long ago I was in Bombay, or Mumbai, among the awful slums between the airport and the city. Children live in stinking, ghastly shacks, held up by sticks, reeking with human excrement, fleas, and lice. Yet you'll see children coming out of the hovel to play tag and hopscotch with a lighthearted air. Their ability to enjoy the basics of life seems greater than that of a spoiled rich kid the day after Christmas, whining and smashing his new toys out of boredom.

How do you maintain a sense of Christian compassion in your work? In India you saw thousands of patients regularly with the same afflictions. After examining three thousand abused hands, how can you maintain your compassion?

I don't know that I do it very well. I probably remember a person's hands better than his or her face. I'll recognize someone and say right off, "You've lost some more of your ring finger." In India I did learn the importance of a sense of touch. Sometimes when we were treating a serious case and had prescribed some drug, the relatives of the patient would go and purchase the medicine, then come back and ask me to give it to the patient "with my good hands." They believed the medicine was more able to help the patient if it was given by the hand of the physician. Interesting, isn't it, that Jesus always touched his patients?

The Christian way of multiplying is the biological way, not the arithmetical way: one becomes two and two becomes four and four becomes eight. I have seen good Christian medical works in India gradually lose their original mission. They become institutionalized, with a building and staff to support, and soon they have to charge their patients fees. To make the work more self-supporting, they branch out into specialized surgery techniques. Soon they're doing brain surgery with all sorts of sophisticated equipment, and the people they originally came to reach—the poor, malnourished Indians—cannot afford the hospital. Christian witness shines when a young person goes out to work among villagers, working with their sanitation, treating diarrheal disease, improving nutrition, educating on childbirth. Eventually more good is done through this kind of personal ministry, I believe.

Jesus Christ did not have to touch people as he healed them. He could easily, with that same power, have waved a magic wand. In fact, a wand would have reached more people than a touch. He could have divided the crowd into groups—paralyzed people over there, febrile people here, people with leprosy there—and raised his hands to heal each group en masse, but he chose not to. No, his mission was to people, individual people who happened to have a disease. They came to him because they had a disease, but he touched them because they were human beings and because he loved them. You can't readily demonstrate love to a crowd. Love is person to person.

–TWO–

THE CONTAGIOUS HUMILITY OF PAUL BRAND

PAUL SMITH

Paul Smith has been the senior pastor of West Side Presbyterian Church in Seattle, WA since 1981. He previously served a church in McKeesport, PA. Paul has a BA in literature from Wheaton College, MDiv from Gordon-Conwell Theological Seminary, and DMin from Trinity Evangelical Divinity School. He has been active in renewal ministries within the church, and is the author of several books including *Jesus, Meet Him Again for the First Time, Enjoying God Forever,* and *God's Plan for Our Good.* Paul and his wife Carreen have raised four children and are now enjoying six grandchildren.

Our first encounter with Dr. Paul Brand at Westside came on a summer day in 1986. Vacation Bible School was going on, and there was plenty of distraction. My secretary looked up from her work to see a slightly rumpled older couple standing politely in front of her. "We're Paul and Margaret Brand," Paul said, "and we wonder if you can help us." The names did not register, and her first thought was, "Oh my, I suppose this dear couple needs a handout." It was our church, however, that was about to receive a "handout," one which has enriched us immeasurably.

Paul and Margaret had just retired and were moving into a small cottage on a bluff overlooking Puget Sound about a mile from our church. It became my privilege to become their pastor—Paul's for the next seventeen years until his death. In all honesty, however, I must say that I could never quite pull off the mental gymnastics necessary to convince myself of the charade. What I know is that he became an enormous encouragement, support, mentor, and role model for me. In her biography, *Ten Fingers for God,* Dorothy Clarke Wilson describes how Paul felt about his retirement after such a sterling career. Biological growth may come to an early climax, but, he pointed out, "there is another dimension of life (call it wisdom?) that involves the integration of knowledge and history and experience and can come only later in life."[1] If any of us thought Paul's energy was spent and he might have little left to give, we need not have feared. He firmly believed that all his life to date had been preparing him for this final phase of activity known as retirement, and "that may well be the most creative and productive of all." This was certainly true for us, as he and Margaret contributed immeasurably to our lives. When my own "retirement" comes, I hope I shall remember this compelling outlook on the whole of life, one of countless lessons learned from Paul.

I have often felt, since coming to know Paul, that I should wear a little bracelet with the letters WWPBD. So often, when facing a significant challenge, I have found myself asking, "What Would Paul Brand Do?" In fact, I often asked him this question directly, and he contributed invaluable counsel. I never told Paul about the bracelet idea, however. He would have been terribly disappointed. He would have been quick to remind me that the only adequate role model was Jesus Christ. But so long as we do not confuse the two, a tangible, even fallible model, is of great value, as the Apostle Paul acknowledged in 1 Corinthians 11:1.

And Paul would never have confused the two. My most fundamental and abiding observation about Paul Brand was his genuine humility, and that his true greatness lay in that humility. Saint Augustine purportedly said, "Humility is the foundation of all the other virtues. Hence, in the soul in which this virtue does not exist, there cannot be any other virtue except in mere appearance." Paul Brand accomplished many remarkable things in his lifetime. A good number of these are well known to readers of the best-selling books he wrote with Philip Yancey. The story of how Brand discovered that the source of tissue damage for leprosy patients lay in shallow nerve damage which destroyed the protective pain response is well known, and changed medical treatment and revolutionized the way we view pain. Medical experts worldwide praise his pioneering hand surgery techniques. He has been regularly consulted by the World Health Organization. His lucid and informative writing has inspired Christians and drawn the admiration of scientists and those who simply enjoy a good story. All these extraordinary accomplishments are magnified in the eyes of those who have met and worked with Dr. Brand by his sincere humility. But like Saint Augustine, I would go even further and say that it is not so surprising that he has done all this and remained humble. Rather—and I say this for the benefit of every potential servant of Jesus Christ—I believe his humility is the compelling force that lies behind those accomplishments.

Some readers may have heard the story behind Dr. Brand's receipt of the highest honor below knighthood granted by the British monarchy. His wife, helpmate and accomplished colleague, Margaret, was preparing a pair of Paul's trousers for the laundry one day when she found a letter in one of his pockets. Curious, she opened it to read, "It is the good pleasure of Her Majesty Queen Elizabeth II to confer upon you the honor of Commander of the British Empire." Paul had not even mentioned it to her. "Did you answer it? What did you say?" "Well," Paul replied, "it's not my business to interfere with the Queen's good pleasure, is it?"

Paul was not able to return to England for the investiture, however, so it was determined that the high commissioner or his deputy would present the award in Madras. Since the queen

---

1   Dorothy Clarke Wilson, *Ten Fingers for God* (Grand Rapids: Zondervan, 1989), 286.

would not be present, Paul assumed it would be an informal affair. As the plane was late, he arrived at the government compound in Madras wearing a rumpled traveling suit, only to find flags flying and the room crowded with dignitaries. His equally unprepared escort was horrified, but Paul told him, "If they insist on making a fuss over us, they'll just have to take us as we are." It was the sort of response which unmistakably revealed Paul's humility. But by humility I don't just mean Paul's rumpled appearance and unassuming manner. Nor that the man consistently underplayed his accomplishments. He did not. Their significance was unavoidably obvious, but he seldom seemed to consider them at all. What he did consider was the people who might be helped by his discoveries. This is one way in which I believe his humility drove his accomplishments. Paul's mother had encouraged him to consider a career in medicine, but loving to work with his hands, at first he took up construction instead. His ambition was to return to South India and fulfill his father's original dream of building houses in the Kolli Hills. But his deep concern for the hurt of people around him drove him to give himself to improve their lives. This was particularly obvious after a visit to the leprosy sanatorium in Chingleput put him face-to-face with the deep suffering of victims of this dreaded disease. His heart was captured by their suffering, and his subsequent accomplishments were a by-product of his compassion.

One could not watch Paul Brand and fail to see this. When our young daughter ran into a tree at a church retreat and broke her finger, Paul held her hand gently and reassured her as he examined the injury. That quiet compassion translated almost immediately into relief from the pain and a nearly instant end to the tears. Both he and his wife, Margaret, an accomplished eye surgeon who pioneered new techniques which she was regularly called upon to teach to surgeons around the world, never put themselves forward or sought out those who might admire them. Rather, they consistently sought out those in the congregation who were the least attractive, had the least status, or who perhaps showed signs of physical, mental, or psychological stress or disorders, and would simply touch and talk to them, taking a deep and genuine interest in them.

In his book *Mere Christianity*, C. S. Lewis might have been describing Paul Brand when he wrote:

> Do not imagine that if you meet a really humble man he will be what most people call "humble" nowadays: he will not be a sort of greasy, smarmy person, who is always telling you that, of course, he is nobody. Probably all you will think about him is that he seemed a cheerful, intelligent chap who took a real interest in what *you* said to *him*. If you do dislike him it will be because you feel a little envious of anyone who seems to enjoy life so easily. He will not be thinking about humility: he will not be thinking about himself at all.[2]

One Sunday, Dr. Brand stopped to chat with me about the sermon after the service, as he regularly did. I was working on a series of messages and he asked what was coming up. "I'm

---

2   C. S. Lewis, *Mere Christianity* (New York: Macmillan, 1958), 99.

sorry I'm going to have to miss the next couple of Sundays," he said with genuine remorse, "but I have to be out of town. I guess I'll just have to get copies when I get back."

"Oh, where are you going?" I asked.

"Well, I have some speaking engagements," he said. "I'll be out of the country for a few weeks."

"Will you be traveling back to India?" I asked.

"No, I'll actually be in Europe this time."

I wouldn't let him go, and after several more questions finally learned that he was traveling to Geneva, Switzerland, where he had been asked to give a major address to the World Health Organization. But his real concern was that he would miss Sunday worship with us.

With all the acclaim and honors Paul Brand received, one might wonder if his apparent humility was genuine or if he had simply learned to project a modest image. But the question betrays a failure to grasp the heart of true humility. It was that bedrock humility which made him who he was. Not only did it inspire his compassion and drive him to serve anyone in need, but it was also that humility which drove his intellect.

Paul certainly had compelling models of selflessness in his parents. In a spirit much like that of Mother Teresa, Jesse and Evelyn Brand had moved into a remote and disease-ridden area of southern India known as Kolli Hills (or Kolli Malai, which means literally "Mountains of Death"). With minimal training they simply responded to the needs they found there, providing basic but essential medical care despite the considerable risks to their own health, building with their own hands a clinic, a school, and a church, and taking in abandoned children. But the "Mountains of Death" showed no mercy in response to their compassion. At age forty-four, Jesse Brand died of blackwater fever, a virulent complication of malaria. Evelyn, "Granny Brand" to the locals, never faltered, returning to serve the people who needed her care. Despite enormous obstacles, "Granny Brand" refused to retire, moving deeper into the hills and continuing her mission until her body finally gave out at age ninety-five.

But that example alone does not inspire humility. In fact, had he thought much about such "selflessness" he most likely would not have been particularly attracted to it. We may admire selflessness in others, but we are not naturally inclined to expect joy in sacrificing ourselves for others. The inspiration comes not from considering "selflessness" as a state of mind or a character trait. Rather, genuine selflessness grows naturally from becoming so deeply absorbed in the world around you and all its questions and possibilities that you don't really think about yourself at all.

As Paul talked about his father, you were struck by the elder Brand's boundless curiosity about God's creation.

> My father tutored me on the mysteries of the natural world: the termites he had foiled by building our house on stilts capped with upside-down frying pans, the sticky-toed geckos that clung to my bedroom walls, the agile tailor bird that stitched together leaves with its beak, using bits of grass stalk as a stitching thread.
>
> Once, Dad took me to a termite colony, its tall mounds standing in rows like organ pipes, and cut out a large window to show me the arched columns and

winding passageways within. We lay on our stomachs together, chins propped on our hands, and watched the insects scurry to repair their fine architecture. Ten thousand legs worked together as if commanded by a single brain, all frantic except the queen, big and round as a sausage, who lay oblivious, pumping out eggs.[3]

You cannot read anything written by Paul Brand without recognizing that his considerable intellect was driven by the vast humility of one who found it a grand adventure to uncover and expose the Master-Creator's work. Early in his medical training, considering the possibility of neurosurgery, he undertook a project to dissect and expose the twelve cranial nerves of the head and follow them to their site of origin in the brain. Dr. Brand became rhapsodic in describing the delicate network of nerves he uncovered in the process, and the ways they convey stunningly diverse information to the brain. But what drove him was not his own achievement in this complex task of exploration. Rather, as he observed, "Nowhere are the Creator's fingerprints more visible than in the brain, where mind and body come together."[4] He concluded, "I came away from my dissection project awed by the economy and elegance of the system that transcribes the vast phenomena of the material world."[5]

That same humility inspired his entire career. As he learned more and more about the ways in which pain contributed immeasurably to the health and well-being of the body, he saw this often unappreciated feature of the nervous system as an extraordinary feat of engineering. "The dazzling complexity of the pain network astounded me. I began studying pain out of simple curiosity, having no idea I was accumulating a foundation for my life's work. I came away from that early research with an enduring sense of awe and gratitude for the very sensation most people view with resentment."[6]

Most people probably do not think of intellectual accomplishment as being inspired by humility. But if you truly believe, as Paul did, that all he was doing was discovering what God had accomplished, then you understand how that belief might inspire the sort of insatiable desire for discovery that compelled him. "I have come to realize that every patient of mine," he once said, "every newborn baby, in every cell of its body, has a basic knowledge about how to survive and how to heal that exceeds anything that I shall ever know. That knowledge is the gift of God, who has made our bodies more perfectly than we could ever have devised." It is that humility that drove Paul's intellectual accomplishments. "The best physicians are the humblest ones," he said, "those who listen closely to the body and work to assist it in what it is already instinctively doing for itself."[7]

In fact, only true humility can generate great learning. Arrogance stunts growth because one assumes one has little to learn. In his autobiographical book about pain, Dr. Brand wrote:

3   Paul Brand and Philip Yancey, *Pain: The Gift Nobody Wants* (New York: HarperCollins, 1993), 16.
4   Ibid., 48.
5   Ibid., 49.
6   Ibid., 64.
7   Ibid., 242.

The process of following patients through the whole rehabilitation cycle ultimately challenged my approach toward medicine. Somewhere, perhaps in medical school, doctors acquire an attitude that seems suspiciously like hubris: "Oh, you've come just in time. Count on me. I think I'll be able to save you." Working at Karigiri stripped away that hubris. We could not "save" leprosy patients. We could arrest the disease, yes, and repair some of the damage. But every leprosy patient we treated had to go back and, against overwhelming odds, attempt to build a new life. I began to see my chief contribution as one I had not studied in medical school: to join with my patients as a partner in the task of restoring dignity to a broken spirit. That is the true meaning of rehabilitation.[8]

That same humility allowed him to constantly grow and revise his approach as a surgeon. Admitting some pride in his surgical abilities, he told of coming to recognize that surgery was a radical correction, sometimes necessary, but never preferable to the natural healing instincts of the body. "No matter how skillfully I might operate," he said, "I will always leave a wound and spilled blood and torn tissue ... If I can persuade the body to correct itself without surgery, then every local cell can devote itself to work toward solving the original problem, not any new ones I might introduce."[9]

Paul spoke often and publically of what he learned from others. It was Margaret, he often told us, who excelled in medical school and worked alongside him in bringing hope and healing to the people of rural India. She taught him a compassion which his scientific mind might have missed. He also seemed to have no problem admitting he had been wrong, and making the necessary adjustments to get it right. He was constantly learning from co-workers, fellow surgeons, nurses, hospice workers, and certainly from his patients. If you honestly believe you have much to learn, you don't mind who your source is. As Ezra Taft Benson, a prominent member of President Eisenhower's cabinet once said, "Pride is concerned with who is right. Humility is concerned with what is right."

We regularly saw this spirit during the better part of the two decades in which Dr. Brand served with us at West Side. But he never wore his humility with pride, as most of us are wont to do. It was always genuine and self-effacing. Once, while serving on our missions committee, Paul listened sympathetically to the lament of a young missionary couple who were being recalled from the field because of concerns about the adjustment of their young children. The couple was in tears, describing what they saw as a great failure—a revelation of their inadequacy for the role they yearned to play in world missions. When their emotional account came to an end, Paul said quietly, "I wish someone had sent us home to parent our children when we were on the mission field." All of Paul and Margaret's children have grown up to be wonderful people who continue to make worthwhile contributions. But Paul was admitting his own feelings of inadequacy as a parent and wanting to encourage this young family with a lesson he had to learn the hard way: that even a high-profile Christian calling could not substitute for the primary responsibility of parenting.

8   Ibid., 159.
9   Ibid., 84.

Paul's compassion and interest in others, combined with his boundless curiosity towards the natural world, was contagious. One weekday during the lunch hour we hosted the meeting of the local chapter of Rotary International, a secular organization which brings together business and professional leaders to serve the community. Knowing that one of their goals was providing humanitarian service, one of our members responsible for the program had invited Dr. Brand to speak. He was not known, of course, to the local business community, but most members came for the benefits of networking with other business leaders. I sat at the head table with Dr. Brand and others, and observed the demeanor of the group as they finished their luncheon conversations, glanced anxiously at their watches, and hoped that the speaker, whoever he was, did not take too much of their valuable time before they were free to resume their important lives. Dr. Brand was introduced as an international expert on "Hansen's disease" and their restless inattention betrayed their lack of knowledge of or interest in the topic.

But Paul showed no sign of noticing this. When the introduction was complete, Paul, wearing his trademark gray wool suit and burgundy sweater, rose and began to tell the story of his life, the horrendous ravages of leprosy, and his wonder in discovering the unexpected and indispensable value of pain. I watched in amusement as person after person in the audience turned toward the dais from their private conversations, put down their notepads or other preoccupations, and became totally engrossed in the wonder, the sensitivity, and the joy exhibited by this choice servant of the Lord. Had he offered them the opportunity, I am quite certain the majority of them would have enthusiastically accompanied him to India the next week to contribute what they could to his work among people whom under normal circumstances they would have ignored as irrelevant to their lives and personal success.

I watched a similar transformation of disinterested high school chemistry students who were irresistibly drawn into the childlike curiosity and excitement of this man who never lost the sense of privilege that was his in rediscovering the fascinating and intricate wonders God had built into creation. And it was indeed childlike, which is what made this great man so compelling. Jesus would have understood it, as would King David for that matter. It was David's Psalm 8 that Jesus quoted when scandalized adults criticized the childlike behavior of those who celebrated the first Palm Sunday: "Have you never read, 'From the lips of children and infants you, Lord, have called forth your praise'?" (Matt 21:16).

One Palm Sunday Paul was assisting me in worship. I must sincerely tell you I loved it when he did this. I know I always preached better because of the compelling sense that God was present. On this particular Sunday our children's "Joyful Sound" choir had received palm branches and were preparing to enter the sanctuary during the processional hymn, "All Glory, Laud, and Honor." Paul saw the stash of palm branches at the door and on a whim, just before we entered, snatched one up and stuck it in his lapel as we walked to the front of the auditorium. Of course it was much too large and partially obscured his face, so when he had taken his place up front, he took it out, broke off a more manageable piece, and returned it to his lapel, much to the delight of the congregation. It was one of his gifts to us that you simply could not avoid being caught up in his enthusiasm, transparency, and engaging humility. I will always be inspired by the image of Paul, beaming over the top of an outsized palm branch, when I am tempted to believe that a great man must stand on his dignity and never play the fool.

One never had the impression that Paul Brand was "showing off" his learning or accomplishments, nor that he had to. What always impressed you was his excitement to help you see and appreciate what excited him. He didn't have to defer your compliments by saying, "to God be the glory." The glory of God was evident in everything he said and did. The astute social observer John Ruskin once said:

> I believe that the first test of a great man is his humility. I don't mean by humility, doubt of power. But really great men have a curious feeling that the greatness is not of them, but through them. And they see something divine in every other man and are endlessly, foolishly, incredibly merciful.[10]

This was Paul Brand, and I loved him, and he was an inspiration to me. I have not chosen here to speak primarily of Paul's humility as one of many character traits which might describe the man. I have chosen to speak of Paul's humility because I have come to believe that it was the driving force that made him the person he became—the person who brought healing, hope, dignity, inspiration, delight, and yes, life itself to countless thousands of people. If Paul were here to comment on what I have written, I do not believe he would challenge what I have said about the boundless power of humility. He would only dispute his own true humility, being fully aware of the battle with pride which threatens to undo every great accomplishment and compromise the life of great and small alike. For pride, as C. S. Lewis was fond of pointing out, is the sin which will keep us out of heaven.

In one of his lesser known writings, the *Arthurian Torso*, C. S. Lewis wrote a commentary on the poetry of Charles Williams concerning the legend of King Arthur and the Holy Grail. The work contains this typically lighthearted but insightful Lewisian observation on humility and pride:

> *Of course* the whole thing is a kind of make believe or fancy-dress ball. Not only official greatness, as of kings or judges, but what we call real greatness, the greatness of Shakespeare, Erasmus, and Montaigne, is, from a certain point of view, illusory. What then? What but to thank God for the "excellent absurdity" which enables us, if it so happen, to play great parts without pride and little ones without dejection, rejecting nothing through that false modesty which is only another form of pride, and never, when we occupy for a moment the centre of the stage, forgetting that the play would have gone off just as well without us.[11]

There is no question that Dr. Paul Brand accomplished great things. There will be no way to calculate, this side of heaven, the tremendous impact which his learning and skills have

---

10   John Ruskin, *The Works of John Ruskin*, ed. E. T. Cook and Alexander Wedderburn, 39 vols. (1903–12), 5:331.
11   C. S. Lewis, "Williams and the Arthuriad," in *Arthurian Torso*, ed. Charles Williams and C. S. Lewis (London: Oxford University Press, 1948), 329.

had on the lives of countless people—particularly those with the least hope and opportunity. But to see those accomplishments in isolation from his fundamental Christlike character would be to miss entirely the weight and significance of Paul Brand's life.

I cannot tell you Paul Brand's full legacy to our generation. I leave that to others more knowledgeable and astute than I. What I *can* tell you, without a shadow of a doubt, is that I am a better man for having known him.

–THREE–

HOW RALPH WINTER ENGINEERED WORLD MISSIONS

GREG PARSONS

Greg H. Parsons is global director of the U.S. Center for World Mission (www.uscwm.org). He and his wife Kathleen have been on staff there since 1982. He received a PhD on the life and early missiology of Ralph D. Winter. Greg is also the Ralph D. Winter Associate Professor of Intercultural Studies at the William Carey International University (www.wciu.edu) and supervises the Winter and Donald McGavran Archives and frontier research center. Greg has a regular column in the USCWM periodical, *Mission Frontiers* (www.missionfrontiers.org) and serves on its editorial board, as well as that of the William Carey Library.

Ralph and Roberta Winter founded the USCWM in 1976 and WCIU in 1977.

In my junior year of college, I sat with my friend Doug Houck in an auditorium at Stanford University. About two dozen students from our church in San Jose had driven up to participate in a student missions event.

Ralph D. Winter was standing on the poorly lit stage, showing hand-drawn overhead slides and the status of Christianity in three great regions of the world: among Muslims, Hindus, and Chinese. Black and white circles had been drawn proportionate to populations of each bloc. Tiny circles within those large circles showed the very few Christians in those parts of the world.

It had been a long day, and Doug and I were wide awake and spellbound—we had never heard this before! We were already committed to Christian missions. We produced a detailed insert on missions for our church newsletter. We were reading a newly released book called *Operation World*, praying for each country, following notes in that book regarding items for praise and prayer—but we hadn't heard any of this before.

At the time, Ralph Winter was on an unpaid sabbatical from Fuller Seminary's School of World Mission, where he had taught for eight years. A few weeks after this presentation, he and his wife, Roberta, would start the U. S. Center for World Mission on a well-used campus just three miles northeast of Fuller in Pasadena. What he was talking about that day at Stanford captured the attention of the missions world.

Years before, Ralph and Roberta, with their four daughters, had served with the Mam (pronounced "mom") tribal people in the highlands of Guatemala for ten years. The Mam lived at the edge of starvation. None had completed more than three years of school. They had no ordained pastors, opportunities for education, or the money to study. Not only did the missionaries bring spiritual assistance, but they also provided agricultural, medical, economic, and educational help. Men needed work, especially the pastors, who were all part-time and normally not paid.

Roberta described their living conditions:

> Their one-room huts were made of mud with dirt floors and three stones strategically placed in the middle of the floor to serve as a fireplace-stove. Their clothes (of which they had only one change) were patched and repatched; in fact, where the women carried their babies on their back, the patch itself was very often patched. The Mam diet was almost completely corn with a bit of black beans once a week perhaps and a tiny bit of meat for a very special and somewhat rare occasion. They had no milk, no eggs, no other vegetables or fruit ... They raised chickens but could not afford to eat either their eggs or the chickens themselves.[1]

There were established leaders and churches in the area, but they were not recognized by those outside local fellowships. Winter and Jim Emery, a missionary who had arrived five years earlier, set out to change that. Both were engineers by training—the kind that constantly "tinker" to improve anything around them. The usual training model of enrolling young, unproven men and women in residential programs—often at great distance and cost—was not working. The local seminary was too far away and expensive, so Winter and Emery, and later Ross Kinsler, began to find ways to get training to the existing leaders.

What they started in the highlands of Guatemala would become known as Theological Education by Extension (TEE). Instead of gathering pastors in one location that was difficult to reach, expensive to maintain, and cut off from family and existing ministry, Winter and Emery brought the training to the church leaders. The idea was not totally original, but they helped popularize TEE throughout Latin American and on other continents. At its peak, some 100,000 students were involved worldwide. In some places the program remains effective, such as in India, where it is called The Association for Theological Education by Extension (TAFTEE) and now trains more than 13,000 students.

Ralph's father, Hugo, was an honest and honorable father, a leader in his church, and a self-taught engineer who helped build the Los Angeles freeway system. He worked his way up the chain of command in the L.A. Planning Department and was responsible for the

---

1   Roberta H. Winter, "Winter Initiatives" (unpublished document, September 31, 2000), 20.

department that designed bridges by the time Ralph was twelve years old. He worked with leaders in more than seventy cities to plan the routes the new freeway system would take. Ralph's mother, Hazel, was also a serious Christian, yet the opposite of Hugo in many ways. Hazel was outgoing, affectionate, and emotional, but also quite sharp.

As children, Ralph was close to his older brother Paul, who also became an engineer. One opportunity to use their budding engineering skills came when the fireworks catalog arrived each year. They would add up their savings and figure out how to get "as much bang for their buck" as possible! But occasionally plans went awry, such as when their calculations were a little off and an explosion singed Ralph's eyebrows.

Ralph worked with diligence at any project or activity he put his mind to. Paul described him as "competitive," and whatever project Ralph undertook, he possessed the ability of "seeing right through to basic principles."

David, Ralph's other brother, was six years younger than Paul. David later recalled the role Ralph played in his life:

> When I was just starting college … I was just sort of drifting and [Ralph] … came to me and said, "Dave, you are just messing around. You need to get away from here. You need to leave family and friends and have … an adventure … You need to go to Prairie Bible Institute." He was very persuasive and I was also intimidated by his vision, his ideas … I came back from that year a different person.[2]

Spiritual commitment came early for Ralph and, as with other things, once that sunk in, he focused on it with great intensity and commitment. In his late seventies he recalled:

> I early caught on to the fact that I could learn more, learn faster and retain longer by directly concerning myself with the concerns of God for His Kingdom and for His righteousness … The will of God in this imperfect world was central early in my thinking.[3]

One of Ralph's teenage friends was a boy named Dan Fuller. They met at Lake Avenue Congregational Church in Pasadena. Dan was the son of Charles and Grace Fuller. Charles E. Fuller had become a nationwide radio broadcaster with programs like *The Pilgrim Hour* and *The Old Fashioned Revival Hour*. These shows were carried on the Mutual Broadcasting System and had larger audiences than even Bob Hope! Charles later founded Fuller Seminary.

Both boys were influenced by Lake Avenue and its commitment to the Bible and world outreach. Many missionaries were sent out by the church. The boys were also involved in the nationwide Christian Endeavor youth movement and the Navigators. The first was a high school church program that was run by the young people themselves, with adults helping

---

2   Comments by David Winter at Ralph Winter's memorial, June 28, 2009.
3   Ralph D. Winter, "Autobiography," (speech, Lake Avenue Church, Bakers Square breakfast group, Pasadena, October 7, 2003).

guide the group from the background. Youths took turns leading meetings, forcing Ralph and Dan, who were somewhat introverted, to learn valuable communication skills.

The Navigators focused on Bible study and discipleship. Ralph and Dan were involved in a "Navs" high school program called "Dunamis" (the Greek word for might or power), where they gathered to study the Bible and memorize verses. Ralph memorized five hundred, and Dan doubled that figure!

Dan Fuller later reflected:

> I really enjoyed being around Ralph. He always had something interesting to say, some new idea … I think that eighty percent of the direction that my life has taken comes from that picnic at the Winter's house when I decided to send my application to Princeton … He felt the importance of learning Inductive Bible Study … And that's the thing that I gave my whole life to … and I owe it to Ralph.[4]

Ralph was, above all things, an innovator. He was always thinking up new ideas and sharing them with anyone he could. No matter what he was involved in, he was always mobilizing people to whatever he was thinking about or working on at the time.

Ralph visited Guatemala for the first time while he and Roberta were in language school in Costa Rica. He wrote to his parents in the fall of 1957 about his anticipated role as a field missionary:

> I've felt and responded to the call of the ministry and missions. I have surely much more certainly felt and responded to what I believe is a call (no matter what everyone else may think) to the studied application of modest ingenuity to the Christian cause in general … Yet while the inventor's role is partially recognized in the secular world it is not about to be in the ecclesiastical.[5]

Winter brought that "studied application of modest ingenuity" to bear on an astonishing range of activities to help the mission and the Mam people.

He perceived that the poor economic condition of the Mam was related—in part—to their land inheritance system whereby land was divided up between sons, with the youngest receiving a larger portion so he could care for his aging parents. By the time the Winters arrived, plots had been subdivided so often that they were now small, scattered, and far from the farmers' homes. Since almost no churches could support their pastors, in order to make a living, a pastor might have to walk hours between farms, church, and home. They could not even consider crossing the mountains to establish new churches.

The Winters helped the Mam in ways that concentrated resources. Since there was no way to meet the most basic needs of the people by selling one another goods or services, they sought to produce and sell desirable products to markets *outside* the Mam area. Winter tried a number of things, including helping them establish and run small, portable businesses.

---

4   Daniel Fuller, interview with the author, March 7, 2005.
5   Letter from Ralph D. Winter to Hugo and Hazel Winter, fall 1957.

These businesses were intended to help sustain pastors and give them the freedom to expand their ministries and allow the pastor/businessman to travel as necessary. The largest of the ventures was a furniture-making business, producing folding chairs, pews, and later closets and doors for housing developments. These were sold to the second largest city in the country, Quetzaltenango, fifteen miles away.

Other businesses included itinerant photography with a photo lab, a weaving business using the best available colorfast thread, a print shop with mimeograph machines, and silk-screening services. Winter and his colleagues also taught basic dentistry and built a fluorescent-light assembly factory. Winter also taught several men to drive a jeep, which became the first "ambulance" service for the mission clinic.

Winter taught church leaders the skills to run the businesses, including accounting and the need to invest back into their businesses. Any money that was invested had to be paid back, so that it could be put into another project. It would take a few business cycles to see them get paid off, but every business eventually had to make a profit or was shut down. There was no room for long-term subsidies. This reinvestment of funds was crucial for building businesses and solving endemic problems.

The missionaries set up not only production but also distribution for textiles. As they began to make and sell products, the Winters hoped that Mam women could earn enough to pay to have corn milled at a local mill and use their time for weaving or other profitable activities. This didn't work; husbands simply took the money their wives had made, leaving the women with an extra job and little to show for it.[6]

While most Mam were not formally educated beyond three grades of school, they were bright, eager to learn, and worked hard. They were soon running these businesses, accounting for thousands of dollars a month down to the penny. Some of the businesses failed. But they increased the ability of the pastors to serve their churches and provide for their families.

The village near the Winters' home had about two hundred inhabitants, with a regional "market" population of close to one thousand. At the request of the mayor and town leadership, Winter also started a local junior high school that is still in operation. They started the Inter-American school, an international Christian school, also still operating.

Yet they saw that many of the leaders in the area did not have enough schooling to qualify for TEE training and, eventually, ordination. The Winters and dozens of missionaries from several missions across the entire region helped produce curriculum which allowed adults to pass proficiency tests and move forward in their education. The first year of this curriculum, more than a thousand students participated.

Ralph and Roberta sought to live out their faith in practical ways, including in how they handled money. As noted, Ralph taught Mam businessmen accounting. Another practical way they sought to apply their faith was by not spending money on nonessentials such as soda pop. In Guatemala, they knew that if the Mam followed that lead of the outsiders and purchased Coke, it would literally take food out of the mouths of their families, not to mention rot their teeth.

---

6   Roberta Winter, "Winter Initiatives," 26.

Even worse problems were already being caused by alcohol. When women made money from their weaving business, the men would take it for drink. So Ralph and Roberta opposed alcohol consumption as well, since supporting it in any way would contribute to damaging marriages, families, and Mam society. They recognized that the Bible does not forbid a glass of wine at dinner, but they were attentive to the larger consequences of their example.

Ralph's work came to the attention of Donald McGavran, head of the Fuller School of World Mission. He was probably the best-known missions strategist in the West in the late 1950s to 1970s. Ralph and Roberta were invited to teach at Fuller.

The faculty learned a great deal from the students, by design. They called students "associates." The typical associate was a missionary with at least four years of mission experience. International students were leaders in their respective countries. Faculty and associates would meet regularly to discuss ideas, often totally unconnected to any particular assignment. When asked by professors at other institutions how many students the SWM had, Winter, half joking, would reply, "Four to five," pause for a shocked reaction, and add, "but we have one hundred teachers." He would add that he was not sure what the students learned, but that he and the other faculty learned a great deal about the world where the students had served as missionaries.

Winter reflected back on those years in 2004:

> The new school was a growing beehive of serious thinking and critical evaluation of missionary methods and strategies. It was great! Those years were full of gushing insight and floods of information from every corner of the earth. A thousand missionaries passed through my classes while I was busy researching, evaluating and teaching about the major moves forward of the Christian faith in the last 2,000 years.[7]

Winter and McGavran were asked to be plenary presenters at a meeting, called by Billy Graham, of some 2,500 Christian leaders in Lausanne, Switzerland, in 1974. The event promoted three important ideas, the last of which Winter was perhaps the leading spokesman:

1. A statement of evangelical commitment called the "Lausanne Covenant," crafted by John Stott and with input from theologians and leaders from around the world.

2. A clear recognition by evangelicals of the need to expand their work to include more social issues. The attempt here was to end the unbiblical and artificial split between only telling people about Jesus and helping them in practical ways.

---

7   From "The Introduction to the Reprint of Mission Frontiers 1979–1981," 1. Reprinted in *Frontiers in Mission: Discovering and Surmounting Barriers to the Missio Dei*, Second Edition (Pasadena: William Carey International University Press, 2005), 4.

3. Winter and others argued the need to take the gospel to "unreached people groups," or ethnic enclaves in which there were as yet few, if any, serious believers in Christ.

Winter used to say that among these thousand experienced missionaries who came through his classroom, none arrived from fields to which they had not been sent! The thousands of cultures where missionaries had not yet gone were mostly concentrated within three blocs—Muslim, Hindu, and Buddhist.

What I heard Winter say that Friday night at Stanford was a more refined version of what he had just presented at Lausanne. Beyond the fact that the message of Jesus Christ had not yet taken root in these large blocs, an underlying challenge for Christians was to find ways of communicating the message that made sense to those who heard it.

It wasn't that missionaries hadn't tried or that they had always failed. On the contrary, success itself created new needs where the church was growing. There just wasn't much experience in some parts of the world. Christians had gone to India and seen people come to Christ, but few Hindus seemed to respond. They had gone to the Middle East, but ended up working with Christians in established churches and hardly touched Muslims.

These ideas drew the Winters away from Fuller and toward something new that was only slowly coming into focus.

Winter was also intrigued by religious orders, like the Jesuits and Franciscans, and all they had managed to accomplish over the centuries Winter believed God was raising up people within the church to found organizations that worked outside usual church ministry to tackle major problems. The organization Ralph and Roberta were about to begin was also such an organization, which would implement many of Winter's ideas and apply them in a systematic way to world missions.

Although he was just a professor with no financial backing, Ralph and Roberta took the option to purchase a campus in Pasadena with just $100, even though a well-funded Eastern cult was occupying the property and wanted to buy it outright. That gripping story, as told by Ralph, is found in the book Roberta wrote, called *Once More around Jericho*, later revised as *I Will Do a New Thing*:[8]

All these new insights illuminated new opportunities, obstacles and problems which cried out to be taken into account as soon as possible. However, a school as a school was not quite the proper place for idea implementation. Furthermore, I have considered myself a scholar-activist. Even before the Fuller Theological Seminary School of World Mission existed I had been drawn to problem solving. When I moved from my Caltech background in engineering to Cornell for a doctorate in linguistics, anthropology and mathematical statistics, people said, "Why are you leaving engineering?" I answered "I am moving from civil

---

8   Roberta H. Winter, *Once More around Jericho: The Story of the U.S. Center for World Mission* (Pasadena: William Carey Library, 1979); and Roberta H. Winter, *I Will Do a New Thing: The U.S. Center for World Mission and Beyond* (Pasadena: William Carey Library, 1987). This was updated in 2011 with material edited from draft chapters Roberta wrote before she died.

engineering to social engineering." When, after that degree, I then completed theological seminary I told people I was moving "from social engineering to Christian social engineering." When I became a missionary I was now in Christian mission engineering.[9]

Winter had seen the need for "an indissoluble connection" between serious academic inquiry and the implementation of those ideas in the real world, "if only to test them rather than mindlessly teaching them." His goal was nothing less than to solve whatever problems were impeding the spread of the gospel to areas of the world that had not yet been reached.[10]

The focus of the U. S. Center for World Mission (USCWM) was on cultural groups where the message of the gospel was not yet clear enough for people to respond. A number of the other things Winter started either became a part of the USCWM or flowed into it, including the publishers of this book.

I have never seen a couple that worked together so seamlessly. This began when they were first married, just before Winter started his PhD studies. Even after their daughters were born, Roberta was very involved. Yet all the girls remember that time fondly. Ralph was always available. Each of the girls felt they could "interrupt" him anytime and he would drop everything, giving them full attention.

As they got older, they also felt fully involved in the work. Ralph and Roberta believed that it was wrong to merely let children play and learn in school. They needed to be involved in productive activities commensurate with their age and abilities. When they were between the ages of eight and thirteen, all four girls were involved in the work of the William Carey Library Publishers. The girls were co-owners and helped pack books and stamp "errata" on back covers. When books arrived from the printer, it was all hands on deck! Ralph would put a box on a skateboard and the youngest, Tricia, would roll it down the driveway of their home into the garage—where the business started. The oldest, Beth, acted as the publisher's customer service "department." Later, Linda helped with bookkeeping, and Becky managed the mailroom.

Ralph and Roberta probably could have done that work faster, especially in the early days. But they felt it was important to give the girls a sense that they could be involved in important ministry.

Just a year after starting the U.S. Center, the Winters also founded William Carey International University (WCIU). The ambition of this institution, located on the U.S. Center campus, was, among other things, to apply the lessons learned through TEE, and other experiments, in new ways. WCIU would award degrees that outside institutions would recognize. By promoting distance learning, now made easier through the Internet, WCIU allows qualified and dedicated Christian leaders to study without needing to leave their families or "deculturize" from their home environments. Winter suggested that such

---

9   From "The Introduction to the Reprint of Mission Frontiers 1979–1981," 1. Reprinted in *Frontiers In Mission: Discovering and Surmounting Barriers to the Missio Dei*, Second Edition (Pasadena: William Carey International University Press, 2005), 4.

10   Ralph D. Winter, introduction to *Mission Frontiers 1979–1981* (reprint, 2004), 1. http://www. ralphwinter.org/A/view.htm?id=4&part=1&section=1.

methods would allow "exactly the same educational results by working at a distance" and thus develop "superior leaders."[11]

As a student Winter observed that Christians seemed to avoid the sciences, and scientists avoided issues of faith. He became fascinated in studying what Roberta described as "things not taught in secular schools about the relationship of the story of the Faith and the unfolding of Western civilization."[12] He had learned at Caltech about the academic achievements of great scientists such as Isaac Newton, Michael Faraday, William Thompson (Lord Kelvin), James Clerk Maxwell, and Sir Humphrey Davy. But Caltech did not mention that each of them were also men of faith. He discovered to his surprise that Newton had spent twenty years studying the life of the Apostle Paul. Faraday was an ordained preacher who taught from the Bible every Sunday.

As always, Ralph sought to share these ideas with others. Why, he wondered, was this separation so pervasive? Even when science was taught at Christian colleges, there was no clear connection with the faith of those involved.

Ralph wondered, "What would a regular 'secular' history course look like if also studied from 'God's' perspective?" He had surmised that fifteen out of seventeen evangelical students were in secular schools. He decided to prepare history lessons from a Christian perspective and meet with a handful of willing students at the University of Southern California USC each week. Winter learned a great deal from this experiment, and this led to an ongoing, as yet unfulfilled, vision to meld together faith and "secular" disciplines. Later he wrote:

> God has given us two "books." 1) the Bible which is a Book of Revelation, and 2) nature, which is His Book of Creation. He does not want us to slight either one. Yet the sad situation is that, in general, one major human tradition (the scientific community) is studying the second and despising the first, and another human tradition (the church community) is studying the first and ignoring the second. Yet, both are essential in understanding God and His will ... The Bible itself affirms the second, "The heavens declare the glory of God and the firmament displays His handiwork (and) there is no speech or language where their voice is not heard."[13]

In many ways, this holistic view of Christian thought was an outworking of Winter's own expanding studies. He attended seven different schools (including Cal Tech, Columbia, Cornell, and Princeton Seminary), and earned degrees in civil engineering, teaching English as a second language, linguistics, anthropology, mathematical statistics, and finally theology.

While at Princeton, Winter discovered the work of Kenneth Scott Latourette, the respected mission historian at Yale. When he later returned in more depth to Latourette's works, he was enthralled. Latourette captured an amazing amount of information in what was eventually eighty books. Winter loved the fact that as he chronicled the expansion of Christianity he

---

11 Ibid., 4.
12 Roberta Winter, "Winter Initiatives," 7.
13 Ralph D. Winter, "Ten Frontiers of Perspective" (seminar, August 20, 1999; revised January 21, 2003), 8.

described the impact of Christianity on cultures and how those cultures impacted Christian thought.

> Winter began to teach church history at Fuller, though he preferred to call it "the expansion of Christianity." Whatever he called it, Winter's class was engaging. One student recalled: In his first lecture he picked up the chalk and drew the cross of Christ in the middle of the blackboard. He said, "Let's not start the history of Christianity in 32 A.D." He walked to the farthest left hand corner of the blackboard, which stretched across the entire wall behind him, and he said, "Let's start with Abraham." And he wrote the year 2000 B.C. on the blackboard. "What is this!" I thought. Then Dr. Winter made the connection between Abraham and Jesus Christ's Great Commission, and then he connected all the history of the Bible and all of the Psalms into one unity of the Bible, "I will bless you and you will be a blessing to all the families of the earth." I had never heard of the Bible as a single story, and never heard anyone suggest a unity based on the Great Commission that began with God's call to Abraham, "blessed to be a blessing." Then Dr. Winter said, "This course is about what God did with the Bible in history."[14]

Then Winter would teach "the expanding story" up to current events.

So that the School of World Mission could offer a PhD, they needed a professional association and a journal. Winter therefore helped found both the American Missiological Society and the *Missiology* journal, both of which still thrive.

One of Winter's best-known legacies, one that expresses the holistic passion by which he saw life, is the study course (and book) called *Perspectives on the World Christian Movement*. Each week a different instructor exposes students to a broad range of experiences, ideas, and insights, building off material in that week's reading. Some students are still in high school, while others are senior citizens, businessmen or businesswomen, or people in full-time ministry. In 2011 almost ten thousand students took the course at over two hundred locations.

Winter believed in lifelong learning. A little box from Amazon.com, sometimes not so little, would show up at his home every other day or so. The box would contain books on science, history, and other subjects. Over one three-month period, when Winter was eighty-three, he acquired sixty new books this way! The rate was about a book every other day for many years.

Winter strongly believed it was not enough just to study or know the Bible; we also had to study the world around us. While his study of science dated at least to his Caltech days, it took on a new flavor when Roberta was diagnosed with multiple myeloma in 1996. In the process of research and treatment, he began to reflect more deeply on theological issues related to the work of God and Satan in the world. He questioned whether some standard views of God and evil were really biblical, and tried to fit his theological understanding (however speculatively) better with recent discoveries in science.

---

14 Email from Bob Blincoe to the author on August 31, 2010, 1–2.

Winter wondered if the conventional interpretation of Genesis 1 was correct in his article, "The Embarrassingly Delayed Education of Ralph D. Winter":

> Eight years after Wheaton's decision, the widely respected department chair of Old Testament Studies at Dallas Theological Seminary, Merrill Unger, went into print (*Bibliotheca Sacra*, 1958) with a highly unconventional view of Genesis 1:1,2, namely, that Genesis 1:1 was a new beginning not THE beginning, that is, Genesis Chapter 1 is the beginning of *the human story* and not the beginning of *the universe*.[15]

Noticing that predators first appeared in the Cambrian Period, Winter wondered if evil spiritual powers were already at that stage involved in nature:

> Has the slow progression of increasingly complex life forms been the work of obedient angels—while the violent, predatory life forms have been the contrary effect of angels whose rebellion caused the distortion and violence first appearing in the Cambrian Period? Is that why, when Satan appeared much later in the Garden, he already had a lengthy "crime record"? Was his "fall" when the Cambrian Period began 500 million years earlier, thus explaining the unremitting destruction, suffering and wildly diverse, violent animal life for the next 500 million years?[16]

Winter was working towards a perspective that would challenge Christians who merely accepted "fate" or were too quickly resigned to "God's mysterious will" to see the hand of Satan as something they could actively resist.

> If this scenario is by any chance correct, then there is clearly no contradiction between the Bible and the latest thinking of contemporary paleontology and paleoneurology … The simplest forms of life may very well have begun to appear 4 billion years ago. Then, after 3.5 billion years of angelic labor and intensive learning prior to the Cambrian Explosion, the labor of angels who were all good, (and, under God's guidance, tinkering with DNA) life forms would develop to a threshold where already larger animals (not vicious nor predatory) would finally appear.[17]

Winter said he believed that God could have created the universe in an instant, and that it could have been created to look older than it was. But he asked, "Why would he?" This kind of speculation impacted our theology and how we live out our faith. He looked askance at the common perspective that malevolent evil is part of God's direct or "decreed" will. His

---

15   Ralph D. Winter, "The Embarrassingly Delayed Education of Ralph D. Winter," 1. The reference about Genesis is from Merrill F. Unger, "Rethinking the Genesis Account of Creation," *Bibliotheca Sacra* 115 (January–March 1958): 27–35; Merrill F. Unger, *Unger's Bible Handbook* (Chicago: Moody Press, 1967).

16   Ibid., 2.

17   Ibid., 3–4.

theory attempted to address the concerns of non-Christians who couldn't believe in a God who allows so much evil.

Winter would say, "We can praise God *in* all things but not rejoice and praise God *for* all things. We can be confident and rest in the idea that with God, 'all things work together for good' [Rom 8:28 KJV], without believing that all things are his initiative."

> This scenario is the very opposite of sitting back and assuming that God does all things both good and bad. Rather, it explains the urgent and momentous obligation to distinguish evil from good and to fight all evil and every evil with everything in our command (not just using First Century knowledge).

> This includes healing the sick, rescuing those who are suffering for any reason, preventing disease and malice, and eliminating or eradicating sources of evil and disease. It requires us to engage meaningfully in the global battle against human slavery, corruption in government and private enterprise, family breakdown and so forth.[18]

Even many on Winter's staff, wondered how this new thinking fit with reaching people with the gospel. He explained, "You don't have to agree with me," and "This is not an official USCWM position." Many of his documents are specifically noted as being speculative or inquisitive and not intended to communicate that he had the answer or that this was his final position on these issues.

Certainly this new concern was partly inspired by Roberta's suffering and death. Bruce Koch, curriculum specialist with the Perspectives program, replied to an entry in the twenty-four-hour prayer room log which Winter had made:

> If we are to see a movement of Christ followers within every people, we have to address the basic question of "what keeps them from accepting and following God?" The struggle for the revelation of the glory of God to the nations involves a lot of things. We want people to know his power, his creativity, his wisdom, his compassion, his mercy, his justice, etc. But for many, no matter how much we extol the excellences of our God, the question remains, "If God is sovereign and loving, why is there so much evil and suffering in the world?" Bottom line— people will not give their allegiance to God unless they are convinced he is good.

> So my answer is simply this: If we are serious about closure … then we have to tackle the fundamental question of evil. I am convinced that Dr. Winter's musings are contributing a great deal more than any of us realize to the completion of the Great Commission discipling mandate and the wider mandate to engage in the battle against Satan and his minions in order to reveal [God's] glory to all peoples.[19]

---

18   Ibid., 5–6.
19   Bruce Koch's reply to Dr. Winter's entry in the prayer log, June 30, 2005.

As Paul Smith said in chapter 2 about Dr. Brand, since Winter's death on May 20, 2009, I have often asked myself, "What would Winter do or say?" Perhaps I was overly influenced by him. While I didn't always agree with the way he tried to get things done, I disagreed with few of his ideas about missions or science or even theology. Some were just theories. And while I just finished a PhD researching Winter's life and early missiology, I haven't read all of what he wrote!

Missionary physicians like Brand work to restore human bodies and spirits as a witness to God's original creation and in the hope of his ultimate restoration of all things. One could ask: Why should missionaries care that men and women have a limb amputated? What difference does that make to their eternal souls? Dr. Winter also believed that God is interested in more than just "salvation" in the sense of how to get to heaven. Missions is the story of God—including mysteries not revealed, and the mystery revealed in Jesus Christ. And it is the story of human beings being restored and reconnected to our Creator.

Ralph Winter thus "studiously applied" his (allegedly) "modest ingenuity" over a long and productive career, until his death in 2009. I have learned a great deal from him.

–FOUR–

MARX, THE MOB, AND MISSIONS

BILL PREVETTE

Bill Prevette is a missionary with the Assemblies of God (USA) and has worked internationally with youth and children at risk since 1985. His ministry began in urban Los Angeles with youth involved in gang-related activity. He and his family moved to Southeast Asia in 1989. They have lived and worked in Thailand, Cambodia, and Romania. Bill completed his PhD at the Oxford Centre for Mission Studies and now lives in Oxford, UK where he serves as a research tutor in practitioner research, mentoring doctoral candidates from Asia, Africa, Latin America, and Eastern Europe. Bill also continues to work internationally with young leaders, churches, and faith-based organizations focusing on Child Theology and human trafficking. He is the author of *Child, Church and Compassion: Towards Child Theology in Romania*.

© 2012 Bill Prevette

Cambodia can be beautiful, if you walk along the dusty paths at sunrise. Majestic stratocumulus clouds march across the horizon. Rice paddies reflect an iridescent green that shimmers in the sideways light. Tall, isolated palm trees punctuate the sky. Working as the director for a large faith-based agency in Cambodia during the late 1990s, I found the beauty of the dawn seem to fade in the sun and spread its scorching heat onto what was still a terribly shattered country. Cambodia remained scarred by Pol Pot's Killing Fields and the genocide of the late 1970s. The Vietnamese then invaded and occupied the country for a decade, but did little to rebuild the country. Hundreds of thousands of unexploded land mines still remained buried in those peaceful-looking fields. I often met children begging in local markets who were missing legs and arms, their innocence lost to a past that literally refused to remain buried. The beauty was fragile.

In Cambodia I would experience chaos and instability that reflected my own also-troubled past. I had arrived with great hopes of helping to change the situation in the country, but it was through Cambodia's chaos that I came to better understand the faith to which God calls us, and the fact that faith seeking understanding often means embracing struggle and uncertainty.

Our agency had built a number of primary schools, two children's homes, three health care clinics, an English learning center, and a small Bible college. With all the needs around me, I began to work seventy, even eighty, hours a week in a highly stressful environment. By the summer of 1997 our family was desperately in need of a break, so we made plans to leave for a few days of rest and relaxation in Thailand. We made arrangements to catch the afternoon flight to Bangkok on July 3.

That morning Fred, a Filipino coworker from the Bible college, ran through our gates, pale and frightened. "Tanks are coming into the city! It looks like they are coming to attack the government offices!" I assured him that this must be another day of routine government demonstrations. The whistle of incoming artillery silenced my comments as tank rounds landed near our home. The sharp report of small firearms was heard in all directions as soldiers advanced on armed government buildings. Phnom Penh was soon engulfed in a firefight between troops loyal to the government and those seeking violent change. Three days of fighting destroyed much of the inner city, demolished newly built businesses on the city's outskirts, and ruined rekindled hopes of national reconstruction. Though I could not foresee it, this chaotic event also set the stage for a deep and much-needed healing in my emotional and spiritual life.

I was an unlikely person to be representing the gospel of Jesus in Cambodia. My childhood had left me with interior land mines of a different sort. My attempts to build life over unstable emotional terrain had, in the past, led me into some dark places. God had radically intervened in my life, but transformation proved a gradual and painful process.

SEPARATION FROM FAMILY

I don't remember my biological father. He had been a cardiac surgeon and died of a heart attack at a young age. My mother earned a minimal salary working as a nurse while raising my brother and me in Winston-Salem, North Carolina. She would not accept help from her siblings who offered to assist her financially, saying stoically, "Every tub has to sit on its own bottom." Eventually, financial constraints and a violent incident with one of our caregivers convinced Mom that her two boys needed more supervision than she could provide. She reluctantly placed us in the Children's Home of North Carolina on June 10, 1963. I was nine years old.

The Children's Home was founded in 1909 by the United Methodist Church of North Carolina to care for boys and girls in need. When we arrived, there were about three hundred children from five to eighteen living at the home. We were divided into "cottages" by age; my brother and I were separated from this point on. The environment was one of strict discipline and a strong work ethic.

My memories of the home are mixed. I had one or two houseparents who were kind and caring, but others were harshly abusive. Religion was "stuffed down our throats" as we were required to attend various church services. The first time a houseparent physically beat me with a belt he said, "Jesus loves you and you need this." I developed serious doubts about church and religion. Salvation of a sort was offered through a fourth-grade teacher who saw I was troubled and encouraged me to read and write. This dear lady had the patience to tutor me after school, and she nurtured a love of books and knowledge that has seen me through to this day.

But reading certain books could also get a kid into trouble in the pre–civil rights South! When I was thirteen years old, I read Harper Lee's *To Kill a Mockingbird* and, like many readers, I was drawn to the courageous and justice-seeking character of Atticus Finch. When I challenged one of my houseparents for making a derogatory remark about African-Americans who lived across town, I got the beating of my life. The next Sunday this same man was up reading the Bible in our church services. I decided then that I did not want anything to do with these bigoted and hypocritical "Christians."

FROM CAMPUS ACTIVIST TO DHARMA BUM

By the time I was fifteen I knew that I had to get away from the Children's Home as quickly as possible. I chafed at the abuse and argued with the authority figures as I worked hard to qualify for a place in university. Two years later I was accepted into the University of North Carolina at Chapel Hill. The university was an intellectual hub for radicals and popular causes, and I quickly fell in with older students associated with the Students for a Democratic Society (SDS), Vets against the War, and neo-Marxists. It didn't take long for me to become well acquainted with LSD as well.

The values I had been taught and the university counterculture seemed at first to engage in an internal tug-of-war. I declared a premed major, thinking I would become a doctor like my father. But my studies morphed to include interests in political science, philosophy, and chemistry (admittedly, a bad combination for a young and arrogant anarchist in the making!). My reading ranged from biology and physics to Marx, Nietzsche, Sartre, and existential philosophy. As I jettisoned my Methodist upbringing, I developed an interest in Eastern spirituality, reading Allen Ginsberg, Alan Watts, and others who espoused Zen philosophy and Eastern mysticism.

In spite of my intense intellectual curiosity, I became increasingly dissatisfied with formal education and university life. I set out for California thinking I would take a year away from college and return to graduate school after I had seen more of the world. I left Chapel Hill with a fifty-pound backpack and began hitchhiking to the Rocky Mountains. My path intersected that of another "Dharma bum,"[1] as we liked to think of ourselves, and we decided to join forces. By the time Mike and I reached the West Coast we had decided to hike the

---

1   *The Dharma Bums* (New York: Viking Press) is a 1958 novel by beat generation author Jack Kerouac, who had also written *On the Road*, which my generation found inspirational.

Pacific Crest Trail from northern California to Canada. We set up preplanned food drops at specific locations where interstate highways intersected the "Trail," and spent the better part of five months hiking and climbing one of the most amazing pieces of real estate in North America. We shared many good books over the miles; *Walden* and *Civil Disobedience* by Henry David Thoreau were two of our favorites. Mike also introduced me to *The Hobbit* and *Lord of the Rings* (it is just as well that I had no clue that J. R. R. Tolkien was a Christian).

Our mutual interest in Zen spirituality inspired us to take a vow of "poverty, simplicity, and chastity." This was no small feat for a couple of twenty-two-year-old kids in the mid-1970s. The rhetoric of the counterculture and antiwar movement was giving way to the emergence of the conspicuous consumerism and licentiousness that would define the "baby-boomer generation" for the next several decades. The mountains shielded us from the burgeoning tidal wave of materialism—at least for a while.

We finished our trek as the first snows of autumn were dusting the Canadian peaks. During our many campfire dinners together, Mike shared his dream of building a forty-foot oceangoing sailboat and asked me to help him construct the boat and fund the project. All the adventures in the world seemed within reach and the only answer I could imagine was "Why not!?" We went different directions to earn some necessary cash; Mike went to the Yukon with its wealthy gas and timber resources, and I found work in Big Sky, Montana as a climbing and skiing guide. We met up the following summer in Victoria, British Columbia. Together we built Mike's forty-foot trimaran and to get the boat seaworthy, we conducted sailing trials around Vancouver Island. Mike set off to circumnavigate the globe later that year. That was the last I heard from him, but he left me with the realization that if I wanted to build my own boat and sail around the world, I could.

I moved north to the Queen Charlotte Islands of Canada to build custom sailing yachts and I worked as a lumberjack. The following winter I worked on the Alaska Pipeline. As with most of the work I was beginning to enjoy, it was highly lucrative. My Zen commitment to "simplicity" faded as I joined the rush for more material goods. My emerging ambitions included becoming a millionaire by the age of thirty, owning a custom home near a major ski resort and, for good measure, building my own offshore racing yacht. I had a dogged perseverance to work hard to accomplish my goals, and my life was now shaped by pure hedonism, adrenaline, and exhilaration. If anyone had asked me what I thought about God at this point in my life, I would have said, "I don't believe in God; but if there is a god, he helps those who help themselves to ALL they can get!"

PIRATES OF THE CARIBBEAN

Then a woman named Ky entered my life. I met this lady, in some ways my opposite, while working at the Alyeska Ski Resort not far from Anchorage, Alaska. She had grown up in a normal Californian family, loved horses and other animals, and had a compassionate, if not somewhat naive, nature. Although when we met she was still healing from a broken relationship and I had little room in my heart for commitments to anyone other than myself, I was drawn to her goodness and must have sensed that she had something I was missing. After a period of serious flirtation, we began living together, as was common for couples of our generation. She dreamed of building a romantic relationship and a shared life with me while I continued on my personal quest for acquisitions.

I heard that a former acquaintance had established a business designing and building racing yachts in the Caribbean. Contacting him resulted in an exotic new phase of our lives and a change of latitude. While I perceived advantages to living along a "cocaine and cash highway" of islands that stretched from South America to Florida, Ky thought tropical paradise would be a nice change from the cold, dark Alaskan winters. We relocated to lush Saint Vincent of the Grenadines to build ourselves a boat. But my intensity and workaholic habits blinded me to the natural beauty around us. I became obsessed with the task at hand and showed little consideration for my coworkers or Ky. I became a screaming control freak. I yelled and cursed at the men working in the boatyard, often berated them, and threatened to throw them off the job. In hindsight, it was a wonder one of them did not put a knife in my back.

Even after we finally launched our beautiful, custom-built, forty-foot sailboat—*Dragonfly*—I was dissatisfied and wanted more. I began to meet people who were involved in moving guns, money, and drugs through the Caribbean. I plotted how to find the money to build a sixty-foot yacht and got acquainted with the men who had the means and materials to make this happen. Ky finally gave up on her dreams, left me to my own devices, and returned home to California.

DARKENING OF THE DREAM

Ancient mariners often labeled the margins of their known world by writing on maps, "Here there be monsters!" I began sailing *Dragonfly* toward my own far edges (and monsters) when I began offering charters around the Caribbean. Saint Martin provided a good base for operations, as it was a playground for the rich and famous from Europe and the East Coast of the United States. I made connections with unethically wealthy people and learned how to set up "front businesses" for laundering money. I flew in and out of Miami and offered to move any commodity or product for a price. I thought I had hit the "big time." Lyrics from one of my favorite Jimmy Buffett songs sum up this phase of my life fairly accurately: "I made enough money to buy Miami, but I pissed it away so fast." The more I consumed, the greater became my addiction to hedonism and power.

In the summer of 1982 I helped sail a classic *Sparkman & Stephens* yacht, let us call her *Mystic*, from the Caribbean to Martha's Vineyard. The yacht was due for a major overhaul at a shipyard there, and its owner, "Vinny," who treasured it greatly, flew to Europe and left me in charge.

As you might imagine, the logistics of lifting a twenty-ton yacht out of the water are complex and expensive. On this occasion we had a disaster; the marine railway malfunctioned and the lifting equipment failed. To our horror, the shipyard owner and I watched *Mystic* plunge from the shipping cradle into Vineyard Haven Harbor. She sank to a depth of fifteen feet; her magnificent interior, electronics, engine, and period furnishings fully saturated and altogether ruined by the salt water.

On receiving news of this calamity, "Vinny" immediately flew to the scene and was murderous with rage; no financial settlement would quench his Italian temper. I felt as if I had become a character in *Good Fellas* or *The Sopranos*. It became clear this situation was unraveling and someone was going to be seriously hurt. It dawned on my cocaine-saturated brain that if I continued in this lifestyle, I was likely to end up either with a bullet behind the ear or spending the rest of life looking over my shoulder. I needed to find a way out of this situation, or there would be no turning back.

Desperately racking my brain for solutions, I remembered the words of a mature and sober friend: "Bill, with your willingness to work hard, you can build a good career and make plenty of money legitimately. You don't need to bend the rules to be successful." For some reason Bob had shown an interest in my life from our first meeting in 1977. I called Bob from Vineyard Haven, told him of my fears, and asked his advice. His answer was quick and to the point. "Get yourself on the first plane you can! I think you know where this is headed. For God's sake, use your head—come here and we will talk." This time I listened.

Bob's invitation was the "ticket out of Dodge" I needed. I told my "friends" that I was going to take a few days to go to the West Coast and clear my head. I had no idea if I would be back, but I knew I had to get away from this scene and was glad to get out of this situation in one piece. I flew to Seattle, where Bob welcomed me into his home. He offered me honest employment remodeling one of his factory warehouses. He told me I would be working alongside a concrete contractor. Since the opportunity gave me "safe, mundane" space to sort out my next move, I gratefully took the job.

A STRANGE LETTER AND NEW FRIEND

Occasionally during these stressful months, I called Ky. She had been chasing her own monsters, living in a New Age community in the Santa Cruz Mountains of California, experimenting with mental telepathy and psychic massage. Ky had always been drawn to spiritual encounters, but as far as I was concerned, all religion and spirituality, no matter what the source, was a sham. On our last call she said she had "found Jesus."

I scoffed and ridiculed her. "Sure, everybody finds Jesus—just check out your local jail—but what difference does it make to any of them?" I ended the call in anger. In my experience, Christians were hypocritical, deceived simpletons who wouldn't think for themselves. But despite my ridicule, Ky began to pray that I too would have a reckoning with the living God.

Shortly after arriving in Seattle, a letter came from Ky. She had sent it to Martha's Vineyard, the last known address she had for me, and it had been forwarded. I was surprised to hear from her, and opening the letter brought additional consternation as it was written in a language that sounded strange to my ears:

Praise God, Hallelujah! How are you, Bill? We were in church tonight and our pastor gave a word of knowledge. He said, "Someone is praying for a man named Bill and he is going to come to know Christ through a man named Bob." I was so excited to hear this because several of us are praying for you regularly. I don't know what is going on with you, but I believe that our friend Bob is going to have an influence on your life for Christ. Are you planning a trip to see Bob in Seattle? Our church is going to keep praying for you because you need God's love and grace.

What bizarre code was this? I knew Ky was involved in something she described as a "Bible-believing, Pentecostal church." Weren't these the people who handle snakes and speak in strange tongues? The letter made no sense. Ky was in Marin County, California; neither of us had seen Bob in years or spoken of him in our intermittent phone conversations. The letter was dated the day before *Mystic* sank. How could prayer make any difference to anybody or anything? How did Ky know I was going to Seattle before I did? And what in the world was a "word of knowledge"? These were strange words indeed. I surmised that Ky's psychic practices were bearing fruit.

Sitting in Bob's living room, I cautiously showed him the letter. Bob is a quiet and committed Catholic. His response did little to discredit Ky or vindicate me: "Bill, the providence of God is sometimes difficult to understand." I was determined to know if Ky had joined a cult. Maybe I should fly to San Francisco to get her out of this "Assembly of God" sect. I booked a ticket for the following Friday.

That week I met Lee, a concrete contractor hired to engineer the new floor structure for the factory warehouse. Lee was a giant of man and he worked like a human locomotive; he was able to carry 150 pounds of plywood on one shoulder while climbing a ladder. Yet he seemed intensely happy, with a deep laugh that matched his stature. I asked him if he was using some form of drugs. He laughed and said he had something better than drugs, but didn't tell me his secret.

Our days together doing concrete work were physically demanding with long, hard hours digging earth, building forms, and tying heavy steel bar with wire to support the concrete. Lee and his crew worked at an amazing pace; it was hard to keep up with them. Unlike many general contractors where swearing and verbal abuse is common, I noticed that Lee treated the men on his crew like family. They seemed to have a genuine bond on the job, using their coffee and meal breaks for quiet conversation. What was going on with these men?

AN ENCOUNTER WITH "THE LEAST OF THESE"

One afternoon Lee asked me to join him for lunch. We climbed into his large truck, but instead of heading for the restaurant, Lee drove into one of the rougher areas of downtown Seattle. Before I realized what he was up to, he had parked the truck next to several drunken men lying on the street and was offering to take them to lunch with us.

"What are you doing? These guys are a damn mess!" I shouted.

"God loves these people, and so do I. We are going to help them," Lee replied in a matter-of-fact tone.

"Are you nuts? If God loves these people, he sure picked a lousy way to show them," I snapped back.

Lee's response was completely unexpected. He grabbed me by the lapels of my coat and stood me up in the street. For the first time in my life, I looked into the eyes of true righteous indignation. "Hey, you don't know God, so don't tell me what God loves." He finished loading the men into his pickup, and we headed to the Seattle Union Gospel Mission where they received a hot lunch. I was stunned, but I was not about to give in gracefully to Lee's claims of faith.

I lectured Lee on Nietzsche's theory of power and Marx's assessment of poverty. Lee responded simply with Jesus, the Apostle Paul, and God's love, quoting Saint Matthew and the book of Romans. He obviously knew the Bible well. Our intense discussion continued throughout the afternoon. As I became more and more angry and frustrated, Lee continued to insist that God loved everyone, especially the broken—and he audaciously asserted that God loved me! It was like arguing with a wall. Lee's faith was firm and he had the lifestyle to attest to his convictions; I was beginning to fear I had met a "true believer."

The next days were spent arguing steadily while pouring ninety yards of concrete. Lee was resolute. I said it was impossible for human beings to even know if there was a God, let alone know him personally. Lee countered with these remarkable words: "Bill, you *can* know if God is real, but you have to ask him to show you in a way that you will understand. If you are willing to ask God with sincerity, then I believe you too can know God and his Son, Jesus Christ."

I was furious at his certainty. How could anyone know God? Lee's claims sounded as farfetched as Ky's! I pulled her letter from my hip pocket and handed it to Lee. After slowly reading the letter, he looked up at me with a huge grin on his face. "Praise God, brother. God is working in your life. Don't you see it? You are not here by accident!"

I felt hemmed in by Jesus fanatics. Boarding my flight to San Francisco later that Friday night, I was on a mission to get Ky out of this cult she called a church. As she drove me from the airport to a special evening service, I did not share all that had taken place in Seattle. I let her think I was in full agreement to attend the service, but I was forming a twisted plan in my head. I had been to enough church services as a child to know how these meetings operated. Someone, usually the pastor, would speak and then ask people to come forward and "receive Jesus as their Lord and Savior." At that point in the meeting, I would walk to the front of the church, knock the pastor to the ground and tell those gathered in the building what idiots they were to be listening to this drivel.

DIVINE INTERVENTION

The church service was as I imagined: lots of enthusiastic singing and hallelujahs, energetic preaching, and finally the expected "altar call" for sinners to pray and repent. As people began to move forward, I took the opportunity to carry out my plan, joining the swarm of passionate seekers at the front of the sanctuary. I waited patiently for the pastor to stand before me so I could make my move. As he stepped into position, the preacher looked me straight in the eye and said with calm boldness, "Young man, you are playing games with God, but God sees your heart, and he is not playing games with you." He then turned and moved on.

If I could have moved my arms at that moment, I think I would have torn the man's head off his shoulders! Instead, I felt as if my entire body was locked in place. I was shaking with anger, but I could not lift my arms. What was happening to me? I felt embarrassed and confused. I wanted to run from the building, but the best I could do was shuffle back to my seat and stare at the floor. "This place has to be a cult; there is no natural explanation for what has just happened to me," I thought.

During the remainder of the extended weekend visit, Ky took every opportunity to immerse me in her newfound faith. There were other church meetings, a Full Gospel Businessmen's breakfast, the Sunday church service, and even Christian stations playing over her car radio. I kept calling Ky a "Jesus fanatic." I was introduced to a number of men who gladly dialogued with me regarding their theories of God. Many had experienced the counterculture of San Francisco in the 1960s and shared stories similar to mine. They had a different approach than my friend Lee; they formulated their arguments from the words of Christian philosophers like C. S. Lewis, Francis Schaeffer, G. K. Chesterton, and A. W. Tozer. I felt I could relate to them intellectually. We debated for hours about the concept of "reasonable faith." Was it possible to have experience, knowledge, and a rational encounter with the living God revealed in Christ? These men said it was. Through their voices, I kept hearing Lee's challenge back in Seattle: "Bill, you can know if God is real, but you have to ask him to show you in a way that you will understand."

Finally, on Sunday afternoon I came to a breaking point. With my fists in the air, I challenged God. Not knowing what else to do, I shouted to the heavens, "None of this has ever worked for me! If you are real, then show me in a way I can understand, and I will believe that Jesus is the Son of God; otherwise, I just can't believe in something I don't understand!"

At that moment, I experienced two things as never before: first, a kindness and love enveloped me that was overwhelming; second, a sense of conviction or remorse that I did not think was possible. I fell to the ground and began to weep like a child. I felt as if I was watching my life play out in slow motion before me. My eyes and heart were opened to my wrong thinking, wrong decisions, wrong actions, and wrong words that had caused pain to so many. I became aware of my own deep needs and wounds that I had never fully acknowledged. I was swept away by the holiness and love of God. Months later, as I became more familiar with Scripture, I would identify with an experience Paul mentions: "I know a man who, fourteen years ago, was seized by Christ and swept in ecstasy to the heights of heaven. I really don't know if this took place in the body or out of it; only God knows" (2 Cor 12:2,3 *The Message*).

I remained on the floor of Ky's apartment and wept for several hours. She became concerned; over the years she had become familiar with my anger, but she did not know what to make of my ongoing tears. She trundled me into her VW bug and sought help at the church's Sunday evening prayer meeting. The associate pastor led me in prayer and on Sunday, October 24, 1982, I was ushered into the kingdom of God. With the deepest part of my being I knew that Jesus had become a reality in my life. The knowledge of the Holy was now burning in my soul. God had been revealed as my Father, and he accepted me as a son who had finally recognized home.

REBIRTH

When I tell this story, I am often asked, "How did you go from this conversion experience to becoming a missionary, and then a doctoral research tutor in Oxford?" Perhaps, one day, that story will become a book on its own, but for now I will trace some of the highlights.

Ky and I were discipled and nurtured by a strong local church community (yes, the same church where I plotted to assault the pastor). I was encouraged to spend time formally studying the Bible. Eager to do something meaningful with my spare time, I began to volunteer at Teen Challenge, working with at-risk youth who were addicted to drugs and other life-controlling problems. Tough, troubled young people were easy for me to relate to! I found I had much to offer those who were good at pushing the limits and had not learned to work with systems of authority. Teen Challenge introduced me to ministry in the urban context and nurtured a budding interest in community development work.

Our church also had a strong commitment to global missions and often invited missionaries to speak. I will never forget meeting Dr. Mark Buntain, a Pentecostal missionary who had spent thirty years working with the poor in Calcutta. His life exuded a passion for the good news of Christ; it was a passion demonstrated in the full giving of his life to others. Similar to Saint Francis, he preached the gospel at all times and when necessary used words. I was attracted to the integration of medical care and education, social and civic engagement in his ministry. Missionary stories inspired me; I wanted to experience the power of the gospel in cultures different from my own.

Within a year of coming to faith, Ky and I married and accepted an invitation to work short term with a missionary in Southeast Asia. He led a number of programs helping youth on the streets in Indonesia and Malaysia. I read every mission biography I could find and vigorously pursued the formal study of mission, earning an MA in international development from Fuller Theological Seminary. I discovered the writings of Dr. Ralph Winter, a historian and missiologist. Winter gave me new insights into mission structures, the role of the church in shaping history, and a new appreciation for the social dynamics of mission. His words, along with others who worked in international development, deepened my desire to work in holistic mission, serving children and youth at risk.

We relocated to Thailand in 1989 to work as missionaries. I gained new insight by reading *Pain: The Gift Nobody Wants*, coauthored by Phillip Yancey and Dr. Paul Brand. I was working in a large Bangkok slum at the time; it was home to thousands of people. Many young children tried to earn a meager living by selling cheap candy and flowers on the crowded streets. I wanted to honor God and I had committed myself to serving the poor, but I grappled with the pain and injustice around us. I struggled to see God working in and through such neglected lives and painful situations. Often, as I worked along the fetid canals of the slum, I wondered if the work we were doing was having any meaningful impact. Brand and Yancey's book helped lead me to a deeper awareness of God's grace in difficult places.

The quarter century since my conversion has taught me that faith is the pursuit of understanding, not only in some abstract intellectual sense, not merely by reading and thinking, but working in concrete ways that honor God. This comes in praying, serving alongside the poor and exploited, preaching the gospel in both word and deed, and rebuilding communities. Ky and I have lived in five nations and worked in twenty. We have built or administrated health clinics, churches, schools, and small colleges. I currently serve as a research tutor at the Oxford Centre for Mission Studies. In seeking to know God we have been led by him to put faith into action and work for the transformation of individual people and society at large. But I have learned that the "gift of pain" is an integral component in understanding God's ways.

PAIN AND UNDERSTANDING

When I began this chapter, I said the chaos of Cambodia taught me about embracing uncertainty. During the military coup in July of 1997, five thousand foreigners were evacuated from Phnom Penh. I remained in Cambodia at the request of our agency and was placed under house arrest for a number of days. Work and ministry suddenly ceased and I fell into the arms of God, experiencing the symptoms of burnout, and learning another lesson about "faith seeking understanding."

As you may have gathered, my conversion experience was not the only aspect of my life that embodied radical commitment. I engaged most challenges with intensity and passion. Conversion did not bring instant clarity to the motives that had driven me to pursue recognition and success. I dove headlong into missions, not taking adequate time to contemplate my interior pain and "shadows," or to seek the Holy Spirit's revelation. With the benefit of hindsight, Anne Dillard's warning about "monster shadows of the soul," that is to say, illusions that control our lives, makes a great deal of sense to me now.

God used the coup to bring my frantic pace of work to a screeching halt. House arrest forced me into a time of silence and stillness. I sensed God showing me that my driven lifestyle had become a mask for unresolved pain. My obsessive patterns expressed a longing and concern for image more than character. God invited me to embrace this pain rather than run from it.

Embracing personal pain and the pain of others lies, I think, at the heart of Anselm's concept of "faith seeking understanding." We must allow ourselves to meaningfully encounter the suffering that is so central to the human condition. But action is not enough; contemplation and reflection are needed to unmask the illusions that keep our pain hidden. In confronting interior "shadows," I found the strength to move through them. For years I had carried the haunting feeling that I was never doing enough. Recognizing this as a "shadow of the soul," I came to understand that addiction to work had to do with a faulty understanding of God and his unconditional love for me as a person. This discovery of truth led to a rebirth of intimacy with God, family, and community. I made a commitment to live more openly and transparently while embracing the struggles of my heart, mind, and soul.

"Faith seeking understanding" invites us to ask hard questions when grappling with God. Living in faith is messy, and we may never get all the answers. I still don't completely understand why my mother experienced so much heartache and had to put us in a children's home, why people claiming to bear the name of Christ abused me, or why Cambodian children lost limbs from buried land mines. However, I have learned that life in the kingdom of God is not so much about certitude as about fidelity.

As we live in faith, we learn to embrace pain, puzzlement, and promise. Our understanding of God is limited, fragile, subject to our fallen nature and our proclivity to make mistakes. "We see through a glass, darkly" (1 Cor 13:12 KJV). Should we expect to experience seasons of doubt and perplexity after becoming a Christian? I now believe these seasons are normative for those wanting to know God with both heart and mind. We must experience some confusion for faith to grow. Ambiguity and mystery are intrinsic to the human condition and develop our yearning to make sense of the world. We learn, through our shared faith, the reality that everything in human existence—including our love for God, one another, and children—is colored to some degree by human ambiguity. The more we love, the more our faith is vulnerable to the reality that not all is well with the present world (Jer 45).

Cambodia taught me the importance of contemplation and reflection. I thank God for the "gift of pain" we experienced there. When we moved to Romania, I decided to pursue a PhD investigating the factors that motivate people of faith to engage with children and youth in crisis. That work helped shape some of the ideas I have described here. When faith authentically seeks understanding, one can expect to experience sacred space, what the Celts used to call "thin places," where we are cast more fully into God's grace. Living in the kingdom of God means being prepared to live with some temporary chaos. There we learn to appreciate the value of uncertainty, paradox, and confusion. Even in our "understanding," we are constantly surprised and disturbed by the work of God.

PART II:
CHRIST IN CULTURE

–FIVE–

EGG FLOWER SOUP AND CHERRY BLOSSOMS: A WOMAN'S LIFE GLIMPSED THROUGH WORLD RELIGIONS

MIRIAM ADENEY

Miriam Adeney is professor of global and urban ministries at Seattle Pacific University and teaching fellow at Regent College. She is the author of *Daughters of Islam; God's Foreign Policy: Practical Ways to Help the World's Poor, A Time for Risking: Priorities for Women, How to Write: A Christian Writer's Guide*, and *Kingdom Without Borders: The Untold Story of Global Christianity.*

BUILDING BRIDGES WITH MUSLIM WOMEN

Egg flower soup. Crab cakes. Garlic shrimp. Cashew chicken. Lychees in syrup. When I met my husband, the world of Chinese dinners opened to me. His parents had married in China in the 1930s and had three children there. They departed under duress in 1950. But in their hearts they never left. The rest of their lives were spent among Chinese in Hong Kong, Singapore, and Berkeley, California. Whenever I was with them, whether in the U.S., in Asia, or even in Europe, we were immersed in a Chinese community—and Chinese dinners. Whatever continent we inhabited, we migrated to those round tables draped with red cloths and surrounded by convivial noise and the aroma of egg flower soup.

I was raised not in Asia but in Oregon, in a Christian family that practiced stewardship, service, and witness. Anthropology drew me into a PhD. Ever since then, I have been teaching, writing, and consulting, a calling that has taken me to five continents. World Religions is one course I have taught for decades. Yet I have never set down my notes in writing. In this essay, I will try to remedy that, to weave a few of those notes with a little of my life.

All religions contain glimpses of beauty and truth, I believe. Yet the good news that the Creator of the cosmos has come close to us personally and transformingly in Jesus is something more. The appendix lists some bridges to this good news specific to each religion. These are a core component of my course. In this essay I will offer a few more tastes of that course, serving up one theme in each faith that has touched my own life.

BUDDHISM: PAIN

Life hurts. I have suffered my share. Beyond personal losses, I am troubled by global hunger, HIV/AIDS, deaths in childbirth, and the abuse and denial of opportunities suffered by millions. On my mind now are Iranian Christians in prison. One pastor's wife has just agonized through her fourth miscarriage while penned up in a cell. Sometimes the pain of the world seems too much to bear.

Buddhism offers a way forward. If I can see that suffering is pervasive, if I can recognize that it is exacerbated by my own desires, and if I can learn to quench my desires, then peace will come. In a nutshell, this sums up the first three "Noble Truths." My Thai friend Chaiyun Ukosakul, who became a Christian as an adult, summarizes what he was taught: "When I am angry, a tiger grows in my heart. But when I am enlightened, the tiger dies."

Buddhism invites me to let things go. I must not cling to things, or relationships, or truths. I must hold everything in an open hand. It is all passing away anyway. When I was in Indonesia a few years ago, I climbed up a huge stone structure called Borobodor. Built more than a thousand years ago, this monument is as large as a city block. On the lower levels, the stone carvings were intricate, elaborate, lyrical, mellifluous retellings of episodes from the life of the Buddha. As I rose higher, I saw that the carving became sparer, until at the top the decoration was minimal. The closed domed pinnacle is said to contain emptiness. And that is the destination I seek, according to Buddhism. That is my goal as I shuffle off unnecessary desires. When I no longer drag baggage around, how much lighter I will feel.

A decade ago, the Prime Minister of Thailand was named Kukrit Pramoj. He was also a famous novelist. Once he wrote a short Buddhist reflection on the gospel.[1] The main character in Pramoj's story was a blind man named Bartimaus. Every day Bartimaus made his way to the outdoor market, tapping along with his walking stick. There he sat down. Vendors greeted him and dropped a little food in his bowl. Birds sang. Children laughed. A woman named Ruth befriended him, and over time they fell in love.

---

1   Kukrit Pramoj, "The Hell which Heaven Forgot," *Practical Anthropology* 13 (May–June 1966): 129–39.

Then Bartimaus heard that Jesus was coming through town and that Jesus could heal the blind. "Have mercy on me, and heal my eyes!" Bartimaus called out.

Jesus did.

Suddenly Bartimaus' tranquil routine was shattered. He saw the sewage and the flies, the vendors' faces lined with weariness and resentment, the children dressed in rags, their skin pocked with sores. Ruth had been through a terrible fire, he knew. Now he saw the gross burn that oozed where her face should have been, and could not stand to look at her.

Later he saw Jesus crucified. Then he fell to his knees and cried, "Oh God, give me back my blindness!"

This is a Buddhist response to the gospel, according to Kukrit Pramoj. At bottom, life is ugly. It is like a muddy pond. We can't do much about the mud. But we *can* aim to shoot up from the bottom like water lilies and lie clean on the top.

That appeals to me. If there were no God, or if God had not reached out to us, I might be a Buddhist. The faith offers a way to live with some degree of peace in a painful world.

But the amazing news is that there is a God, and he has cared so strongly for us that he chose to walk with dusty feet right to the painful, bloody cross, where he died and later rose in power for us.

This is not tranquility. This is passion. Desire. Love. And it is what makes my own love possible. I cannot manufacture love on my own. But I *can* receive it and pass it on.

Deep in my heart I sense that I am not just a candle flame, or a drop of water, or a temporary psychophysical event, which are common Buddhist metaphors for human beings. Nor do those images describe the people around me. We have lasting value. Jesus told a story to make that point. In this parable a shepherd rounded up ninety-nine sheep. Just one sheep was missing. Yet the shepherd went out into the dark and the cold to search for the one that was lost. That one sheep mattered. Jesus made it clear that every one of us counts. Each person is important.

I think also of a Japanese haiku poet named Issa. Although he had several children, they died, one after another. When the neighbors came to comfort him, they offered a bit of Buddhist philosophy: "After all," they said to Issa, "this is a world of dew."

What did they mean? Dew appears on the grass in the morning, then disappears. Our children arrive, and later they may disappear. None of this should upset us. That's life.

But when Issa was alone, he wrote a poem:

> The world of dew
> Is a world of dew
> And yet! And yet![2]

His children were not dew. They mattered enormously. His grief nearly crushed him. Buddhists are made for love, just like everybody else.

Of all the faiths, Buddhism tempts me. It offers a way to live with dignity in a pretty ugly world. Desires can enslave. Buddhism is right about that. Yet when I open myself to receive

---

2   Michael Griffiths, *Take off Your Shoes* (London: Overseas Missionary Fellowship, 1971), 40.

God's love, a current flows through me that pushes to be passed on to others. I can dare to care. I can invest in relationships. I can make lasting commitments because God has made a lasting commitment to me. Day by day I can be energized to love my family (at least most of the time!), my work, my country, even strangers. This is what I am designed for and it is what I long to do. Although emptiness tempts me, I was made for love.

Still Buddhism calls me beyond glib optimism and cheap cheerfulness, not only to experience God's grace but also to sit in silence with those who suffer and to weep with those who weep.

JAPANESE RELIGION: BEAUTY

In the Willamette Valley, oceans of white and pink fruit orchards waft fragrance into the air. I am visiting my parents in the Oregon town where I grew up. In the fields round about, lambs bounce past grazing mothers, their gangly legs kicking and their flattish tails flopping. A quail scurries across a back road. A bevy of chicks bob in a line behind her. Bees pollinate. Although half a world away, Gerard Manley Hopkins described it well:

> Nothing is so beautiful as spring—
> When weeds, in wheels, shoot long and lovely and lush.
> Thrush's eggs look little low heavens, and thrush
> Through the echoing timber does so rinse and ring
> The ear, it strikes like lightnings to hear him sing.[3]

Such beauty is a theme not only in Hopkins' England and in my Willamette Valley but also in Japanese religion. As I write this in March 2011, an earthquake and tsunami have smashed Japan. Yet the sensitivity to the beauty of nature which is a classic Japanese value will help them regain equilibrium in the hard days ahead.

No culture has emphasized beauty more. Think of gardens, even gardens of gravel and moss. Cherry trees. A few flowers in a vase. The tea ceremony. The arrangement of food on a plate. The graceful movements of the geishas. Amid the combination of traditions that constitute Japanese religion, beauty is a significant component.

Consider *The Tale of Genji*, a foundational piece of literature written over a thousand years ago.[4] Nobel prize-winning speeches, novels and poetry, high school essays, and *manga* all cite *Genji*. It is even commemorated on the two-thousand-yen banknote. In this epic tale, as in much Japanese literature, the transience of beauty provokes lament. *Mono no aware* (the grief of things) refers to our sadness as we realize how fleeting nature's beauty is. Yet this is a cathartic, cleansing, even ennobling sadness. In the presence of beauty, we are roused to long, to ache, to yearn for something more. Briefly we glimpse it. Tragically, we cannot live

---

3   Gerard Manley Hopkins, "Spring," in *Hopkins: Poems and Prose*, ed. Peter Washington (New York: Knopf, 1995), 25.
4   My thoughts on beauty in Japan have been enriched by Roger Lowther, "Beauty through Japanese Eyes: *The Tale of Genji* as a Window to Japan," *Japan Harvest* (Winter 2011): 28–31.

in this beauty because we ourselves introduce ugliness. In the presence of beauty we shiver, pierced by intimations of our preciousness and also of our lostness. Genji dies alone. This happens two-thirds of the way through the book. The rest of the story explores a world where beauty has been lost, like the world after Eden. Reading *The Tale of Genji* as a Christian, Roger Lowther reflects:

> Born the son of the Emperor, [Genji] dies in despair. Moved by the death of this "Shining Prince," I can't but help think of the greatest "Man of Sorrows," the son of the emperor of all emperors, king of all kings, who also died completely alone in the end. If we move too quickly to the resurrection of Jesus, we miss the power and beauty of the image. Just as Jesus wept at the death of his friend Lazarus minutes before raising him from the dead, so we too can find deep heartfelt *mono no aware* in Jesus' suffering. Perhaps the Japanese heart can teach us how to feel the journey of our Savior in a renewed way.[5]

The Tale of Genji intensifies beauty through contrasts, as does other Japanese literature like Matsuo Basho's simple haiku poem:

> By the old pond
> A frog leaps
> The sound of water[6]

Such contrasts wake us up. What about the contrasts in the gospel? Death and life. Brokenness and wholeness. Word made flesh. Strength from weakness. Illumination from jars of clay. A king born in a barn. The Creator of the cosmos choosing to be a baby. "What could be more beautiful than Jesus' light shining into the darkness of Christmas night?" Lowther asks. "What could be more beautiful than life for humanity coming out of the death of the Son of God?"[7] These jarring contrasts can start us moving toward worship of the One who is truly lovely.

I resonate with this because I myself take time for beauty. Near my home is the Edmonds ferry dock. A multistoried white ship, the ferry furrows through the water. Seagulls whirl and dip and caterwaul. Beachcombers stroll. Divers' buoys hint at mysteries beneath. A sailboat flits past. A container ship from Asia muscles through the channel between forested islands on the horizon. Jagged, snow-covered mountains stab the sky in the distance. Soft waves feather the shore nearby. A pleasant briny smell invades my nostrils. A breeze reminds me that this is sweater weather—or raincoat weather.

Coming in, the ferry connotes summer to me, travel to the islands, friends, fun, beaches, water play. Going out, it connotes loss, the irrevocable end of possibilities. But stay here long enough—Look up!—and there it is again. Rhythms recur. That, too, is beautiful. I go to the dock for the beauty, including the yearning that is awakened.

---

5   Ibid., 30.
6   Ibid.
7   Ibid., 31.

HINDUISM: SOUL

From untruth lead me to the truth,
From darkness lead me to the light,
From death lead me to immortality.[8]

Hinduism is complex and confusing. British colonizers helped create it, squeezing many local religions into one orderly system. In *Kingdom without Borders*, my book about global Christianity, I divided contemporary Hindus into three categories: *dharmic*, *Dalit*, and "dot.com." Only the *dharmic* pay much attention to the teachings. Low-caste *Dalits* have little reason to love the doctrines. Yet the faith does own ancient poetic holy books (*Vedas*), historic theologian-philosophers, widely popular religious epics, bodies of worship songs, and a great splash of religious festivals.

Through all these sources a key theme resonates: We are souls. We are not passing phenomena, not candle flames or drops of water. Each of us is eternal. Each of us has a destiny. We are not machines. We are not just consumers or producers. We are souls, born to rise to union with the great Soul. Spirituality is the foundation for everything that exists.

How then can we experience union with God? Perhaps by placing flowers in front of an elephant statue? Or by wandering naked through the street? By reciting Scripture? By worshiping in a trance? By immersion in the Ganges River? By fasting? Or by orgies? Through myriad gods and methods, Hindus pursue God, soul to soul.

Bhakti (devotion to God) may be expressed through songs, quietness, recitation, or other spiritual approaches, usually channeled to a specific god. Christians from such background may have special sensitivities in illumination and inspiration. Practicing the presence of God is a discipline that some of them model. They know how to go deep, how to lose themselves, how to worship. (Of course many Hindus are so rattled by Bollywood that they know little about meditation.)

Karma remains a burden, however. Our virtue must be greater than our faults or we will never progress spiritually. Anger, selfishness, lust, pride, and laziness detonate our store of merit again and again. We live out the myth of Sisyphus, eternally rolling a stone up a mountain. Karma also means that poor, sick, or low-class people may be blamed for their own troubles.

Yet those who have allowed Jesus to take on their *karmic* burden have blessed me.

Their spirituality is a vibrant thing as they worship Jesus—the truth, the light, and the life, the answer to their prayer:

From the untruth lead me to the truth
From darkness lead me to light,
From death lead me to immortality.

---

8   Brhadaranyaka Upanishad, Yajur Veda, I.iii.28, quoted in *Tell it Well* by John Seamands (Kansas City: Beason Hill Press, 1981), 166.

ISLAM: WORD

When I was a little girl, I would wake up in the morning and shuffle sleepy-eyed down the stairs and into the kitchen. There I would often see my Dad sitting at the table, reading the Bible—and memorizing it.

As I turned thirteen, having memorized verses and psalms all my childhood, I dared myself: "Why not memorize a book of the Bible?" That summer it was my job to paint the interior woodwork upstairs, the moldings, baseboards, window frames, and sills. As I lugged a paint can and brush from one spot to another, I also toted along a Bible and memorized the book of James. Other books followed. If I have any serenity or smile today, it is because my roots go down into the Word.

For Muslims, too, the word of God is important. God is not an abstract entity like Confucius' Tao or the Hindus' great Soul. God is a person who communicates. God speaks. He speaks magnificently. He speaks to us. He speaks with clear applications. And we can take his word into our hearts and souls and worship him as those words come out of our mouths, as "the speech of God passes into the storehouse of memory and into the currency of our lips."[9]

Muslims believe Christians and Jews have corrupted the Old and New Testaments, but they also believe that large parts of those Scriptures came from God. This includes the Pentateuch, the Psalms, and the Gospels. Therefore Christians are called "People of the Book (from God)."

The Muslim Scripture, the Qur'an, was written five hundred years after Christ. Many Muslims memorize and recite parts of it. It makes sense for Christians in such contexts to memorize Scripture. I think of two single women in Pakistan who over thirty years helped six hundred Muslims come to faith in Jesus. Every new believer was expected to memorize thirty-four key verses from the Gospel of John. Illiterates asked others to teach them. The result was that simple field laborers knew what they believed and became flaming evangelists.

Standing above us all, Scripture connects us with people throughout time and space. It critiques us:

> For the word of God is alive and active.
> Sharper than any double-edged sword,
> it penetrates even to dividing soul and spirit, joints and marrow;
> it judges the thoughts and attitudes of the heart. (Heb 4:12)

And it affirms us:

> As the rain and the snow
> come down from heaven,
> and do not return to it
> without watering the earth
> and making it bud and flourish,
> so that it yields seed for the sower and bread for the eater,

---

9   Kenneth Cragg, *The House of Islam* (Encino: Dickenson Publishing Co., 1975), 41.

so is my word that goes out from my mouth:
It will not return to me empty,
but will accomplish what I desire. (Isa 55:10,11)

A few years ago I stumbled into a choir that performs Christian classics. My first term we sang Bach's *B Minor Mass*. Then came Brahms' *Requiem*. Then Haydn's *Creation*, along with some sacred music by Rutter and Mozart. I have always loved ensemble work, where unity rests on diversity, where each part must defer to the others. Yet when I was introduced to these great classic works, it was a series of new worlds. I was poleaxed. Who would have guessed that at my age such magnificent galaxies lay in wait to be discovered, and that they would open to *me*? That every Monday night I could drive to a church basement in my grubbies and harmonize full-throated about glorious gospel truths with strong, confident sopranos and resonant basses? I still shake my head in wonder.

Take Brahms' *Requiem*, written in memory of his mother. The lyrics are all Scripture. The second movement opens with a march in a minor key, twenty-two measures of loud, deep, slow orchestral chords. Then the choir joins in lament: "All flesh is grass, and all the goodness of man is grass. The grass withers and the flower fades." Loud and soft this is repeated. Underneath, the ominous rhythm reverberates. A gentle interlude counsels patience as we wait for rain to water the grass. The sad, resigned, despairing truth returns: "All flesh is grass, and all the goodness of man is grass. The grass withers and the flower fades."

Suddenly we shout, "However!" followed by a pregnant pause. Then Isaiah's words roll on: "the word of the Lord continues forever." The last word, "forever," extends over four full measures at top volume.[10]

An exuberant, full-speed-ahead dance explodes: "The redeemed of the Lord shall return and come rejoicing to Zion" with everlasting joy upon their heads and gladness their portion. Tears and sighing will flee away.

Pain is pervasive in this world, as Buddhists have pointed out. *However*, there is something more, namely the everlasting word of the Lord. This gives us a foundation on which to build—and to dance. Muslims agree. The word of God grounds us and guides us. In Muslim communities, the call from the minaret sounds throughout the neighborhood five times a day:

Allahu Akbar!
Come to prayer,
God is great,
Prayer is better than sleep.

Crashing into early morning dreams, the call may jangle in the foreign visitor's ears like sounding brass or a clanging cymbal. But Muslims rise and respond to the God who speaks. Tongue, larynx, uvula, lungs, and voicebox resonate. Body energy pours toward God. Ideas

---

10 We sang in German language, in which "however" is *aber*, and "forever" is *ewigkeit*, which fit the music better than the English words do.

are channeled by physical acts of standing and bowing, listening and speaking. Recited in a group, the words nourish the community of faith.

Wonderful as God's poetry and law and interpersonal communication are, the word of God is even more. Incredibly, for a period of time "the word became a human being, and, full of grace and truth, lived among us" (John 1:14 GNT). God's communication is so dynamic that God himself chose to live in our world of pain, stretched to its extremes on the cross, and erupted with power to generate new beginnings. Muslim Scripture omits this. Jesus the Lord is our core difference, and it is huge. Nevertheless, Scriptures are a beginning bridge to Muslims—the precious gift of a God who communicates.

PRIMAL RELIGIONS: STORY

Instead of philosophical propositions, stories shape primal religionists' worldviews. These are not mere tales. The myths explore ultimate questions metaphorically. Where did we come from? Where are we going? What is a healthy society? How is justice restored? How can pain be endured? Taken all together, the mythological cycle rolls out a cosmic story. This is reenacted regularly in rituals.

Stories matter to me. One of the strongest apologetic arguments for my faith has been the stories that I have seen lived out all over the world. These are not perfect stories. The failures of stupidity are almost as bad as the failures of morals. Yet I also encounter love, joy, peace, long suffering, gentleness, goodness, faith, meekness, and balance energizing pilgrims on their journeys and making a difference in communities.

God loves stories. The Bible is not primarily doctrines but the stories of people who encountered God and responded, well or badly. The specifics of these stories touch people. In *The New Faces of Christianity: Believing the Bible in the Global South*, Philip Jenkins notes Bible themes that move people in poorer countries:

> Robbers on the roads, streets full of crippled and sick, the struggle to pay gouging tax and debt collectors, demanding landlords ... immanent national collapse ... personality cults of dictators ... judgments on the rich and haughty ... sowing and reaping and shepherding ... feasts of plenty and wells that never go dry ... deliverance from evil.[11]

These details come from stories. Jesus not only told stories but lived one when he stepped into ours.

This was high drama. All the powers of darkness conspired against him, but Jesus, "having disarmed the powers and authorities ... made a public spectacle of them, triumphing over them by the cross" (Col 2:15).

---

11   Philip Jenkins, *The New Faces of Christianity: Believing the Bible in the Global South* (New York: Oxford University Press, 2006), quoted in Joel Carpenter, "Back to the Bible," *Books and Culture* 13, no. 3 (2007): 23.

The third member of the Trinity also has been present in the world of stories—from the beginning, when the Spirit brooded over creation (Gen 1:2), to Acts 2, when the Spirit dynamized Jesus' people to live out their stories, to our time.

What is the setting for these stories? A holistic context, God's world, not a place of fragmented compartments but a place where the heavens declare the glory of God, where the trees of the field praise him, where the stones cry out his glory, where everything that has breath will honor him.

The themes of creation, cosmic struggle, spirit power, and holistic integration of the physical and spiritual world are important to those who come from primal religions. So is a circular worldview. This was pointed out to me by Terry LeBlanc, who heads the First Nations organization known as the North American Institute for Indigenous Theological Studies (NAIITS). In a public paper I had described Christians' linear understanding of the movement from Eden to the final kingdom. Terry gently critiqued this monovision. He reminded me of the circles of the seasons, and of the generations, and of the spiral of the process of learning, and of the rise and fall and renewal of many things. Ever since then, I have been seeing the promise of spring as autumn leaves fall, and sunrises in sunsets, and the traits of my grandparents in my grandson. We are marching in a line, true, but we are also comforted by circles. No matter the ups and downs of our lives, Easter erupts every year. Count on it.

Stories have played a big role in my life and my faith. People say that I tell them well. I also love to collect good stories about God's people. Now I am helping indigenous writers in various countries collect their own.

CHINESE RELIGION: COMMUNITY

At the beginning of human history, God said, "It is not good for the man to be alone" (Gen 2:18). This makes sense to Chinese. Individualism is not admired. Group success is the goal. Tasty dinners celebrate that. The core group is the family, but work and recreational groups matter too. Group identity expands to the nation of China. From the Middle Kingdom, which saw itself surrounded by barbarians, to the superpower today, Chinese continue to identify with the great potential of their people. Even overseas Chinese feel that kinship.

My first book—How to Write: A Christian Writer's Guide—was published in Asia because that is where I was living. The publisher was a Chinese press in Singapore. When I received my first copy, I lovingly and proudly stroked the cover. Then I turned it over. What a shock I received. The blurb on the back cover began with these words: "Miriam Adeney, daughter-in-law of David Adeney ... "

As an individualistic American, I was annoyed. What kind of description was that? I was my own person! Now that I have lived longer in Asia, however, I appreciate the blurb. I have come to value community deeply. I see that it does take a village to raise a child, or to promote a book.

Confucianism undergirds the focus on community. For Confucius, religion's primary concern was proper social relationships, which give order to society and provide a framework for progress and well-being. Confucius listed five key relationships, including ruler and subject, and husband and wife, but his special focus was on the father-son relationship. In general, elders and leaders should be respected. Individuals should defer to the common good. Collaboration should be practiced.

Now, as we enter the second decade of the twenty-first century, we are aware that China's annual economic growth has been at least 8 percent, and sometimes as high as 14 percent, for more than twenty years. An emphasis on community, cooperation, and networking has been essential to achieve this. Similarly, the Chinese church's massive, unprecedented growth to at least 80 million Christians would not have happened in an individualistic society. Comradeship and connections also serve Chinese missions, an increasingly significant force on the global scene.

Yet there is a danger. The good things we value can become idols. Chinese value their families, their social networks, and their heritage. Accepting other groups as equals can be hard. This has implications for mission. Chinese have birthed a powerful "Back to Jerusalem" mission movement. Yet over the past thirty years few of their missionaries to Muslim China have learned the local language. "To the indigenous people, these Chinese missionaries appear to be just one more arm of the imperialistic Han," comments an observer. "Find me a Han Chinese who loves God more than he loves China," a Uighur seeker recently exclaimed.

A Chinese Christian leader from Malaysia wrote in a student paper:

> Chinese often pride themselves on their rich cultural heritage, their high moral values, their sense of filial piety and their respect for elders. Western culture appears decadent in comparison. While there is great admiration for Western progress in science and technology, the Chinese often feel that the West has nothing more to teach them. And they certainly do not wish to be polluted by a culture that is "inferior." This racial pride may be consciously or unconsciously nursed by Chinese Christians as well. There is the fear of losing our "Chinese-ness."

> Yet the Bible calls us to humble ourselves before God. It is not our racial or cultural heritage that gives us a place in God's kingdom. It is purely grace. In pointing out the weaknesses of Western culture, we must not fail to recognize that there are shortcomings in our own.

Although a Chinese sense of communal identity may be an idol for some, it has been a blessing to me. Networks of Chinese have provided a home for me in Malaysia, Indonesia, Hong Kong, the Philippines, Thailand, Singapore, and even as far away as Mali and the United Arab Emirates. I echo God's words, "It is not good for the man to be alone." We were created to live in communities of meaning. No people have shown me that better than my Chinese friends, stretching chopsticks across the table to share one more morsel with a friend.

WHY DO I BELIEVE?

I have explored what pain, beauty, soul, word, story, and community mean to me, and how God has spoken to me in those areas. During my formative years, a robust view of Christianity and cultures was nurtured by Wheaton College, as well as by publications from the Summer Institute of Linguistics, case studies flowing out of the Institute of Church Growth at Fuller Theological Seminary, and the journal *Practical Anthropology* sponsored by the United Bible Society.

Beyond the themes in this essay, I could discuss the intricate designs within nature, or the mystery of personality, or the explanatory power of the doctrine that humans are simultaneously in God's image and also sinners, a paradigm that helps make sense of societies. I could discuss the life, death, and resurrection of Jesus, or the community of his followers spread throughout time and space, fallible yet spiritually alive, morally sharpened, and energized to serve, or the mystical witness of the Scripture and the Spirit in my soul. As an anthropologist/missiologist, it has been my great privilege to explore God's world. This paper serves up a sample of what I have tasted.

BRIDGES TO CHRISTIAN FAITH IN OTHER RELIGIONS

BRIDGES TO BUDDHISTS

1. Respect quest for transcendence
2. Empathize with suffering
3. Love comes from love
4. Individuals matter
5. Committed relationships can be built
6. Moderation
7. God's care for animals and plants
8. Power to reach *dharma* ideals
9. Shame rather than guilt
10. Symbols, not propositions
11. Christ as teacher and Christ as power

BRIDGES TO JAPANESE

1. Empathize with suffering
2. Love is possible, because God loves
3. Appreciate beauty
4. Moderation, discipline, self-control
5. Shame rather than guilt
6. Metaphor and indirect communication

7. Group belongingness, empathy, interdependence, reciprocity
8. Spiritual insight is gradual
9. Buddhist ideals
10. Patriotism, how Japanese Christians have built society in education, art, and in serving communities with special needs

BRIDGES TO HINDUS

1. Awe before the Transcendent
2. Many satisfactions are illusory
3. *Bhakti*
4. Self-knowledge
5. Unity with the cosmos
6. Self-denial
7. Sacrifice
8. Karma
9. Family in Scripture, family in the church
10. Drama, song, dance
11. Spiritual study centers
12. Christ as power

BRIDGES TO MUSLIMS

1. God
2. Prayer
3. Jesus the Prophet
4. Scripture: Torah, Psalms, Proverbs, Gospels
5. Jesus' death—God's generosity and provision of a sacrifice, Jesus' loyalty and concern for God's honor
6. Spiritual blessing, *baraka*
7. Personal ethics: honor, modesty, trustworthiness, raising godly children
8. Social ethics: justice and righteousness
9. Stewardship of the earth
10. Muslim civilizations' contributions
11. Prophet Muhammad's contributions—monotheism, political, literary, and ethical
12. Repentance for Western sins: Crusades, imperialism, stereotyping of Arabs, disrespect for parents, extreme individualism, media that promotes pornography

BRIDGES TO PRIMAL RELIGIONISTS

1. God created the world and has interacted powerfully throughout history
2. God in Christ died to conquer the power of all other spirits
3. The Spirit of God can live in us
4. The church provides holistic community
5. Metaphors and stories, including motifs from the local repertoire of mythology
6. Discernment of local believers in order to avoid syncretism

BRIDGES TO CHINESE

1. Seeking the Ultimate—Tao
2. Appreciating order in physical and social worlds
3. Appreciating family
4. Appreciating the supernatural
5. Sensitivity to suffering
6. Sensitivity to need for renewal and cleansing
7. Sensitivity to need for celebration
8. Appreciating literacy
9. Appreciating metaphor
10. Appreciating civilization and long-term goals

–SIX–

INDIA'S SEARCH FOR JESUS

IVAN SATYAVRATA

Ivan Satyavrata presently serves as senior pastor of the Assembly of God Church, a church of about four thousand people with a significant social outreach, providing education and basic nutrition for several thousand children in and around the city of Kolkata, India. His interests include issues relating to the Christian witness to people of other faiths and the Christian response to social issues, especially human trafficking. He presently also serves as international deputy director for the Lausanne Movement in South Asia. He has authored two books: *The Holy Spirit: Lord and Life-giver* and *God Has Not Left Himself without Witness*. Ivan's wife, Elizabeth [also called Sheila], and sons, Rahul and Rohan, are the pride and joy of his life.

Our family has been blessed to live for twenty-one years on a twenty-one-acre college campus on the outskirts of the city of Bangalore. One morning I was up unusually early and wound my way to the back of the campus as the first rays of the sun peeped over the horizon. You cannot get closer to nature than that in any part of urban India, and I always delighted in the experience of the sunrise or sunset. I eagerly breathed in the crisp, early morning air as I walked and prayed, thanking God for the gift of the new day and seeking his strength and guidance for the tasks that lay ahead.

As I began to pour my heart out in prayer I became aware of the earliest sounds of a waking world: the familiar music of birds singing, the chickens and cows from the farm next door, the sound of the occasional automobile and, in the midst of this cacophony, the sounds of religious devotion. First the drums, cymbals, and chants from the temple in a nearby village; then the distant strains of the Muslim *maulvi*'s rising call to prayer from the mosque; and finally the sounds of worship from our own chapel as early risers gathered for morning prayers. A question that I had struggled with from my earliest years as a believer came back to me afresh: Does the all-powerful, all-knowing, all-present God hear the cries of sincere people of other faiths? How does he respond to the prayers of those who call out to a God whose name they do not know?

Only a small minority of my neighbors and friends during my childhood, school, and early college years were Christians. Through marriage, two of my extended family members have come from other faiths: one, a devout Muslim, and the other, Zoroastrian. One has since come to faith in Christ and is a radiant believer, the other is open but not yet a professing Christ follower.

I spent much of my time in the first few years of my ministry on the streets and crowded slums of one of the most densely populated cities in the world, Mumbai (Bombay). On the way home in a crowded local train after spending several hours preaching and witnessing on the streets, as a young believer I would see the tens of thousands who streamed in and out at every station and wonder: What place does God have in the lives of all of these people? How many of them have heard a clear presentation of the gospel of Christ? And if they have not, are they out of reach of God's grace? What do they know and believe about God, and how does their God awareness impact their response to Christ?

India is the birthplace of at least four major religions and also home to many of the other living religions of the world. Hinduism, the *sanatana dharma*—the quintessential religion, without beginning or end—is indisputably rooted in India's soil and permeates all of Indian society and culture. The Hindu civilization can trace its origins to at least 5000 BC. Jainism was an early spin-off from Hinduism and like Buddhism emerged in India during the first millennium before Christ. Sikhism, what is now the world's fifth-largest religion, was born in India in the fifteenth century.

Although Christianity was born outside of India, the Eastern Orthodox tradition in India today traces its origin to the Apostle Thomas himself. Islam too, though Mideastern in origin, came to India early in the seventh century and spread rapidly. India today has the second largest population of Muslims in the world, a politically significant minority community. Judaism and Zoroastrianism are two ancient religions which found welcome reception in India. This is not to mention myriad reformed Hindu sects, guru movements, and syncretistic and quasi-religious cults. India is thus a land of many religions, a nation with a soul, a soul with a seemingly insatiable thirst for reality, on a quest for truth, in search of God.

This thirst is perhaps best captured in a verse from the *Upanishads*, which represent the highest expression of Hindu philosophical wisdom:

> Lead me from the unreal to the Real;
> Lead me from darkness to Light;
> Lead me from death to Immortality[1]

This cry from the soul of India has been echoed through the centuries and has been variously expressed in the writings of many sages venerated by the Hindus. **Swami Vivekananda** (1863–1902) was one of the most influential Hindu voices of the nineteenth century, responsible for both the revival and growing global influence of Hinduism in the

---

1   Brhadaranyaka Upanishad, Yajur Veda, I.iii.28.

modern era. In his adolescent years Vivekananda was obsessed with the idea of seeing God. His study of various Western philosophers provided him no answers. He wondered if anyone had ever actually experienced God directly, and began seeking out holy men and religious teachers, asking them the burning question of his heart: "Have you seen God?"

His search took him to the banks of the River Ganges, where he met Maharshi Devendranath Tagore, father of the poet Rabindranath Tagore and the leader of the reformed Hindu sect, the Brahmo Samaj. He asked him, "Sir, have you seen God?" This great spiritual guru too seemed to evade the question. Finally one day Vivekananda went to meet Sri Ramakrishna Paramhansa, a somewhat eccentric priest of the Kali temple in Calcutta. When he was posed with the question, this practically illiterate priest gave him a straightforward reply: "Yes, I have seen God. I have seen him more tangibly than I see you. I have talked with him more intimately than I am talking to you." That was it—Vivekananda stayed at his feet and became Ramakrishna's disciple for life, eventually founding a religious organization after his guru's name called "The Ramakrishna Mission."

Sometime later Vivekananda wrote a poem entitled "Quest for God," of which the following is an excerpt:

> O'er hill and dale and mountain range, in temple, church, and mosque,
> In Vedas, Bible, Al Koran I had searched for Thee in vain.

> Like a child in the wildest forest lost I have cried and cried alone,
> "Where art Thou gone, my God, my love?" The echo answered, "gone."

> And days and nights and years then passed a fire was in the brain,
> I knew not when day changed in night the heart seemed rent in twain.
> I laid me down on Ganges's shore, exposed to sun and rain;
> With burning tears I laid the dust and wailed with waters' roar.

> I called on all the holy names of every clime and creed.
> "Show me the way, in mercy, ye Great ones who have reached the goal."[2]

This poem reflects not just the intensity of Vivekananda's search for God, but also gives us a glimpse of the soul of a nation. But perhaps no one has articulated India's search more eloquently or with greater intensity and passion than India's revered poet laureate, **Rabindranath Tagore** (1861–1941). Tagore's *Gitanjali* (Song Offerings), written originally in Bengali and translated into English by the poet himself, received worldwide acclaim and earned him the Nobel Prize for literature in 1913. While his poems from *Gitanjali* are variously interpreted, they are reminiscent of a great Indian tradition called the *bhakti* tradition.

The *bhakti* cult in Hinduism first emerged in the seventh century as a popular reaction to the impersonal monistic philosophical school in Hinduism. *Bhakti* devotees worship God

---

as a loving, personal being distinct from his creation, and their worship finds deep emotional expression, often accompanied by devotional lyrics, music, and dance. Salvation according to *bhakti* is through surrender and sincere and fervent devotion to the deity. Separation from the loved one, waiting, searching, mourning, and lamenting over the absence of the Supreme Lover are all common themes in the *bhakti* tradition. The search for God is often painful and the destination elusive in the path of *bhakti* devotion.

Gitanjali is a string of devotional poems in which love is a major theme that connects all the verses. God in *Gitanjali* has no name or abode and cannot be identified with any specific Indian god. He has his own form and personality. He is referred to as "you," "thou," or "thee." At times he is shown as a loving Father who cares for his children, and at other times as a Lover who is waiting for reciprocation from his own creation. The search motif is, however, prominent, of which the following is a classic illustration:

> I have been seeking and searching God for as long as I can remember, for many many lives, from the very beginning of existence. Once in a while, I have seen him by the side of a faraway star, and I have rejoiced and danced that the distance, although great, is not impossible to reach. And I have traveled and reached to the star; but by the time I reached the star, God has moved to another star. And it has been going on for centuries. The challenge is so great that I go on hoping against hope. I have to find him, I am so absorbed in the search. The very search is so intriguing, so mysterious, so enchanting, that God has become almost an excuse, the search has become itself the goal.

Tagore goes on to describe how he arrives at the doorway of God's house in a faraway star, but then is struck by a fear of what lies behind the doorway and, hence, turns around and flees. But "searching for God" has now become his very life, and so he continues his search again, looking again in every direction, enjoying the journey itself—the pilgrimage. While Tagore's thoughts are clearly steeped in Hindu tradition, his poems reflect a free spirit shaped by Christian ideas as well. This was due to the influence of the Brahmo Samaj—a reformed Hindu sect deeply nourished by Christian sources—with which his family was closely associated. Thus on one occasion this great muse-philosopher of India and venerated composer of the Indian national anthem made this fascinating confession:

> Do you know I have often felt that if we were not Hindus ... I should like my people to be Christians? Indeed, it is a great pity that Europeans have come to us as imperialists rather than as Christians and so have deprived our people of their true contact with the religion of Jesus Christ ... What a mental torture it is to know that men are capable of loving each other and adding to one another's joy, and yet would not![3]

---

3   Krishna Dutta and Andrew Robinson, ed., *Selected Letters of Rabindranath Tagore* (Cambridge: Cambridge University Press, 1997), 199.

This admission from the pen of one whose heart was so closely attuned to the soul of India finds interesting resonance in the writings of a number of followers of Christ who began their journey towards truth with their feet firmly planted within the Hindu tradition.

Keshub Chunder Sen (1838–1884) was one of the foremost leaders of the Brahmo Samaj and a key figure in the development of Indian Christian theology.[4] He was in many ways the archetypical model of the Hindu seeker after Christ. Sen's response to the person and message of Christ evolved through various stages, with Christ moving progressively closer to the centre of his religious experience. He was convinced that the indigenous instincts and aspirations of the Hindu tradition were satisfied by the coming of Christ. He thus appeals to his fellow countrymen to direct their devotion to Christ in fulfillment of their deepest spiritual hunger:

> Behold Christ cometh to us as an Asiatic in race, as a Hindu in faith, as a kinsman and a brother, and he demands your heart's affection. Will you not give him your affection? He comes to fulfil and perfect that religion of communion for which India has been panting, as the hart panteth after the waterbrooks.[5]

Krishna Mohan Banerjea (1813–1885) was a pioneer of indigenous theology and an early representative of a progressive class of high-caste Bengalis called the *bhadralok*, who attempted to accommodate their traditional Hindu culture to the Western lifestyle of the British. He was converted under the influence of the Scottish Presbyterian missionary educator Alexander Duff. Banerjea was a statesman, linguist, historian, social reformer, and national civil rights leader. He found pointers to Christ in the teachings on sacrifice in the Rig Veda, India's oldest scripture, and especially in Prajapati, the Lord of Creation who sacrifices himself for the world, as a prefigure of Christ. According to Banerjea, Jesus alone fulfilled the ideal of the vedic Prajapati:

> The position of *Prajapati*, himself the priest and himself the victim, no member of that [Hindu] Pantheon has dared to occupy. His throne is vacant, and his crown without an owner. No one now can claim that crown and that throne in the hearts of Hindus, who are true to the original teaching of the Vedas, so rightfully as the historical Jesus.[6]

A final impassioned appeal boldly and imaginatively invites Hindu readers to consider his message as the "voice" of their ancestors, the vedic seers:

---

4   Although Sen's journey towards Christ stopped short of his becoming a professing Christian, his importance is based on the fact that many of the conceptions and categories used by subsequent Indian Christian thinkers were first stated by him.

5   Keshub Chunder Sen, "Who Is Christ?" in *Keshub Chunder Sen*, ed. D. C. Scott (Madras: Christian Literature Society, 1979), 215–16.

6   Krishna Mohan Banerjea, *The Relation between Christianity and Hinduism* (Calcutta: Oxford Mission Press, 1881), reprinted in T. V. Philip, *Krishna Mohan Banerjea: Christian Apologist* (Madras: Christian Literature Society, 1982), 197.

It is the voice also of your primitive ancestors calling upon you in the voice of their Vedas … not to waver in your duty to acknowledge and embrace the true *Prajapati*, the true *Purusha* begotten before the worlds, who died that you might live, who by death hath vanquished death, and brought life and immortality to light through the Gospel … You will find in Him everything worthy of your lineage, worthy of your antiquity, worthy of your traditions.[7]

Nehemiah Goreh (1825–1895) was a high-caste Brahmin by birth and a Sanskrit scholar of considerable stature. The public testimony of Goreh's conversion showed his emotional attachment to his ancestral religion and his deep roots in the Sanskrit philosophical tradition, although he shared it with characteristic reserve and humility.[8] Despite his markedly negative attitude towards Hinduism, Goreh loved his ancestral culture and Hindu fellow countrymen. He was convinced that the light of God in general revelation had prepared the sincere Hindu to appreciate and accept the truths of Christian faith:

> Providence has certainly prepared *us*, the Hindus, to receive Christianity, in a way in which, it seems to me, no other nation—excepting the Jews, of course—has been prepared. Most erroneous as is the teaching of such books as the *Bhagavadgita*, the *Bhagvata*, etc., yet they have taught us something of *ananyabhakti* (undivided devotedness to God), of *vairagya* (giving up the world), of *namrata* (humility), of *ksama* (forbearance), etc., which enables us to appreciate the precepts of Christianity.[9]

Goreh believed that certain concepts in orthodox Hinduism, such as the possibility of miracles and the idea of incarnation, could legitimately be regarded as a *preparatio evangelii* (preparation for the gospel) within Hinduism. Goreh illustrates from his own experience, for instance, how Hinduism prepared him for the idea of a divine incarnation:

> I never found fault *in idea* with its [Hinduism's] teaching that God becomes Incarnate. Indeed, many stories of Krishna and Rama, whom the Hindu religion teaches to be incarnations of God, used to be very affecting to us … And thus our countrymen have been prepared, to some extent, to appreciate and accept the truths of Christianity.[10]

Goreh thus viewed Christ as the fulfillment of the "anticipations and yearnings" of his Hindu ancestors. He concluded that search for unity with God, which his ancestors aspired

---

7   Banerjea, *Christianity and Hinduism*, 200.

8   He is sometimes regarded as one of the most deeply versed in the Hindu tradition of all Indian Christians. Robin Boyd, *An Introduction to Indian Christian Theology* (Delhi: ISPCK, 1991), 40.

9   Nehemiah Goreh, *Proofs of the Divinity of Our Lord*, 75, quoted in Boyd, *Indian Christian Theology*, 55.

10   Goreh, *Proofs*, 76–77, quoted in Boyd, *Indian Christian Theology*, 56.

after for centuries, finds its true realization in the Christian experience of union with God through Christ.[11]

The Hindu *bhakti* tradition I made reference to earlier has held a great attraction for Indian Christians because of its conception of God as a loving, personal being distinct from his creation, who bestows grace upon his creatures and can be worshiped with feelings of deep love and personal devotion. Several of the proponents of this school were poet-mystics. The best-known Christian *bhakti* poet was **Narayan Vaman Tilak** (1862–1919), a high-caste Hindu convert and a renowned poet-saint and activist. Tilak came to an end of his spiritual search after studying the New Testament, when he found himself irresistibly attracted to Christ and convinced that Christ was the Guru whom India and the world was looking for. Tilak believed that "if Christ could be presented to India in His naked beauty, free from the disguises of Western organisation, Western doctrines and Western forms of worship, India would acknowledge Him as the supreme Guru, and lay her richest homage at His feet."[12]

Tilak saw expressed in the older Hindu devotional literature, especially the *bhakti* poet-saints of India, a deep longing after God, illustrated in his own claim to have "come to the feet of Christ over the bridge of Tukaram."[13] Tukaram was a sixteenth century Marathi poet-saint, highly revered in Tilak's home province of Maharashtra, whose devotional poetry captured the restless longing of a soul desperate for God and ignited a passionate desire for deep intimacy with God. Based on his personal spiritual pilgrimage, Tilak explained how the teaching of *bhakti* saints like Tukaram and Jnanesvara positively influenced his movement towards Christ:

> The traditional way of union with the Supreme through *bhakti*, which Hindu mystics have conceived and Hindu devotees experienced, may be summed up in the four words, *samipata* (nearness), *salokata* (association), *Sarupata* (likeness), and *sayujyta* (yokedness or union); this has helped me to enter into the meaning of that series of Christ's sayings—"Come after Me," "Take My yoke upon you," "Become like unto Me," "Abide in Me."[14]

For Tilak Christ was the One who actually satisfied the search and quenched the thirst so poignantly expressed in the Hindu *bhakti* tradition of India.

Another illustration of India's search for God finding fulfilment in Christ comes to us in the life experience of **Sadhu Sundar Singh** (1889–1929). From his earliest years Sundar Singh's mother had ingrained in him the need to seek earnestly after the greatest treasure on earth, peace of mind and heart. His deep spiritual thirst led him to earnestly search the

---

11   Nehemiah Goreh, *Objections*, 41–42, quoted in Boyd, *Indian Christian Theology*, 54. See http://www.spiritual-short-stories.com/spiritual-short-story-252-Searching+for+God.html.

12   J. C. Winslow, *Narayan Vaman Tilak: The Christian Poet of Maharashtra* (Calcutta: Association Press, 1930), 118.

13   *Dnyanodaya* (24 May 1917), 162; Quoted in Philip Constable, "The Scottish Missionaries, 'Protestant Hinduism' and the Scottish sense of Empire in Nineteenth- and Early Twentieth-century India," *The Scottish Historical Review* Vol 86, 2:222 (Oct 2007), 310.

14   Ibid., 56–57.

Granth (the Sikh scriptures), the Qur'an, and the sacred books of the Hindus. Sundar Singh's pre-Christian spiritual consciousness was nourished by *bhakti* influences which aroused in him a deep longing for an authentic experience of mystical communion with God. According to Sundar Singh's testimony, his quest was satisfied in a mystical encounter with the "risen" Christ. It happened early one morning when he prayed desperately for God to reveal himself and show him the way of salvation, failing which he would commit suicide. He waited in anticipation of a vision of Buddha, or Krishna, or some other avatar. Instead he suddenly became conscious of a bright radiance which entered and filled the room:

> I opened the door to see where it came from, but all was dark outside. I returned inside, and the light increased in intensity and took the form of a globe of light above the ground, and in this light there appeared, not the form I expected, but the Living Christ whom I had counted as dead. To all eternity I shall never forget His glorious and loving face, nor the few words which He spoke: "Why do you persecute me? See, I have died on the Cross for you and for the whole world." These words were burned into my heart as by lightning, and I fell on the ground before Him. My heart was filled with inexpressible joy and peace, and my whole life was entirely changed. Then the old Sundar Singh died and a new Sundar Singh, to serve the Living Christ, was born.[15]

Sundar Singh claimed that from this moment onwards the peace and joy that had been the object of his lifelong quest became his most precious possession. He thereafter became a devoted follower of Christ and an ardent evangelist who traveled all over India and even abroad in the service of the gospel.

Sundar Singh believed that the light of truth was present in some measure in all religions. For him, all religions were provisional but legitimate expressions of the human search for God. Hindu religious experience thus also represented an authentic expression of mankind's search for truth. There were many sincere seekers after truth among the ancient sages and teachers of Hinduism, and many devotees who had received some measure of light:

> Among its teachers were many real seekers after truth, and bhaktas, or devotees, who had received some measure of light from that God Who "left not Himself without witness" among the nations (Acts 14:16,17) ... In the world today it would be difficult to find a people more engrossed in religious observances than the Hindus.[16]

According to Sundar Singh, human beings experience spiritual restlessness and a deep sense of alienation apart from God. The love of God both places this deep longing for communion with God within the soul of man, and makes provision for it to be fulfilled.

---

15   Sundar Singh, *With and Without Christ* (London: Harper & Brothers, 1929), reprinted in T. D. Francis, *The Christian Witness of Sadhu Sundar Singh: A Collection of His Writings* (Madras: Christian Literature Society, 1993), 399.
16   Sundar Singh, *The Search after Reality*, reprinted in Francis, *Sadhu Sundar Singh*, 141–42.

He illustrates this in the following testimony of a seeker: "I realized that this impulse and this satisfaction of heart had both come from the Living Christ, in whom all my restless strivings have now found rest."[17] For Sundar Singh, the impulse for union with God within the *bhakti* mystical consciousness was a preparation for Christ, evidence that "every race, in every age, has in some form or other shown its deep craving for God," and that the individual soul is "burdened by the sense of its separation from the Eternal God."[18] A recurring theme in his thought is that this deep and natural craving in the human heart can only be satisfied in God:

> From our experience we know how strong is the desire for God that is born in our hearts. As the hart is distressed till it finds the water-spring in the jungle, so the heart of man thirsts for God, and is restless till it finds Him. Although, in many ways, man tries to satisfy this inborn longing of his heart, yet his desire is never satisfied till he finds God.[19]

I have attempted thus far to illustrate the soul cry of a nation that has sought after a vision of the true and living God through all of its recorded history. Its cumulative religious memory, consisting of tomes of sacred literature, countless temples and pilgrimage centres, and myriad religious sects and movements bear living testimony to its ongoing, insatiable spiritual thirst. These various age-old expressions of God awareness have not always been wholly pure, spiritually wholesome, or morally consistent. In fact, exploitative priestcraft, fearful superstition, oppressive social practices, and even dark, occultic rituals have also been an integral part of the Indian religious tradition all through its history.

The intent of this article, however, has been neither to offer a critique of any aspect of India's religious life, nor to propose answers to vital theological questions that emerge in our encounter with India's richly diverse religious traditions. My purpose rather has been to provide a glimpse of the lesser-known "other side" of the soul of a nation that is desperately searching for God. The Gospel of John records an occasion when a group of Greeks came to the disciples with a simple request: "We would like to see Jesus" (John 12:21). Two thousand years later, in this amazing land with a mosaic of religions and diverse cultures, the cry is essentially the same: "We would like to see Jesus."

There is perhaps no nation in the world where the hunger for God is as intense or widely manifest as India. We see truth amidst deception, goodness alongside revolting evil, and light shining through the darkness. The varied expressions of religious hunger in the religions and cultures of India present helpful "landing strips": points of contact which may be used to communicate Christ with people of other faiths. What can we do to help part the curtain, to remove obstacles, to build bridges rather than walls, so that the people who walk in darkness may see the great light of Jesus?

---

17 Francis, *Sadhu Sundar Singh*, 360.
18 Ibid., 140.
19 Ibid., 197.

I think we can do no better in this regard than to closely heed the gems of wise counsel from the lips of the most famous Indian who ever lived, the revered father of the Indian nation, **Mahatma Gandhi** (1869–1948). In an oft-cited incident, the American missionary-evangelist Dr. E. Stanley Jones, a friend of Gandhi, once asked Gandhi: "How can we make Christianity naturalized in India, not a foreign thing, identified with a foreign government and a foreign people, but a part of the national life of India and contributing its power to India's uplift?" Gandhi gave the following clear fourfold response:

> First, I would suggest that all Christians, missionaries and all, begin to live more like Jesus Christ. Second, practice it without adulterating it or toning it down. Third, emphasize love and make it your working force, for love is central in Christianity. Fourth, study the non-Christian religions more sympathetically to find the good that is within them, in order to have a more sympathetic approach to the people.[20]

Jones offers helpful reflections in his commentary on Gandhi's response. He marveled at Gandhi's advice to not adulterate or tone down the gospel message. He noted Gandhi's earnest plea to make love an active force in the communication of the message of Christ, observing that the Mahatma's eyes filled with tears when 1 Corinthians 13 was read to him. Gandhi's final suggestion for a sympathetic posture to non-Christian religions resonated with Jones' own views in this regard. It also strengthens the case for the approach recommended earlier in this article. Jones' most powerfully moving comment, however, comes as a reaction to Gandhi's first response:

> I knew that looking through his eyes were the three hundred millions of India, and speaking through his voice were the millions of the East saying to me, a representative of the West, and through me to the very West itself, if you will come to us in the spirit of your Master we cannot resist you.[21]

India's age-old cry is for an authentic vision of God, a God whom we believe is revealed in his full glory and majesty in the face of Jesus Christ. Gandhi's challenge is a challenge to every Christ follower to present the message of Christ "in the spirit" of Christ. It will not do to "market" the gospel effectively in India—to capture the media and flood the land with the text of the gospel message. The success of the Christian witness in India depends on the extent to which the gospel is effectively "incarnated" in an authentic community of Christ followers. The authentic Christ is more than just a set of propositions—he is the decisive and final self-revelation of God, who reveals himself through his word and Spirit, who still lives in the midst of any truly Spirit-indwelt community of God's people. The living and vibrant witness of such a community is the only response that will truly satisfy the restless soul of a nation earnestly searching for the authentic Christ.

---

20   E. Stanley Jones, "Mahatma Gandhi's Four Points," *Eastern Tidings* 22, no.1 (January 1, 1927): 1.
21   Ibid.

–SEVEN–
AMAZING GRACE FOR CHINA

YUAN ZHIMING

Yuan Zhiming was one of the intellectual leaders behind the democracy movement in China in the late 1980s. He fled China after the Tiananmen Square Massacre and later became a Christian. He is now a popular Chinese evangelist, writer, and film producer, well known among Chinese Christians in the mainland and around the world.

In two books written soon after his conversion, Yuan came to a remarkable understanding of Chinese thought and history. In *Lao vs. the Bible*, Yuan boldly proposed that the ancient classic *Dao De Jing* was not merely the product of human research, but that its author, Lao Zi, had also received some sort of divine revelation. He argued that the Tao Lao Zi wrote about, was another name for God. And that the Sage he described, the incarnation of the Tao, looked a lot like Jesus. Taking Jesus as it unifying center, Yuan then retold the story of Chinese civilization. God had been working in Chinese history for 5,000 years, he argued. The Chinese had long ago revered God, but then turned their backs on Him, and are just now in the process of returning. Yuan's books provoked sharp controversy. I asked Yuan to share his story and insights about Chinese thought and translation. I translated the paper he sent from colloquial and sometimes poetic Chinese.

© 2012 Yuan Zhiming

It is by God's grace alone that I came to be his servant. I have dwelled in the depths of two starkly contrasting worlds—atheism and theism, secular China and Christianity.

I served as a soldier for twelve years in atheist China. For a while I was a political officer in the Peoples' Liberation Army unit stationed around Beijing to protect the capital. Later, attending Peoples' University, I studied Marxist philosophy in pursuit of an MA and PhD. For sixteen years I belonged to the Communist Party, even working as secretary of a local branch. During the 1980s I became a critic of Chinese culture and one of the leaders of the movement to reform China and open it to the outside world. In the wake of the democracy movement and the events of June 4, 1989, at Tiananmen Square, an order for my arrest was issued, and I fled China.

A year after I was baptized at Princeton University, I entered Mississippi Reformed Seminary. After graduating, I became part of the staff of a new Christian magazine called *Overseas Campus*. Later I worked on film projects including such major documentaries as *China's Confession*, *The Cross*, *The Gospel*, and *Beyond*, along with testimonial-type evangelistic DVDs, which were disseminated widely both inside China and overseas. For about a decade, almost every weekend I have preached the gospel around the world, leading some ten thousand people to the Christian faith.

Some old friends and classmates, who are still atheists, don't understand all the change that has come over me. Not surprisingly! To tell the truth, I could never have anticipated becoming what I am today either. As a young man I had many goals in life, such as becoming a philosopher and scholar, but I certainly never thought I'd wind up a Christian, still less a pastor. But in reality this gap between atheism and theism, secular and sacred, is just a shadow of the vast gap that yawns between the divine nature and man, which human beings cannot cross by our own efforts.

When I think about how this great crossing was achieved, I have to give all credit to God. I see that it was not my choice or due to my merits at all, but God's intervention in my life and his intervening grace.

I look back at my conversion from three perspectives.

First, God called me to seek him. From childhood I was curious and a good student. Summer evenings I would watch the distant stars, and in winter the snowflakes silently drifting down from the sky. I have always felt a great love of nature; seeing such things was like meeting a bosom friend in a dream. In middle school I began to think about the meaning of life.

In my early years Marx had a deep influence on me. He said one ought to choose an occupation that allows one to serve humanity. Under his influence I came to view with contempt people who are selfishly ambitious and grasp after position. After middle school I lived in a farming village for two years, reading whatever books I could get my hands on. Later in the army, whenever I had free time, I burrowed into books: literature, philosophy, science, anything I could get my hands on. I began to think about where the universe came from, leading me to write a massive million-word manuscript (never printed) demonstrating the wisdom of atheism. After the Cultural Revolution, when China opened colleges again, I took the high school exam for students who had studied on their own, and tested near the top for the Beijing military district. In 1982, feeling as if I were letting out one long breath of pent-up thought, I published ten or so essays in *People's Daily* and other major publications. The next year, without going to college, I began to study for my master's degree. Before finishing my MA, I started working on a doctorate. Just when I was about to complete my doctorate, which would have come in the summer of 1989, I was forced to leave China.

I recount these facts to show that from early on I loved to dig into the roots of things and was not satisfied with conventional wisdom (I never could quite accept the story that man had come from monkeys, for instance). Seeing that God chose me from my mother's womb, as the psalmist says, apparently he allowed the genes I inherited to give me this unquenchable desire for truth, which would finally lead me back to him.

An amusing incident happened during my years in the Peoples' Liberation Army. My grandmother found two blind fortune-tellers and paid them to tell my fortune. As it happened, both told her, "This grandson of yours is something special. He will keep on rising until he attains the highest position." When my family heard this, they were in a daze of joy. But when I got the news, I laughed and thought, "What does that mean, the highest position? Will I be national chairman? Secretary of the United Nations?" Looking back now, I see I was, indeed, restlessly searching for that which is above, until I found the high God and my search came to an end. So can what we call "destiny" turn out to be the calling of God? Jesus said, "The one who seeks finds" (Matt 7:8). I was a seeker and in the end came to God. This was not my own doing, but his gift.

Sometimes the search can cause a seeker to become proud, supposing that he found what he was looking for by his own wisdom and will power. Looking back, I see that God allows a seeker to go down blind alleys, allowing despair to teach him humility, so that he genuinely turns to God, calls on him, and finally gains from him the true satisfaction that humanity seeks.

In 1989, with the initial, overwhelming success of the democracy movement, then its sudden, crushing failure, with life and death all around me, I came to recognize my sin and limitations. All my old idols had been smashed. The party and leaders in whom I invested so much hope had caused me to lose hope. The fatherland in which I had put my trust, and to which I was deeply committed, suddenly slammed the door in my face. I was an exile. I once believed without wavering in the People's Government, but now—where had that faith gone? I had been proud of my own wisdom, but that too no longer seemed reliable. In the freedom that had suddenly come to us—under the temptation of authority, power, wealth, and sex—my ethics and the morality of us noble-minded reformers all seemed to collapse like a house of cards. Truth, justice, intuitive knowledge, and love—all these sacred and inviolable things—had been unceremoniously trampled in the dirt. Being far from home and not knowing when the exile would end, the impotence and frailty of emotions revealed themselves in ways that I could not deny.

Pushed by divine grace to the edge, I finally began to pay attention to God. And God, the root of all life, began to reveal himself.

In the refugee center in Paris, a pastor gave me a copy of the Bible. Though I had owned a copy of this book, I had never had time or desire to read it. In some surprise, I noted in my diary, "I grew up reading Mao and Marx, and singing 'The East is Red' and 'The Internationale,' but until now, I never thought about reading the Bible!"

Jesus said, "Blessed are the poor in spirit ... those who mourn ... the meek" (Matt 5:3–5). God loved me and so molded me into the person that I am, or rather, made me return to my true form, so I could receive the blessings he wanted to give me all along. This is what "amazing grace" means to me.

Second, the love of God attracted me. It was while I was studying as a visiting scholar at Princeton University that I had my first serious encounter with Christians. At the time my feeling of aimlessness and depression was strong. The saying "Attain the sky and lose the earth" describes my life at that time; although I had all kinds of freedom overseas, I seemed to have lost my home and my roots.

The love of Christians I met caught me by surprise. Not only did they show compassion for physical needs (however insignificant), more important was a feeling of consideration, the warmth one could feel behind the kind actions. They cared for my concerns and prayed for my family continually. The weekend meetings I attended seemed full of joy. Faces seemed to reflect a light, with honesty shining from their eyes. Being around such people, one could be as sincere and unguarded as with a friendly group of children. Although I didn't really understand the sermons, somehow that didn't seem so important; I was conquered by the atmosphere of sincere friendship and honesty. But my reason soon recovered and I thought to myself, "I don't know whether what they believe or delude themselves into thinking is true or false. But if there is a power above this world that causes human kindness to reveal itself like this, I ought to investigate and see what this power might be."

My Christian friends ascribed all the virtue in themselves to Jesus, just as they blamed themselves for their own sins. They thus turned the focus of my attention from themselves to Jesus. They were studying the book of Hebrews at the time, but advised me to read the Gospels first. I started from the Gospel of Matthew. I will never forget how moved and full of joy I felt reading the words of Jesus for the first time. When, in a simple metaphor, he used the sun and the rain to describe the heavenly Father's love; when he pointed to the birds of the air and the wild flowers and exhorted his disciples not to worry about tomorrow; when he told a woman who had committed adultery, "Then neither do I condemn you ... Go now and leave your life of sin" (John 8:11); when on the cross he prayed for those who were killing him, "Father, forgive them, for they do not know what they are doing" (Luke 23:34)—reading such things, my eyes often filled with tears.

What moved me so deeply? When I read Jesus' words, "My sheep listen to my voice" (John 10:27), I said almost without thinking, "Yes, I know I am your sheep!"

Facing Jesus like this, a beam from heaven seemed to pass through (maybe even around) my mind and shine directly into my soul, carrying with it a warmth that is not of this world, transmitting both light and power. When reason slowly regained its strength and tried to test whether what I had just experienced was rational or not, the facts had already brought my reason to the point that it had no choice but to humbly surrender.

Third, God's Spirit gave me new birth. I know well that human wisdom, morality, and will power cannot cause a person to be born again, because these things are all a part of the self. I adored intellect, because it was a powerful tool that served the ego. Precisely for this reason, it could not transform the ego that it served. So my understanding of God was not enough to cause me to believe; faith is something that transcends reason, so it cannot itself depend on reason but must depend on the Spirit of God.

So when Nicodemus said to Jesus, "We know that you are a teacher who has come from God. For no one could perform the signs you are doing if God were not with him" (John 3:2), he was basing this on a kind of reasoning. Although there was nothing wrong with his reasoning, it was not enough to cause him to know God or allow him to be born again (which are really the same thing). Jesus said, "No one can enter the kingdom of God unless they are born of water and the Spirit" (John 3:5).

The Holy Spirit blows like a breeze into the soul. When the soul is awakened by the gentle touch of the Spirit, she sees that she already rests in the bosom of God.

The life of Jesus (his character and words, his blood and flesh) is the wind of the Spirit that wafts over humanity. After I opened the shutters of my heart (I had closed my eyes), I would never be the same.

I discovered my own corruption and ugliness, and could now admit that I was a sinner. I was easily moved to tears, and more easily than before felt gratitude and satisfaction. I began to feel pity for other people's weaknesses. Like threads of mist scattered before a great wind, the hatred and bitterness seemed to be blown out of my heart. I had always despised a life of selfish aggrandizement, but only now really understood what it meant to lose one's self in a holy purpose. All my seemingly noble ideals had been built on corruption, which was why they had seemed so flimsy in the face of calm and storm alike, failure and success. But now God began to work in my life.

The relationship between my wife and I had become terrible; in despair, at times we argued about divorce. We both recognized that we just couldn't get along. While there are still areas in our lives that don't seem to mesh well, we are now able to accept one another, temper one another, and grow together. We now confess our own sins before God, forgive the other's faults, and receive God's love. Before, it was the other way around: we confessed the other's sins, forgave our own faults, and gained pain and bitterness as a reward. Thinking of good friends in Beijing who advised us not to divorce twenty years ago, some have divorced, others separated, while the two of us have held together—I feel this is entirely by the grace of God!

Of course I still have weaknesses and sin. God continually warns me not to look at myself too highly or demand too much from others. But I am deeply aware of living in the light, because unless one lives in the light, one cannot see one's own dark shadow.

CHRISTIANITY AND CHINESE CIVILIZATION

When I entered the Chinese church, I grew concerned: after we Chinese become Christians, are we still Chinese? I asked this because it seemed that a lot of Chinese Christians are intimately familiar with the history of Israel but don't bother to ask about the five thousand years of Chinese history, disdaining to think about it at all. Or they see Chinese civilization and the Christian faith as being somehow in conflict, as if the God that we believe in had no jurisdiction over five millennia of Chinese civilization.

And there does seem to be conflict. Partly the apparent conflict between Christianity and Chinese culture is due to cultural superiority on the part of Chinese, a comrade feeling with the Boxer rebels, who tried to physically drive all foreigners out of China in 1900, or kill them. It is also due to hasty arguments by some popes and theologians that strained the relationship between Christianity and the Chinese people, to the point that any desire to link the two seemed immoral and perverse to those on both sides.

BIBLICAL PRINCIPLES

But the God I trust in is great! He transcends the world of mere human speculations. I didn't want to hide in some corner, cut off from my own society, and enjoy the spiritual isolation. The Christian faith touches on heaven, earth, and everything else. Jesus spoke about the sun, the rain, flowers of the earth, and the birds of the air. He gave us the good news without boundaries! Since all things are his creation, is it really credible that for five thousand years Chinese civilization remained completely outside his control?

I believe that, in fact, God was the God of the Chinese from ancient times. He was also Lord of China and left marks on our civilization as well. One can find traces of God's general revelation in Chinese culture. The ancient Chinese classics, for instance, carry traces of almost all the truths in the first eleven chapters of Genesis.

Biblical theism teaches us that God is the source of all peoples (Acts 17:26), the light of all humanity (John 1:4), and King of all the earth (Ps 47:8). God is not only the God of the Jews, but also of the Gentiles (Rom 3:29).

The biblical concept of revelation tells us that God's general revelation fills the earth (Ps 19), informs cultures (Acts 17:23), and is broadcast into the hearts of men (Rom 1:19), so that we "would seek him and perhaps reach out for him and find him, though he is not far from any one of us" (Acts 17:27).

The biblical view of history shows that God is Lord of all human history (Ps 29:10; Jer 10:10; Acts 14:16). Modern people are all descendants of Noah. Given the common history that the first chapters of Genesis record, one would think it would be possible to find traces of that story in any civilization that is sufficiently ancient.

LAO ZI AND THE BIBLE

The Holy Spirit led me. I noticed a Bible verse: the fruit of the Spirit is love, joy, peace, and so forth (Gal 5:22–23). There is no law against these things, because goodness transcends law. I suddenly remembered a paradoxical saying by the ancient Chinese philosopher Lao Zi: "The greatest virtue is not virtuous, and that is where its virtue lies. Lesser virtue clings to virtue, which is why it is lacking in virtue." In other words, one who belongs to the Way, or Tao, and honors ultimate virtue, need not assiduously keep every ethical rule, because the law has been internalized. But one who assiduously obeys those rules, demonstrates that he has yet to internalize them. This looked like a footnote to what Paul said about the fruit of the Spirit! That insight set me on track.

I had researched Lao Zi's great work, the *Dao Dejing* (the Scripture of the Way and of Virtue) as an atheist. But now, reading it in the light of faith, what I found in the book simply blew me away!

At a minimum the Tao (Way) Lao Zi wrote about seemed to possess the following qualities:

- The Tao is utterly unique, eternally self-existent, regardless of what people know or don't know, believe or fail to believe about it.

- The Tao is Creator of all things, loving and nourishing them.

- Tao is above human wisdom. It transcends mere ethics and phenomenal objects.

- Tao is eternally alive, without death.

- Tao is speaking to humanity with words and using wonderful acts to reveal itself to humanity in a wordless revelation.

- Tao is just, in the midst of all the tragic mysteries of life; Master of life and death who both gives and takes away.

Tao is the Savior of mortals who descends into sin and death. By depending on his own wisdom and moral virtue, man cannot save himself. We must repent, make a U-turn, and enter eternal life, looking to and hoping in the Incarnate Sage.

This Sage (literally "holy man") that Lao Zi also wrote about a great deal comes across as an extraordinary human being.

The ancient Chinese defined the word "holy" here (聖) as "connecting" (presumably to the spirits above). Mencius explained, "That which is truly great and transforms material reality can be called *holy*. That which is holy and beyond our knowing can be called *divine*" (emphasis mine). To put it simply, the Sage reveals the Tao that cannot be intellectually grasped. He is given in common to all mankind, becoming the medium through which God above shows himself to humanity below.

The *Dao Dejing*, a work so concise that a single word in it is as precious as a thousand pieces of gold, nevertheless speaks of this "holy man" in a full third of its eighty-one verses.

The Sage perfectly manifests the Way, whose character he richly reveals. The Sage inherits the light and eternity of the Way of Heaven and comes to save humanity. He holds to the form of the Tao. All people under heaven seek to come to him and receive peace.

He achieves great things but does not stand upon his achievements. While not aggrandizing himself, he achieves greatness, and his word never fades away.

The Sage is aware of his own glory but willingly suffers humiliation. He is not ignorant of the light that shines on him but willingly enters the darkness so that people in all the world can know the One who mediates the Heavenly Way.

He leads people out of their wrongdoings.

He is humble in outward form but holds treasure within.

The sage Lao Zi describes suffers indignation, humiliation, and trial, yet he is great, he is Lord, and he is King.

No one remotely like this has ever appeared in Chinese history. Yet Lao Zi's expressions are full of sincerity and credibility. They are direct and unwavering, frankly expressed, brooking no doubts. Lao Zi didn't say, "Maybe a sage like this will appear," or "Supposing there be a man like that," or "There ought to be such a person." He didn't even say, "Such a sage must exist!" No, he said with remarkable confidence, "Therefore the Sage does this and that."

Lao Zi also often talked about "cultivating the Way." Consider three of his metaphors: The metaphor of light: "The Great Tao entirely belongs to the Light. The Sage inherits this shining light." It is through the appearance of this incarnate Light that humanity returns to the presence of Light itself.

The metaphor of water: "The Tao that is above all other ways moistens and irrigates all things like water, and does not contest with earthly beings." Water is the softest and most yielding of substances, yet also the most powerful. Water willingly flows to the low, humble places that people despise. Lao Zi compared the Way to water in that it fills up low-lying depressions, making what once looked contemptible whole, and what was crooked straight. By it, that which has been abandoned gains new life, and the hungry and thirsty are made satisfied.

The metaphor of mother and child compares Tao to a mother and humanity to her children. Lao Zi exploited this metaphor in three expressions: "There is a Mother," "Return to the Mother," "Eat and drink from the Mother." Who is weaker than an infant? To Lao Zi a person who seems rich in moral virtue is really just a naked child in desperate need of his mother.

My thesis on this subject at the Reformed Seminary, and then the book I later wrote, *Lao Zi vs. the Bible*, inspired a great deal of debate among Chinese theologians.[1]

I continued to research Chinese history. Beginning with the semilegendary sage-kings Yao, Shun, and Yu, and the three earliest dynasties, Xia, Shang, and Zhou, I discovered that God had long been at work in China manifesting his authority. I then wrote a book called *Divine Land: A Record of Repentance*, which was later transposed into a seven-part documentary called *China's Confessions*, retelling the history of China from this perspective.

THE WAY OF REVERENCE IN ANCIENT CHINA

Chinese all know about the Four Books and Five Classics, which served as the basic curriculum for Chinese students from the time of Isaiah to almost the First World War. The Five Classics were written first and contain many expressions of respect for and praise to God. For example in the *Book of Poetry*, the textbook from which Confucius taught his

---

1   *Lao Zi vs. the Bible* (Taipei, Taiwan: Cosmic Light Publishers, 1996). Editor's Note: The English version of the book was published in 2011 and is available on Amazon. I describe some of the debate over Yuan's arguments in my dissertation and make the case that Yuan's points about the Tao and the Sage are justified in relation to both Christian theology and ancient Chinese thought.

disciples, the Taiwanese writer Li Ao counts several hundred mentions of "Heaven" and "*Shang Di*," which were the main synonyms for God in the China of antiquity. The Four Books are much the same. In the most famous of them, the *Analects* of Confucius, China's great teacher says, "If I were to hear about the Way in the morning, and then die that evening, I would die satisfied." What does this mean? First, it implies he knew there was a true Way. Second, it means he recognized that he did not know it yet. Third, it means he understood that it would be worth giving one's life to know the Way. Who today shows such hunger for truth?

One shouldn't underestimate the ancient Chinese. Some claim Confucius was an atheist, but that is simply blind. When he was sick, a student asked him, "Teacher, have you prayed?" Confucius replied, "I've already been praying for a long time." He also said, "If one sins against Heaven, there is no one else he can pray to."

True, Confucius is also famously quoted as saying, "Respect the gods and spirits, but keep your distance from them." Some people use this to try to prove that Confucius didn't believe in God at all. Not so! At the time, this word translated as "god" (神) was used to refer to all sorts of deities: gods of mountains, sea, even the god of the kitchen stove. This is why Lao Zi and Confucius only used the terms "Tao," "*Shang Di*," and "Heaven," rather than a word that meant "gods, in general," to refer to the one and only Most High.

I believe that if these ancient sages—Lao Zi, Confucius, Mo Zi, Zhuang Zi, Mencius—were to meet Jesus, they would declare Jesus to be Lord. Perhaps they are among those Jesus had in mind when he told his disciples: "Blessed are your eyes because they see, and your ears because they hear. For truly I tell you, many prophets and righteous men longed to see what you see but did not see it, and to hear what you hear but did not hear it" (Matt 13:16–17).

There is a great deal of evidence that the ancient Chinese respected God. I cannot give all the details here, but more can be found in my books and documentaries.

Looking at China's five-thousand-year history as a whole then, the trend of the first 2,500 years is reverence for God, while the main trend of the last 2,500 years seems to be rebellion against him. The dividing line can roughly be set at a historical era called the Spring and Autumn or Warring States period.

For the second half of our history, Chinese have looked at the emperor as divine, effectively rendering to Caesar the worship that belongs to God. Dynasties changed, contenders struggled viciously for power, victors becoming kings, and losers outlaws—the tumultuous political history of China has been long and painful. But the ultimate source of that pain, I believe, was alienation from God. The "True Dragon Son of Heaven," as the emperor was called, made himself as God.

Even so, God has always been calling to China. Great thinkers sought him. Dong Zhongshu, the leading Confucian philosopher of the Han dynasty (206 BC–AD 220), and the neo-Confucianists of the Song (960–1279) and Ming (1368–1644) all recognized human sin and looked in every direction for some solution, some exit strategy from the bitterness of Chinese history. It was a pity that in all their searching they failed to find God. They thought they could depend on human moral training to save themselves, and they all failed.

It's not that God was unaware of the hard and rebellious path that the Chinese people were taking. Early on he began to send his servants. At the beginning of the Tang dynasty (618–907), the Nestorian faith already arrived in China, though it failed to sink roots. During the Mongol dynasty (also called the Yuan dynasty, 1271–1368), both Nestorians and Catholics came to China, also failing to sink deep roots. At the end of the Ming and early Qing (1644–1911), Jesuit missionaries like Matteo Ricci, Ferdinand Verbiost, and Adam Schall arrived, shaking up Chinese society, with a prime minister, Xu Guangqi, and several department heads receiving baptism. Yet the Chinese people as a whole stubbornly rejected and opposed God's call.

It is only in the modern era, when the time was ripe, that William Morrison, Hudson Taylor, and others brought Protestant Christianity to China. In 1949 the Chinese Communist Party expelled all missionaries and tried to control, then extinguish, the church. They never realized that in the midst of this persecution the will of God would be fulfilled: the native church would sink deep roots into Chinese soil and grow and thrive. Today Christianity is no longer a foreign religion, and it cannot easily be expelled or extinguished.

THE DIVINE LAND REPENTS AND IS BORN AGAIN

The process by which the Christian faith sunk its roots into Chinese soil and began to spread has been terribly painful. I'm grateful to have the chance to record some of this valuable history in my documentary series, *The Cross*.

Looking at the five millennia of Chinese history as a whole, China seemed to move from dim reverence to abject rebellion. Chinese seemed paradoxically to be painstakingly searching for God, even while stubbornly brushing him off. In the end I believe that, in Jesus Christ, China must return to its truest spiritual roots in God.

After 2,500 years, two general trends stand out: First, those periods in Chinese history that have been best, aside from the ancient sage-kings Confucius admired, all followed Lao Zi's ideas about the Tao and rule by gentleness or "rule without force": the glory years of the Han dynasty, the early days of the Tang (under Tai Zong), and the later revival under Emperor Xuan Zong, and the rule of the great Kang Xi, emperor of the early Qing. As I showed earlier, among the teachers of ancient China, Lao Zi, the originator of Taoist thought, came closest to Christianity. There is a common saying: "When the world is at peace, everyone follows the Tao; when the world is chaotic, the Buddhist school prospers; but when the world descends into turbulent times, the Confucius school is always responsible."

Second, beginning with the Han (206 BC–AD 220), under almost every dynasty, the first generation of leaders seizes territory, the second and third generations build up a civilization in that territory, and before the fourth and fifth generations end, corruption and disintegration set in. One of the last great men of the Qing dynasty, Huang Yanpei, once asked Mao Zedong, when they were in the northern Communist fortress of Yanan, how, having conquered China, he would escape this vicious cycle? Mao Zedong answered: "Rely on the People."

The present, with the economy expanding rapidly and China growing increasingly powerful, is, one might say, one of the best periods in Chinese history. We are also beginning to move into the fourth and fifth generations (the eight-year leadership of today's Communist Party revolves a bit more quickly than in the past), and corruption and danger already threaten.

From a Christian standpoint, the way to end this vicious historical cycle is not merely democratization, though the corruption we see today proves that the democracy movement of 1989 is not at all outmoded. The root of modern democracy is Christian civilization. Until the souls of the Chinese people have been reborn, the Chinese still don't recognize where their own value and dignity lie. And until they confess that all people are sinners who need constraint, "democracy" is just castles in the clouds.

And in Western "Christian" nations, for people who once revered God, having left him further and further behind, all that prosperity, power, freedom, and democracy is no longer a blessing, but become a curse as righteousness degrades into sin.

Chinese like to say the twenty-first century will be China's century. But the Chinese need to return to God. No nation in history, having become powerful, has been able to continue long without faith. England was once called the empire on which the sun never set. At that time missionaries were largely English. Afterwards America became the most powerful nation, and America then sent out the most missionaries. In the twenty-first century I believe God will not allow China to remain powerful without Christian faith. A country with no reverence for God does harm, like Nazi Germany or imperial Japan and Italy, and God will not permit that to persist.

–EIGHT–

A CONVERSATION WITH DON RICHARDSON

Few adventures stories are as improbable as Don Richardson's life. A missionary among cannibals and headhunters (the fascinating subject of his best-selling book, *Peace Child*), Don is a talented storyteller, linguist, and anthropologist. As he showed in his folksy yet intellectually revealing *Eternity in Their Hearts*, Don has the knack of changing how "civilized" peoples think about how God works in the world, almost as much as the Sawi tribe to whom he and his wife Carol introduced modernity. Don spoke by phone from his home in Florida.

© 2012 David Marshall

I. BEGINNINGS

David Marshall: **You've been based in California and Florida. Did New Guinea spoil you for a temperate climate?**

Don Richardson: Yes, I think it did. And it made me enjoy Florida, because other people say, "It's so humid." And I say, "This is humid? You don't know what humidity is—sea level in New Guinea."

You were born in Victoria, BC, right?

I was born in Charlottetown, Prince Edward Island.

Oh! On the other side of the country!

Yes. I was ten years old when we moved from an island in the east to an island in the west of Canada.

So you grew up partly on Vancouver Island?

Yes, from the age of ten on.

How did you know God was calling you to become a missionary?

I became a believer in Jesus at seventeen years of age, through the influence of another teenager, actually about two years older than me—Jim Sadler. I wanted to go climbing in the mountains of Vancouver Island. In fact there were peaks there that had never been climbed. And at fourteen years of age, I needed someone to go with me, because there were cougars and black bears and things out there.

Jim was such a consistent believer and had such a wonderful character [and] compassion, and was a true friend. He would invite me to go to Youth for Christ meetings in Victoria from time to time. I really liked their cheerful singing—I'd been raised Episcopalian. These songs were youthful and joyful, and people sang to God in the second person, instead of just singing about him in the third person.

But I felt uncomfortable with the altar calls at the end of each meeting. I thought, "This is intruding upon my privacy; I'm not sure I like this." But all the people involved were like Jim. And I thought they all had the same thing. What is it? Why do I find myself admiring them? The other teenagers I knew were kind of crass, crude, vulgar …

My father, who died shortly after he deposited us in Victoria, BC, was the epitome of wisdom. I was living by what he taught me, and he taught me a lot of good things—none of it included being born again and trusting Jesus as your Savior. So, I liked this gospel business because of the nice influence it had on the people who believed it, but it was not for me. Because my Dad didn't say anything about it.

So the Holy Spirit needed a redemptive analogy to get past that barrier in my thinking. And he did …

What do you mean by "redemptive analogy"?

It's something in a person's culture, someone in a person's background, that he or she cherishes, feels very close to—something that is unique to him and his group of people in the world. And it is also like a "cultural compass" pointing to Jesus. It links somehow with at least one aspect of the gospel.

What was the redemptive analogy for you?

Jim was getting rather discouraged, because three years he'd spent just climbing mountains each summer and sharing a lot of experiences—ping pong, etc. I still didn't come to the Lord. But he said, "I'm going to invite Don to just one more Youth for Christ meeting, and if he doesn't come to the Lord tonight, you'd better get someone else."

That evening the man who was to going to speak was hidden behind the pulpit. I didn't see him until he was introduced. I was amazed, because Percy Wills from a distance looked almost exactly like my father.

He preached the gospel, and it was as if my father had come back from the grave to say to me through him, "Don, I didn't say anything about this while I was alive with you, but I'm telling you now through this man: this message is true, believe it, and you will not be disloyal to me."

And that's all it took. So when the invitation was given, I raised my hand …

Two weeks later, someone invited me to a camp meeting out in the forest of Vancouver Island. And there for the first time I heard a missionary from Africa speaking about missions and saying, "The greatest privilege any Christian can have is to be selected by God to be his emissary, the first to cross a new frontier somewhere in the world, bringing the knowledge of Jesus to lost people."

I listened, and about twenty minutes into his message I remembered that while I was nine years old, back on the other side of Canada, I prayed asking God to help me find out what I should be when I grew up. People always asked me, "What are you going to be when you grow up?" And I got tired of saying, "I don't know." I prayed and said, "Lord, please help me find out, so I can tell them!" And I said, "I hope it's something really interesting!" I felt peace at the time that he heard me.

I remembered praying that prayer, and suddenly the presence of God was there, and I knew that what this man was talking about was God's answer to me.

II. INTO THE JUNGLE

When I taught at a secular university in Japan, I sometimes gave *Peace Child* to some of my better students to read. It's a great story! How many copies are in print now?

Well over 400,000, maybe getting close to half a million. And that in, last I heard, twenty-seven languages.

What is the most obscure language that it's been translated into?

Latvian. In January, almost a year ago, Christians in Latvia invited me to Riga, the capital city, to teach seventy Latvian students preparing for cross-cultural ministry in the southern part of the Soviet Union.

Among Muslims?

Uh-huh. And they had me fly there to instruct them for four days. On the weekend I spoke in a citywide missions conference, and forty more young Latvian men and women came forward in the invitation …

I noticed it was a missionary named John McCain who originally assigned you to the Sawi people. Did he get into politics later on?

Here's the amazing thing. My colleague John McCain not only had the same name, he even looked like a twin brother. Maybe a little taller, but his facial features were almost identical—and he had the same name. He was from Florida. I don't know whether they were twins and separated …

The Sawi people were cannibals and headhunters, and you also lived among snakes and crocodiles and mosquitoes. I can understand how a young man looking for adventure would want to live in a place like that, but why did your wife go along?

When I knew I was called as a foreign missionary and knew I would probably go to a pretty wild place, I was at seventeen years of age, of course, interested in girls. And I said, "Lord, there's probably not many pretty girls that would be willing to go to the kind of place I think I'm going to some day somewhere in the world. But if you can find for me a young woman who loves you at least as much as I do and is willing to go anywhere you would call us, and if you know she's right for me and I'm right for her, would you please triangulate us together and enable us to recognize each other when we meet." And I said, "And if she could be really pretty, that would be nice too." And God heard that prayer!

Carol Soderstrom from Oklahoma, a pastor's daughter, was called to missionary service from ten years of age. She had met missionaries who were graduates of Prairie Bible Institute in Alberta, Canada. She and her parents— her mother and pastor father—were very impressed, saying, "That school produces people that don't just look for the easy places. They're willing to go where it's tough, and they stick to the job and get the job done."

So they drove her all the way from Oklahoma, when she graduated from high school, to Prairie Bible Institute, as it was called at the time. We were in the same class. By the time we were juniors I really [felt] drawn to her. You couldn't have a lot of dating on that campus; there were limitations. But we fell in love.

I wanted to get married right after graduation. Ebenezer Vine [E.G. Vine], of what is now called World Team, had come to our campus and pleaded for workers to go into the interior of a big island north of Australia called New Guinea. There were tribes in the interior that were completely uncontacted. The Netherlands government had given Ebenezer Vine permission to send missionaries in, as long as they wouldn't require Dutch policemen and soldiers to go with them to protect them. And Mr. Vine said, "No, no, no, we don't need that. Being eaten by cannibals is a missionary's occupational hazard." Carol and I were among a group that volunteered.

Did you have to swallow a few times and pray an extra amount before you brought your kids along?

Well, actually, we were both single when we decided to go.

But when you went to the Sawis.

We didn't go right away, because God called Carol to take three years of nurse's training. That stunned me. I thought, "I've already been in love for two years, now I have to wait another three years—who am I, Jacob?"

But God gave me grace to wait for her. Then we were married … by the time we went out to the field across the Pacific, we had our firstborn son, little Stephen. Now all our colleagues of World Team were working in the mountains among the Dani tribe. In the mountains of New Guinea the people were welcoming. I mean, they had their wars among themselves. But they welcomed these light-skinned strangers who brought steel tools and medicine and other things that the people thought were great. And they were already beginning to respond to the gospel. So there was already a lot of work to be done among the Danis. And the temperature there is pleasant.

I get the feeling from *Lords of the Earth* that you enjoy hiking in the mountains.

I do, I do! And there wasn't even any malaria there! It was going to come in when aircraft began to come in—mosquitoes would hitch a ride. So it was like a garden of Eden, except for the violence of the people. The missionaries said, "You and Carol are welcome to work with us here! There's lots to be done. But," they said, "there is a new tribe that's been discovered in the swamps way to the south. We just want to let you know, if you do feel God wants you to go where no one else has ever gone—there is that tribe."

I felt God whispering to my heart saying, "Don, go to that tribe! They're the ones that I've prepared for you to bear witness among for me." And I said to the Lord, "You know it's hot and humid, there's malaria there, there's crocodiles in the river, there's tropical diseases, and the people are cannibals and headhunters." The Danis who were in the area where World Team was working warred among themselves, but they were not cannibals, nor were they headhunters. They were violent, but that was the end of it. But the Sawi were known to be cannibals *and* headhunters, which is a rare combination.

I said, "Carol is a pastor's daughter from Cincinnati, Ohio," previously Oklahoma. I said, "She's been on a camping trip or two, but never anything like this. So you'll have to give her your own personal assurance, because I can't force her to go with me to that wild place against her will."

God gave her assurance. She said, "I think God wants us to go there." And we went among them with peace. It was like God was saying, "I know they're headhunters, I know they're cannibals—don't worry, I've taken care of everything. Just go among them, and I've got a ministry match made in heaven, waiting for you, and you have to go among them to find it."

I like the way you begin the story of *Peace Child* in their world. Stone Age life was, as Thomas Hobbes put it, "solitary, poor, nasty, brutish, and short." Living among people who had lived that way for so many centuries—did you ever doubt God's love for them, or why he would allow them to live that way for so long?

No. I was convinced that every human being is made in the image of God. And that image of God is there to be restored, redeemed, brought back to relationship with the owner of that image. So there was no question that God loved them. And I knew that he loved Carol and loved Stephen—and we went among them with this assurance.

All the tribes of New Guinea are black-skinned, and some of them had never seen a white-skinned person. But the reports about white-skinned persons called *tuans* were positive, because wherever *tuans* went they brought *ovat*, which means medicine; and *garum* … steel tools to replace stone tools; nylon fishline; fishhooks; etc. So they were saying wistfully, asking other tribes a little closer to civilization, "Are there any spare *tuans* around? We think we'd like to welcome one." Only to have the other tribes responded nastily saying, "A *tuan* live among you? Who do you think you are? They're a scarce commodity. They're choosy where they live—don't get your hopes up, you wretched Sawi!"

Hearing these insulting comments, the Sawi people said, "Perhaps they're right, we'll never be favored." They also said, "Just in case a *tuan* finds out that we live here and decides he wants to come and live among us—when we find out that that *tuan* has chosen us, we will let that *tuan* know in no uncertain terms we choose him. He'll be our *tuan*, we'll be his tribe."

The kind of white people who went among them were apparently not the traders or soldiers so many primitive tribes have experienced.

Yes—policemen, soldiers, or land-grabbers, or loggers …

Why did it help the Sawi tribesmen to get their first experience of the outside world from missionaries?

Well, because we brought the medicine, we brought steel tools. And we didn't give things out—we gave medicine free, but we didn't give hardware out free. Because if you give one man a free steel ax that costs you several dollars, and there's several thousand men—you're in trouble. If you don't give every man a steel ax—which is going to cost you quite a bit—then, "Oh, you don't love us." And it also makes grown men into children. It transforms these men who are able to survive in that wilderness so marvelously—it makes them like dependent beggars. You don't want to do that.

So I had to set a certain number of days for a steel ax, and a certain amount of freshly killed pork from a wild pig for a knife or a machete, and a certain amount of salt for a fish. And the people liked that. And so it was mutual—they'd bring us food, we'd pay them with things they wanted. They'd bring us firewood for our stove, we'd pay them with things they wanted.

In the modern world we've seen a lot of stories like this. Not just primitive tribes—in the democracy movement in 1989, there was a group of Chinese intellectuals who made a TV series called *The River Elegy*. They used the metaphor of the Yellow River that rises in the Western Highlands of Asia and flows to the ocean; they said China is like that river. It's been depending on itself, feeding itself, for thousands of years. But in the modern era, it needs to "flow to the deep blue sea," as they put it, to mix with other nations. And that's what the Sawi people have done through your work.

David, some of the young men are already graduating from university in eastern Indonesia. Some of them are Christian government employees in a Muslim nation, Indonesia.

One of the things that's striking about your story is, here these people are living in New Guinea by themselves. They don't know much about the outside world, they might have seen an airplane flying overhead once in a while …

They thought it was about sixty miles wide.

And then suddenly they're part of the human race. And you're the conduit—someone's going to come and someone's going to be the conduit …

It's inevitable. You just have to pray, "May the most beneficial outside influence get there first."

What is their general status in Indonesia? How are they doing economically? I imagine it's a lot different from when you were living there?

Oh my, yes, very different. Once that former Dutch colony became the easternmost province of Indonesia, it was inevitable that brown-skinned Indonesian people speaking the Indonesian language would come flooding in, bringing the Muslim religion and bringing outside world economics. So I had to train the Sawi about economics, otherwise an Indonesian who looked down upon them as inferior because of their black skin and kinky hair might say, "I wanna buy your chicken," and give them some paper money, that if the tribesman doesn't know the value of different denominations of currency, he might sell a chicken that's worth five hundred rupees, but only get ten rupees, and won't even buy a fishhook for a chicken. [Or] even take over the land. People think to get them in debt, and then ask to have sex with their daughter, to pay a debt. And they introduce sexual diseases …

Does the gospel help you see the experience of different tribes and different peoples around the world as a single unified story?

Yes … I am working on the idea that, just as there was a redemptive analogy for the Sawi—there was a "peace child"—and the Yali through places of refuge, and through the upside down tree in India, I began to think, "What about an all-encompassing redemptive analogy for the scientific mind, for people who demand logic to the nth degree?"

III. GOD AND THE ANTHROPOLOGISTS

Let me ask about the book *Eternity in Their Hearts*. Lots of people have been influenced by your book, including me. Part of the book talks about people around the world who are aware of God. In his recent best seller, *The God Delusion*, Richard Dawkins wrote: "Not surprisingly, since it is founded on local traditions of private revelation rather than evidence, the God Hypothesis comes in many versions. Historians of religion recognize a progression from private tribal animisms, through polytheisms such as those of the Greeks, Romans, and Norsemen, to monotheisms such as Judaism and its derivatives, Christianity and Islam."

Is Dawkins right about the history of religions?

Absolutely not. What he's picking up on is the theory promulgated back in the 1870s by a British anthropologist—one of the first people called an anthropologist—Edmund B. Tylor. And Tylor said, "Well, you know, Charles Darwin is promulgating biological evolution. What about social evolution?

Let's see if we can apply the principles of biological evolution to the social life of mankind!"

He said, "OK, evolution begins with something very simple and gradually works its way to something more complex, more profound. What's the simplest kind of religion? Animism. Animists believe in spirits and ghosts of trees, rocks, rivers. That's the simplest kind of religion, so it had to be first."

Animism coincided with a stage of human development when there were no class strata and everyone was on the same social level. So all the ghosts and spirits were on the same social level in the imaginary supernatural world, Tylor posited. But gradually mankind developed until there was an upper class. So religious leaders said, "Ah, just as we have the upper class and the lower class, the chiefs and the rulers and the headman and the rank-and-file people, there must be something equivalent to that among the spirits as well."

Thus, gradually, polytheism developed as an echo of class stratification in human society. That's why they had a pantheon of gods in Greece and other places. Gradually, one member of the upper class was elevated to the level of a monarch, a king. "Let's add something in the supernatural world that reflects that," [they said]. And that's when monotheism began to develop—the idea of a supreme God corresponding to a monarch.

So Tylor's theory was that there's no development in religion until something in human society suggests it. It's an imaginary thing, but now that we understand the evolutionary process, it's time for religion to be phased out, it's time we moved beyond it.

You talk about a very interesting guy named Andrew Lang.

Yes, Andrew Lang was a student of Edmund B. Tylor. In fact, Tylor called him one of his best students.

Tylor's theory was based upon an armchair thought experiment. It was not put to the test by anyone going out into the jungles to check with animistic peoples to see if Tylor's thoughts corresponded to reality. Well, who was going out to do the research? Who were interacting?

Missionaries.

Missionaries were! Missionaries learning the languages of hundreds of animistic cultures around the world were surprised to find out that, even though they believed in the spirits, they often believed in one supreme God, often called a sky God, who was invisible to human eyes, who lived in the sky as his primary residence but who also was present everywhere. He was Creator of the heavens and the earth but no one created him. They were animistic people who were still on a single social level, and were not supposed to have developed this idea. But the idea was there.

So Andrew Lang began reading these reports, and he realized that his teacher Edmund B. Tylor was wrong. But meanwhile, Tylor's theory was taken over by liberal theologians in Germany and became a basis for scrutinizing the OT in terms of the *Elohim*, and then leading to Yahweh—it was just an application of Tylor's theory to the OT.

So finally anthropologists said, "Look! Missionaries are sending these reports back about what became known as 'native monotheism,' which refutes Tylor's theory, so we'd better go and check it for ourselves." So they did, and they found it, too. And so Tylor's theory was refuted.

Do you see this widespread awareness of the supreme God as an argument for the existence of God that would be valid in a secular venue?

I certainly do. If the Sawi people I lived among wanted to catch a fish in a pool of water, you don't even know if there's fish there because there's a dark red algae in the water; it's like a black tea, you can't see more than a few inches below the surface. But they found out you take the bark of a certain kind of tree, break it off, and hold a couple pieces of bark under the surface of that pool, swish it back and forth so that the white milky substance on the inside of that bark spreads out into the water. There's an acid in it apparently, and fish do not have eyelids. So the acid is hurting their eyes. They have to come to the surface of the pool to ease the pain of the acid on their bare eyes. And while they're swimming around at least partially blinded, with their heads right at the surface of the pool, the Sawi man takes a long stick, flicks them out on the shore, and he's got fish for dinner!

How did they find out? They didn't conduct scientific tests. They'd didn't say, "Hey, let's take fifty different pieces of bark from fifty different species of tree and put them under the water in fifty different pools and see what happens." Someone knows they need food, they need help, and they arrive in this area, and they're guided to find things to survive. But this idea that God is there, it's innate. And people have to try very hard to really dig down and make themselves believe there's no God. Did you see the film *Expelled* by Stein?

Yes.

And Stein asked Richard Dawkins, "Sir, if you meet God, what will you say to him?" And do you remember how Dawkins answered him?

He quoted from Bertrand Russell ...

He quoted Bertrand Russell's saying, "Sir, why did you go to such extreme measures to hide yourself?" Well that implies that if God exists and wants to be recognized, he has to come out and manifest himself to someone like Dawkins, someone like Russell. If I'd been Ben Stein, I'd have asked Richard Dawkins, "OK, so God is responsible to reveal himself to you. Tell me, what sort of a manifestation would you accept as proof? Suppose he appeared to you as a man and said, 'I'm God. Hello, Richard Dawkins.'" Dawkins would say, "Well you're not God, you're just a man." Or suppose he would say, "OK, I'm going to appear as a mile-high man." So suddenly Richard Dawkins is looking at this mile-high man towering above him—would he accept that as proof? No, he'd say this is somebody's state-of-the-art holographic projection! So the point I'm making is that nothing finite can ever be proof of something infinite. So it's a matter of seeing thousands of indications of care, of justice, and of a sense of justice that's in the human heart, that boils over, gets enraged, or can become blasé, feels guilty, knows it should feel outrage when it doesn't.

When I was living in China, I visited a remote Lahu village in southern China with a hill in the middle of town. On top of the hill there was an old wooden church with a bell. When the bell rang, people would come up the hill to church. That church was founded by the Young brothers that you write about. How did all these tribal peoples in Thailand and Burma and southern China—hundreds of thousands of them—become Christians?

They were animistic peoples. When William Marcus Young—and even before him, George Dana Boardman, a colleague of Adoniram Judson—went to the Karen, he found out they not only believed in one supreme God, they even believed that he'd given mankind his sacred writings in a book. The ancestors had had that book and lost it. But one day the true God would send a white brother from the distant West in a ship with white sails to bring another copy of the lost book to them. All the people were waiting, waiting, waiting.

And lo and behold, here came George Dana Boardman, initially to Rangoon. Then he went down to Tavoy in the southern part of Burma. The Karen were in the hills above the city of Tavoy. He arrived in a ship with white sails. And he was a light-skinned person, and he was kind and brotherly. So the Karen, hearing about him, came thronging around the house that he and his wife, Sarah, were moving into ... They said, "We hear you're a white brother from the West. And you're to bring us a book. And the book is supposed to be white also." So Boardman went into his house and picked up his Bible and held it up in front of a crowd of Karen people. And they saw it had a black cover. They all heaved a sigh, "Oh, it's not white, it's a black book. It's not the one."

But then George Dana Boardman opened it and showed them the white pages inside.

Like an Oreo cookie!

Right! So they practically kidnapped George Dana Boardman from the city of Tavoy, saying, "You don't want to stay here. You'd better come up into the hills. We're the people who are really going to welcome you." Thousands of Karen became believers in Jesus Christ as he learned their language and taught them.

So when you talk about redemptive analogies, you're not just talking about some clever devices that missionaries use. You're talking about things that God has done to prepare people.

Yes! Things that are already there, that they own and believe in. They're "cultural compasses," like physical compasses point to magnetic north …

It seems that earlier missionaries were helped by these things, used them, but never thought to extrapolate from their experience to an aspect of God's love that's worldwide and runs down through the ages. They never gave it a name.

IV. ISLAM

Why are you so hostile to Islam?

Well, because the foundations of it are so … unworthy? And violent, and even immoral? The fact that there is a majority of Muslims who are moderate, nice people, good neighbors—and I've got some here where I live—does not attest to the validity of Mohammed and the Koran. They are manifesting a higher level of morality than the one they call a prophet—a morality of [more] good sense and neighborliness than the Koran advocates.

It's not that I'm hostile to Muslims. But I'm hostile to a false prophet—a man who included in the Koran 109 jihad verses, calling for his followers to behead people like you and me. Cut off our fingertips if we don't submit.

There are some verses in the Bible that I'd almost rather were not in there, about doing things to the Canaanites.

You've read *Secrets of the Koran*, and you know how I respond to that.

Let me play devil's advocate for the moment. Some people might say, "If Don Richardson can find redemptive analogies among headhunters in New Guinea, why can't we use the verses in the Koran that talk about the 'Breath of God' and the 'Messiah' to persuade people to Christ?" Or would you oppose that sort of a missionary approach?

There are missionaries who use things like that, and other things I could mention. But there is a problem. Even though Mohammed acknowledged the virgin birth of Jesus and credited him as a prophet, a profound miracle worker, and someone who was going to judge the world at the end of the age, he denied the most important thing—the crucifixion of Jesus. He denied our Lord's atoning death. So there are Muslims that have become Christians because of things such as you just mentioned. But the problem is, more and more Muslims are being taught through the radical Madrassa school system, that don't believe when Christians quote this verse or this verse. Mohammed interpreted reports of the crucifixion of Jesus as the result of the Jews, by means of mistaken identity, crucifying someone else—they thought it was probably Judas getting his just deserts.

But those headhunters in New Guinea—their cultural waters weren't anymore pure than that river they fished from ...

But the thing is, there is nothing in the animistic system that denies the need for the atonement. Hinduism, Buddhism, Judaism acknowledge the need for an atonement. Islam denies it.

Theologically, why would one religion be unique in its opposition to Christianity?

I posit it this way. God seeded the cultures of mankind, beginning thousands of years ago, with redemptive analogies. I made brief reference to the upside down tree in the Vedas. There's an ancient prophesy that "somewhere in the world there's a tree that is upside down because it is rooted in heaven. It goes down from heaven towards the earth ... for the healing of mankind."

David, this is beautiful. Fruit from the branches and healing sap from a wound in the side. This acknowledges the atonement. What a beautiful thing to use for Hindus in India.

This and other things point to a necessary sacrifice. A Sawi father sacrificing the privilege of raising his own son by giving his son away to an enemy father to make peace acknowledges the principle of sacrifice. And the Yali denying himself his perceived right to kill an enemy because that enemy is standing on sacred [ground]. But when Mohammed denied the crucifixion of Jesus, it's like the evil one saw what God had done to prepare the cultures of the world for the redemptive message to be brought at a later time. So the evil one said, "If that's God's strategy, I'm going to neutralize it. I'm going to invent something and spread it out across the earth which will not have a redemptive analogy, which will negate the thing that a redemptive analogy must point to."

But can't you find images of sacrifice in Islam? And can't you find other religions that oppose central Christian doctrines?

Yeah, but Israel still has its Day of Atonement, Yom Kippur. And in Buddhism there are traditions about Arayana Maitreya—the one who suffers, he has wounds in his hands and feet. When you speak of religions, Islam is designed to be unapproachable by the redemptive analogy method. That puts it in a unique category.

Not all Muslims know Mohammed—the supposed prophet—denies the crucifixion of Jesus. A lot of Muslims who don't know that have been brought to the Lord. And then, of course, once they experience the goodness of Christ, it's too late for another Muslim to come in and say, "You became a Christian on the basis of something you shouldn't believe in."

Did your book on the Koran come as a big surprise to a lot of people who had read your other books?

Yes. But a lot of these began to say, "Now it makes sense why Islam is the most difficult system to approach with the gospel." It's like a firewall.

So because the evil one through Mohammed and the Koran raised that firewall, to separate the hearts of Muslims from the gospel of Jesus Christ, we have to find a way to pierce the firewall. What I recommend in *Secrets of the Koran* is, we need to become like Socrates. We have to learn to ask Muslims leading questions that help them to discover on their own the fact that Mohammed discredited himself.

Right after 9/11, there seemed to be more of a defensive tone to *Secrets of the Koran* than your other books. You're thinking about protecting Western civilization even more, maybe, than reaching out with the gospel cross-culturally.

If I have a motivation to protect Western civilization, guess what the main thing is, David? Where are most of the missionaries going out from? Where is most of the support for missionaries coming from?

Isn't there a danger in becoming defensive in tone, rather than being optimistic and outward reaching?

I urge Christians, if you live near a Muslim, invite them to your home! If a Muslim moves into the community, be the one who shows him where the post office is, the bank is, talk to them. And lots of Christians are doing this.

PART III:
CHRIST IN HISTORY

–NINE–

THE FINGERPRINTS OF JESUS

DAVID MARSHALL

David Marshall worked as a missionary and educator in East Asia for thirteen years, combating forced prostitution in Taiwan, and researching Chinese thought. He is the author of five previous books, including *Jesus and the Religions of Man* and *Why the Jesus Seminar Can't Find Jesus and Grandma Marshall Could*. He recently completed a doctorate with the University of Wales, analyzing the work of Yuan Zhiming and creating a Christian model for how world religions relate called Fulfillment Theology. He lives with his wife and two teenage boys in a small town halfway between Seattle and the Cascade Mountains.

"My sheep listen to my voice" (John 10:27). Yuan Zhiming told in chapter 7 how, reading the Gospels, those words expressed his intuition that he had met a real person, whose powerful teachings often brought tears to his eyes. In a sense that response defines a Christian: one who hears the voice of Jesus and is moved to follow. Jesus' words have been translated into thousands of languages, changing history in vast ways.

Why were Jesus' words translated to begin with? For one thing, in the first Gospel, Jesus says, "Go and make disciples of all nations … and surely I am with you always" (Matt 28:19–20). That command launched the mission enterprise, to which men and women like the Brands, the Winters, and Saint Anselm dedicated their lives, and apart from which the modern world cannot be imagined.

I grew up a few minutes' walk from the shore of Puget Sound, in a home where Christianity was taken seriously. But like Anselm, I doubted. I also felt the impulse to cross geographical and cultural boundaries, to "seek out new life and new civilizations," as the black and white box in our living room advised. As an undergraduate at the University of Washington, I argued with my Marxist philosophy professor and read Paul Kurtz on secular humanism. I worked on a Soviet fishing ship off the US West Coast, among sailors who plied the disciples' trade but had not left their nets (caked with cod and hake scales) to follow Jesus. I was full of doubts. Jesus said, "Go," and I was happy to do that. I came to love the sight of terraced rice fields in the mist, the thunder of tropical storms with cicadas playing strings, the taste of a papaya milkshake, even (with some guilt) the smell of incense in Buddhist temples. I read Asian scriptures and studied in a training school for Communist cadres. Taking Jesus' message to the world, I also listened to what the world had to say back.

Did Jesus really want me to pester Communist cadres, prostitutes, or shop owners in a gritty Taipei suburb about religion? Or was "go and preach" inserted later by religious empire builders, unduly influenced perhaps by the hyperactive imperial wanderings of Alexander the Great? Do we hear the true words of Jesus in the Bible at all?

I finished an MA in Chinese religions, then took a teaching position in Japan (surrounded again by people who seemed to have no interest in God) that gave me a lot of time for research. I began reading a group of critics belonging to a group called the Jesus Seminar.

Dr. Robert Funk, founder of the seminar, was a formidable academic: author of Greek grammars, executive director of the Society of Biblical Literature, and chair of the graduate department of religion at Vanderbilt. Comparing himself to Tom Sawyer, who asked other children to help him paint a fence, during the early Reagan years, Funk invited fellow scholars to the Bay Area to discuss what Jesus *really* said and did. Mostly skeptical scholars showed up, were given red, pink, gray, and black beads, and were asked to vote whether Jesus said, probably said, probably did not say, or definitely did not say, a given saying. The seminar concluded that only some 18 percent of the teachings of Jesus in the Gospels actually came from Jesus' mouth.

Funk expressed irritation at students ("untutored sophomores" with "ill-conceived certitudes") who took those words for granted.

But the experts themselves evidently disagreed about what Jesus said and did. Philosopher Raymond Martin wrote a book describing the confusion in biblical studies between "conservatives" like N. T. Wright and John Meier, and Jesus Seminar fellows and other "liberals" like John Crossan, Marcus Borg, and Elizabeth Fiorenza. He concluded on a bewildered note of agnosticism: "One does not enhance one's understanding by pretending to know what one does not know."[1]

If the experts can't find Jesus, where does that leave ordinary Christians? When elephants fight, mice flee to the sidelines. Martin suggested that "nonexperts" lack the "skill and knowledge" even to decide which among the competing sketches of the historical Jesus is most plausible.

Can we hear the voice of Jesus in the Gospels? Is missions based on false premises? Or would Jesus, properly informed of the situation, now tell us:

"Hear my voice? Not at so tender stage of your career. First learn ancient Greek, the language in which the Gospels were written, and Aramaic, my native tongue. Study the Hebrew Scriptures, and the interpretative traditions by which Jewish schools read the Septuagint, in which I was educated. Immerse yourself in redactive criticism, form criticism, and midrash. That will give you some feel for what is at least possible.

---

1   Raymond Martin, *The Elusive Messiah: A Philosophical Overview of the Quest for the Historical Jesus* (Boulder: Westview Press, 2000), 200.

"Write a rocking good dissertation, get hired by a major university, and the Jesus Seminar might give you a seat at the table and a jar of beads. But until the scholars in the room reach consensus, don't go around quoting me!" I found I objected to the aristocratic bent of the conversation.[2] Funk compared himself to Martin Luther, but the actual effect of his work would be to take the Bible out of the hands of common believers and return it to a scholarly elite to monopolize.

More importantly, I think Funk and Martin miss something about human nature and about the words of Jesus, deeper than mere "expertise" and the specialization of knowledge that ordinary readers of the Gospels often pick up on. We don't need voice recognition software or a PhD to recognize the voices of those we love. After immersing myself in world religions, then in biblical criticism, Jesus' voice has come to stand out even more sharply, and I began to see why "untutored sophomores" might sometimes hear the voice of Jesus more clearly than their professors.

In the temperate zone, one can climb a mountain a long ways before clearing the trees and seeing the landscape around the mountain. As other chapters in this book show, the hard work of slogging it up to the summit is ultimately worth it. But Paul said, "God chose the foolish things of the world to shame the wise" (1 Cor 1:27). Reality seems to be of such a character that the strongest climbers must invest everything in its ascent, while like young Anselm in his dream, a child may plant her flag on its upper reaches before us.

FINDING JESUS

Three and half million passengers flood through Shinjuku station in Tokyo, Japan, daily, making it the busiest train station in the world. Last summer my wife and her mother were drifting on one of the tides of humanity that washes through its halls. Suddenly someone sweeping down an opposite current stopped and stared. My wife's best friend from Seattle! How did she notice? My wife is an attractive Japanese woman of average height. She carries no tattoo or punk hairdo, nor does a parrot perch on her shoulder. Yet somehow, in a city of 22 million, thousands of miles from home, in a split second, her friend noticed one face in a surging tide of anonymous humanity.

Maybe you've had a similar "Where's Waldo?" experience, even while reading this book. Those who were privileged to know Paul Brand or Ralph Winter will, I think, recognize the stories Yancey, Smith, and Parsons told in earlier chapters. Friends of Saint Anselm must also have smiled at the anecdotes Eadmer told, like skits at a retirement party that reveal a beloved old teacher's mannerisms and eccentricities.

Yuan Zhiming and Bill Prevette describe the powerful impression Jesus left on them as they read the disciples' accounts of their Master's life and teachings.

When Jesus said, "My sheep listen to my voice" (John 10:27), he implicitly recognized that, like many animals, people have a sophisticated "agency detection system" that allows

---

2   See David Marshall, *Why the Jesus Seminar Can't Find Jesus and Grandma Marshall Could* (Seattle: Kuai Mu, 2005).

us to distinguish sentient from inanimate life—is that rustle in the bush ahead the wind, or a jaguar waiting to pounce? We also have an amazing ability to distinguish people we know, by voice and sight. From the moment an infant contemplates her mother's frown, each of us tests, practices, and refines the art of "reading people," judging the mood, character, and trustworthiness of those around us.

Recognizing a loved one is neither "blind faith" nor rocket science. We know our friends by an intuition more subtle and intuitive than any form of science, but no less rationally persuasive. It is part of the art of being human.

It may be hard to say what tips us off when we read the Gospels. Scholarly focus often falls clumsily on titles—"Messiah," "Living Water," "Son of God." But such monikers, while evocative, do not define Jesus for us. Rather, the person we meet there shows us what such titles weakly express.

Having met him, even "untutored sophomores" cannot easily be argued out of recognition. We are tempted to retort in a paraphrase of Lloyd Benson: "Dr. Funk, I know Jesus. Jesus is a friend of mine, and this cloud of conjectures, this 'virtual Jesus' you conjure up from your clunky recognition software of red and black beads, is less than the sum of One I have come to know as a person."

I think that is a rational response. In one sense, listening to the words of Jesus over his interpreters simply shows traditional scholarly respect for primary sources. Despite useful tidbits given by Josephus and Tacitus, and a lot of popular bluster these days about "alternative gospels,"[3] in fact, when you read Matthew, Mark, Luke, or John, you directly access the only substantial sources for the life of Jesus. And they are much more than a glance in a subway station.

By paying close attention to the patterns that define the Gospels, we see who Jesus is and become more sure of his reality. We also begin to understand how he has changed the world.

THE FINGERPRINTS OF JESUS

I often buy reading glasses at Costco because I forget my old ones on a couch or table somewhere. But even people more careful than I leave small mementos of their passing, sometimes to the gratitude of the police: human fingerprints.

Ridges on the epidermis of our fingers help us feel and grasp solid objects. Each print of those ridges and the troughs between them carries a unique pattern, which since ancient Rome and China have been used to distinguish people. Usually fingerprints are invisible to the naked eye, unless they carry some messy substance, like the blood from a murder weapon.

Read a Gospel, and some events in them "stick out like sore thumbs" and are visual to casual observers. Jesus healed the sick, taught in public, was nailed to a cross by enemies, then rose from the dead. That's the basic story. It's as readily obvious as that my wife is female and has black hair. But they also carry more subtle properties that I believe allow us to positively

---

3   Which I evaluate in David Marshall, *The Truth about Jesus and the "Lost Gospels"* (Eugene, OR: Harvest House, 2007).

identify Jesus. These traits help the Gospels grip the mind of the reader and mark them as unique. They are not the sorts of things a disciple would add intentionally, or in some cases even could invent. I call those hidden traits the "fingerprints of Jesus."

I grew up reading, sometimes memorizing, the Gospels. But it was only after studying other religions and skeptical books on the Gospels that I analyzed the words of Jesus systematically.[4] I found that the first four books in the New Testament generally share fifty traits. I then compared the Gospels to other ancient writings, trumpeted by skeptical scholars as "lost gospels." I was dumbfounded. However "untutored" early Christians might have been about modern critical methods, consciously or not, they seemed to have picked up on differences between the real Gospels and their supposed competitors far better than some critics. For instance, the Jesus Seminar's most famous work is called the *Five Gospels*, and groups the *Gospel of Thomas* with the four in the Bible. But on careful analysis it became obvious that *Thomas* is not a Gospel at all! *Thomas* turned out to weakly share seven of fifty qualities, mostly insignificant similarities, such as that Jesus answers questions in both. One might as well compare a Phantom fighter to a bucket of Kentucky Fried Chicken, because both have wings! But my study only formally confirmed what attentive readers in all eras recognize intuitively: "We know Jesus. Whatever smart-aleck sayings you put in his mouth, this odd gnostic guru clearly never even met Jesus."

In what follows, I will describe five of those traits, like five ink-stained fingerprints. My goal will not just be to show that the Gospels are believable, though I hope the analysis will demonstrate that. I also want to show why these traits are obvious, even if subconsciously, to ordinary readers, allowing us to "hear Jesus' voice." Furthermore, these same traits help explain how the Gospels have "gripped" humanity and moved those who heard his voice to change the world for the better.

The first lines to notice are the one-liners of Jesus.

(1) APHORISMS

On June 16, 1858, Abraham Lincoln, having been nominated to run against Stephen Douglas for the United States Senate in Illinois, stood before a crowd of a thousand fellow Republicans and warned: "A house divided against itself cannot stand. I believe this government cannot endure, permanently half-slave and half-free."

That first short sentence from his "House Divided" speech proved a dagger pointed at the heart of the American union. In seven words, Lincoln succinctly encapsulated unwelcome truth (some say Lincoln lost the election by voicing it) that decades of growing acrimony between the states had revealed: America had become disunited at its deepest level. Some fundamental change, perhaps some terrible payment of dues, must tip the pendulum and bring about either formal disunity, or union on a more just basis.

Lincoln's words were also powerful because everyone knew where the first seven came from. They constituted one of a hundred or so sayings in the Gospels ascribed to Jesus.

---

4   See Marshall, *Grandma Marshall Could.*

Marcus Borg, perhaps the most eminent member of the Jesus Seminar, defined aphorisms as "short, memorable sayings, great 'one-liners.'" For example: "No one can serve two masters" (Matt 6:24; Luke 16:13), "Strain out a gnat but swallow a camel" (Matt 23: 24), "Let the dead bury their own dead" (Matt 8:22; Luke 9:60), "Do not work for the food that spoils, but for food that endures to eternal life" (John 6:27). The aphorisms of Jesus are "memorable crystallizations of insight that invite further insight." Borg argued that the fact that Jesus spoke in parables and aphorisms is "the most certain thing we know" about him.

Most of Jesus' aphorisms, Funk added, have a social point, and many are funny. Funk went so far as to call Jesus a "comic salvant."

The stress should be put on "salvant" (a teacher whose words transform lives salvifically, to coin a term) rather than "comic." Jesus used humor not for cheap laughs, but to bring his audience to understand and act on saving truth. Yet his parables also mediate a gentle, humorous, and healing quality, sometimes with a touch of slapstick: birds perched on mustard trees, camels contorting through the eye of a needle, mountains jumping into the sea. J. R. R. Tolkien discovered in fairy tales a sacramental quality to objects in daily life. G. K. Chesterton said nursery tales "make rivers run with wine only to make us remember, for one wild moment, that they run with water."[5] In the parables of Jesus, as in fairy tales, the wonder and oddity of creation revisits us in new forms. At the same time, as in great fairy tales, Jesus' words give us deeper insight into the nature of reality—conflict and its consequences, moral choices, the ephemeral character of success—even while pointing us to God.

How likely is it that such profound teachings were tossed off by several different unknown first-century ghostwriting scribes? This is like expecting four students chosen at random from a Sunday school class in Appalachia to all write better novels than Leo Tolstoy. Borg recognized that these sayings bring us face to face with the historical Jesus. But this only expresses what most people recognize intuitively: Jesus brings us up short; it is hard not to see him.

(2) THE WEAK

Like billions of others, a poor couple in the little town of Cana scrimped to put together a respectable wedding. At the last moment, the bridegroom invited a famous guru to attend. He showed up with his whole retinue, a crowd of young people who had been traipsing around the country and were hungry, parched, and ready to have a good time. Their presence added luster to the event, no doubt. But the hosts were mortified when on D-Day the wine ran out.[6]

This, John tells us, was Jesus' first miracle: turning water into better wine than the party steward that day (or perhaps anyone, ever) had tasted.

But the act was also typical of what Jesus taught, and how he treated the poor and disenfranchised.

---

5   G. K. Chesterton, *Orthodoxy* (New York: Image/Doubleday, 1990), 54.
6   I read between the lines here, and below, for dramatic effect.

Unlike modern movies that feature blue-collar action heroes like Rocky or John McClane, the heroes of most ancient stories were aristocrats. In the *Iliad* and *Odyssey*, the stories that Greco-Roman children grew up on, a king or prince is always a great warrior and rampages through the ranks of common soldiers until he confronts a worthy opponent of high blood. Alexander the Great, a big fan of Homer, reportedly refused to fight commoners in the Olympics, and fought like Achilles himself in his own wars. Plutarch says his subject Demosthenes came of "small and obscure beginnings," but he means that, while like Plutarch's other subjects—he was born into the upper class—his family lived in a small town. In Roman times, a piece of paper might cost a day's labor. Why waste a whole book on a peasant?

The Gospels are extraordinary in part because they talk about ordinary people: working for a living, struggling to pay taxes, living out of doors, hungry. Jesus was a carpenter's son. His followers were common fishermen with no credentials or illustrious ancestry. He praised a poor old lady who dropped a few coins into the offering, a woman with a bad reputation, a short but crooked official, a blind beggar: such was the Messiah's own cast of heroes.

Jesus confronted the powerful, while often speaking respectfully (but bracingly) to the weak. This is the opposite of our instinct, as creatures of tribe and pack, to suck up to the powerful and take it out on those below us in the pecking order (or, alternatively, patronize them).

All through the Gospels, Funk noted, Jesus "privileged" the sick and infirm, women, children, tax collectors, and Gentiles. He helped a poor family at a wedding banquet, reached out to a Samaritan outcast, and healed a beggar born blind. Jesus' story of the good Samaritan fits this pattern perfectly. Normally Funk thought a gospel story should appear in more than one source before admitting that Jesus really told it. But a Samaritan was a highly improbable hero in a Jewish morality tale; this story has "Jesus" written all over it, Funk recognized.

The contrast with the "gnostic Gospels" is shocking. In the *Gospel of Thomas*, which Jesus Seminar scholars depict as, if anything, a better Gospel than most, "Jesus" warns his disciples, "If you give to charity, you will harm your spirits." While the canonical Gospels overflow with the world's richest ethical teaching, "Thomas" contains just a few weak platitudes, scruffs of pale sagebrush in a desert of bleached sand. The "Jesus" of the *Gospel of Judas* is positively nasty. I sorted through the entire gnostic library and found that less than 1 percent of the corpus consists of even anemic moral teachings: "For the souls that are filled with much evil will not come and go in the air," and "cast away from yourself all lawlessness," being typical examples.

Who hears the voice of Jesus here? Even aside from the fact that the gnostic writings are late, distant, and un-Jewish, they do not confront us with any face we recognize.

When my grandmother, a Pentecostal of little education, spoke the name "Jesus," her eyes lit up, for good reason—she had come to know and love a real person.

(3) CULTURAL TRANSCENDENCE

Mosab Hassan Yousef, son of one of the founders of the terrorist organization Hamas, was raised Muslim but began reading the New Testament after being caught trying to buy guns. He later described what he found:

> When I got to the *Sermon on the Mount*, I thought, Wow, this guy Jesus is really impressive! ... Every verse seemed to touch a deep wound in my life ... Then I read this: "You have heard that it was said, 'Love your neighbor and hate your enemy.' But I tell you: Love your enemies and pray for those who persecute you, that you may be sons of your Father in heaven" (Matt 5:43–45) ... Never before had I heard anything like [this], but I knew that this was the message I had been searching for all my life.[7]

But Mosab admitted that had he read the same passage before his troubles began, he might have dismissed Jesus as crazy and thrown the book away.

Jesus' words were shocking and unreasonable in his own time, and remain so today—impossible for people of all times and cultures to keep. "If someone slaps you on one cheek, turn to them the other also" (Luke 6:29). "Sell everything you have and ... follow me" (Mark 10:21; Luke 12:22). "Anyone who looks at a woman lustfully has already committed adultery with her in his heart" (Matt 5:28). "Be perfect ... as your heavenly Father is perfect" (Matt 5:48). Yet they can also seem shockingly mild: "Anyone who gives you a cup of water in my name because you belong to the Messiah will certainly not lose their reward" (Mark 9:41). "Feed my sheep" (John 21:17).

Borg admitted a "timeless quality" to much of what Jesus said, but assumed that, in general, Jesus' teaching was not for us: "All of Jesus' teaching was directed to his contemporaries, living in their highly particular social world. He had no other audience in mind."[8]

How does Borg know this? In Mark, Jesus promised that a woman who anointed his feet with perfume would be remembered "wherever the gospel is preached throughout the world" (14:9). She has been. In Matthew, Jesus told his disciples to preach the gospel to "all nations" (28:19–20). This book is, in part, testament to how far that message has gone. However, early Christians understood that their little sect, rejected by Jews, scorned by Greeks, and persecuted by Romans, would ultimately play in Peoria and Peking; clearly they recognized its universal trajectory from the get-go. And wherever the gospel has gone, the words of Jesus have spared neither race, gender, nor class.

"No one ever taught like this man." Even after two thousand years, this anonymous voice in the crowd offers a mild statement of the obvious.

---

7   Mosab Hassan Yousef, *Son of Hamas* (Carol Stream, IL: SaltRiver, 2010), 122.
8   Marcus Borg, *Jesus: A New Vision: Spirit, Culture, and the Life of Discipleship* (New York: HarperOne, 1991), 99.

Modern giants of literature and scholarship, surveying a far vaster range of thought, echo the observation. Dickens described the parable of the prodigal son as the best story in literature. Tolstoy spent a lifetime trying to live up to the Sermon on the Mount. Lin Yutang was one of the greatest modern Chinese writers. Lin wrote novels, social criticism, biography, practical philosophy, an anthology of Chinese and Indian literature, and a dictionary, and is celebrated to this day for his gentle insight and humor. He considered Zhuang Zi the greatest prose writer China had produced. Lin grew up in a Presbyterian church in the hills of Fujian province, left Christianity, and studied Buddhism, Taoism, Western, and Indian thought. Towards the end of a life of feeding on, and lucidly explaining great thinkers, though, he concluded, "Jesus taught as no man ever did."[9]

Harvard historian Paula Fredriksen claimed that "these ancient voices" are now remote: "What matters to us, what is meaningful to us, will coincide at best only rarely with what mattered to them."[10] But really Jesus is not only the greatest, but the most accessible of thinkers. In part this is precisely because what mattered in the first century matters now too: family and loneliness, sin and forgiveness, freedom and guilt, life and death, love and betrayal, bread and barbecued fish with friends by a lake. Jesus is also accessible because—as Yuan, Mosaab, Dickens, Chesterton, and Lin saw—he transcended his environment.

(4) WOMEN

A woman was found in bed with the wrong man. It seems the man jumped out the window and ran off. Living in a time when sexual transgression was a serious offense, the woman was dragged out to be stoned. "Hey! I've got a thought," one of the lantern-jawed seminar professors who nabbed the young vixen suddenly remarked. He then sarcastically posed a question that would one day haunt the world: "What would Yeshua ben Yosef do?"

Yeshua was a famous rabble-rouser. He was popular among the sentimental riffraff, rumored to possess powers of black magic. His contempt for tradition and proper authority had begun to trouble respectable people; the crowd knew who held their backs.

"But he'd just let her go!" The girl's uncle, who felt his family's honor had been compromised, whined.

"Maybe, we could, uh, kill two birds with one stone! If he flouts the Law in such a clear-cut case, with all these respected witnesses," the original speaker said, looking at the rest of the mob with a smirk, "we'll have him! This girl," he patted her on the back unnecessarily, "we can deal with later."

"But what if he agrees?"

"That will do just fine! Righteousness will be upheld. And you can forget about Jesus after that. He'll lose credibility with the crowds." He stopped to pick his teeth. "Take my word for it! This plan is a win-win."

---

9   Lin Yutang, *From Pagan to Christian* (New York: World Publishing, 1959), 229.
10   Paula Fredriksen, *Jesus of Nazareth, King of the Jews: A Jewish Life and the Emergence of Christianity* (New York: Vintage, 1999), 40.

The story of the confrontation between Jesus and the lynch mob is striking for its drama, and for the clever trap his enemies set.

Jesus' escape from that trap is even more famous. Jesus mysteriously wrote on the ground for a minute. Then he straightened up, scanned the crowd, and said,

"All right! Go ahead and do what you like!"

Jaws dropped in amazement; no one really expected this.

"Just one thing," Jesus continued, looking the leader in the eye. "Let whoever has never done any wrong throw the first stone."

These words proved to be a "hinge of history," as Thomas Cahill calls such moments. With his answer, Jesus not only saved himself and the girl, but redirected focus onto the character of those in all ages who are quick to "cast stones."

Man remains wolf to man: people tear into one another on the Internet, in court, in bars, in beautiful old churches in Jerusalem. But things have improved for women around the world. Before Jesus said these words, in some places bones in the feet of young girls were crushed so they couldn't leave their husbands. In others, girls were married to older men, then burnt alive when their husbands died.

What changed? I believe nothing improved life for women around the world more than this story, and others like it in the Gospels.

Scholars point out that this passage is a bit of an anomaly. It does not appear in the oldest manuscripts of John, evidently added to the Gospel later—perhaps from Luke. It's the longest such free-floating story in the Gospels, and for this reason some doubt it really happened.

But as with the good Samaritan, nothing better describes Jesus' character than this story. By contrast, a popular Greek guru often foolishly compared to Jesus, Apollonius of Tyana, actually egged on a reluctant crowd in Ephesus to stone an innocent man to death.

Jesus assumed that women should own property. He called religious leaders "hypocrites" because they prayed loudly and cheated widows out of their goods. A rich woman who lavished alabaster on Jesus was rebuked by the crowd, but Jesus told them to pipe down, thus encouraging spontaneous emotion, and for women to control finances. Widows in Jesus' circle didn't stay home and bake cookies, but traveled and supported his ministry.

Jesus healed many women. He raised a twelve-year-old girl from the dead, reminding her parents to feed her afterwards.

Jesus recognized, with Samuel Johnson, that most human happiness comes at home. Marriage was something to celebrate and a symbol of ultimate fulfillment: the kingdom of heaven was like a wedding banquet. Jesus affirmed marriage—"What God has joined together, let no one separate" (Matt 19:6; Mark 10:9)—and rebuked Pharisees for neglecting parents. He even looked out for his mother as he was dying on the cross. But he understood that family feelings can also be used manipulatively to impede higher happiness and loyalties.

Twice women actually reminded Jesus of the limits of the female role, and he called them beyond them. In one case, a woman called out piously, "Blessed is the mother who gave you birth and nursed you" (Luke 11:27). But a woman's place was not limited to the bedroom or nursery, Jesus reminded her: "Blessed rather are those who hear the word of God and obey it" (Luke 11:28).

Jesus and his disciples showed up at the home of sisters Martha and Mary and their brother Lazarus. Martha complained that Mary wasn't helping in the kitchen—apparently Mary was busy talking theology with the men. Jesus responded not by telling Mary, "We are starving! Girl, go help Sis rustle up some grub for the menfolk!" Not so! Rather, "Skip the hors d'oeuvres, pull up a chair, and dig in to the real main course." Mary chose the better part, "and it will not be taken away from her" (John 10:42).

What does that mean, if not the thousands of schools founded for girls around the world by missionaries who heard Jesus' voice?

Jesus also made women (along with minorities, the poor, and lepers) heroes of his stories. He said a poor widow who gave a small offering was more generous than the temple's Grand Poobah benefactors. He praised the faith of a Gentile woman who refused to take no for an answer, seeking help for her sick daughter. He contrasted an international coed who came to study in Solomon International Business College with the obdurate male teachers of his own generation. Yet Jesus was not naive or sentimental; he recognized that women could scheme, manipulate, and oppress with the best of them. His cousin, after all, had literally lost his head at the hands of two such sphinxes.

Nor was Jesus just talk. Jesus Seminar member Walter Wink argued that Jesus' behavior towards women in the Gospels is "astonishing": "In every single encounter with women in the four gospels, Jesus violated the mores of his time ... his behavior towards women ... was without parallel in 'civilized' societies since the rise of patriarchy roughly three thousand years before his birth."[11]

She was the Elizabeth Taylor of Samaria, minus the diamonds. She had married five men in sequence, and was now living with number six. She came to draw water from an ancient well outside the town of Sychar. Ever social, Jesus struck up a conversation. He let her know that he was aware of her history and offered a "spring of water welling up to eternal life" (John 4:14). Impressed by his gentle probing and how completely he nailed her personal history, she served as a channel to bring "living water" to her village.

Shouldn't Jesus have had her stoned to death? (According to Jewish law!) Shouldn't he leave her alone to follow her chosen lifestyle? (According to modern liberals!) Again, Jesus transcended parochial customs, recognizing the real good of the person he met, and offered a life-enhancing middle path.

Missions have improved the lives of billions of women (and men and children) because some heard Jesus' voice and followed.

Jesus' actions serve as a model for those of us who have reached out to people exploited in the sex industry.

As a young man, I visited a village in Thailand with a group of missionaries. The year before, the leader of our band, Art Sandborn, had brought another group. Men and women were put in different huts for the night, then the men were asked, "Want a girl for the evening? Very cheap!"

---

11   Walter Wink, *Engaging the Powers: Discernment and Resistance in A World of Domination* (Minneapolis: Fortress, 1992), 129.

Our team told this village the story of Jesus in drama, while I prayed behind the bamboo hut where they were acting. During prayer, I suddenly seemed to see the village as a little world for which Christ had died, a community to which he called his children to give their lives and save. I later worked to fight forced prostitution. I met many other Christians in the same fight. I remember standing in an alleyway in Taipei translating for a female friend who told a girl working there about the love of Jesus, as tears fell from the girl's eyes.

Studying history, I now believe the Gospels have been the greatest agents for the liberation of women in world history. Rodney Stark suggested that Christianity was popular among Roman women in part because the church protected them from early marriage, dangerous abortions, and promiscuity, and took care of widows and orphans. Vishal and Ruth Mangalwadi have shown that the Gospels did much to liberate women in India. Others have described the vital role Christian missionaries played in liberating women in Africa, Japan, and China.

Analyzing this brilliant stroke alone, the Gospels allow just two options. Either all their contributors, creatures of their time, patriarchs and misogynists as skeptical scholars take them to have been, mysteriously conspired to invent a Jesus utterly at odds with the biases and scruples of millennia of Middle Eastern civilization. Or else Jesus really was a man who acted like this. And the Gospel writers were honest enough to record his true voice and actions, however perplexing they might have found them.

Jesus' sheep do hear his voice—calling them away from the abyss of oppression and selfishness. The Gospels reveal his fingerprints, on the lever that moves the world.

(5) JESUS' MIRACLES

Skeptics often tell me that Christianity only succeeded in the ancient world because people then were so gullible. They didn't understand science, and credulously believed every far-fetched story they heard.

Read the Gospels, though, and this gullibility is not obvious. The Gospels relate hard doubts about Jesus. He's accused of being a commoner, a sinner, a "Samaritan and demon-possessed," of breaking Jewish law, not paying taxes (the same charge they got Al Capone on), lack of education, blasphemy, insanity, and black magic. Modern critics are often kind to Jesus by comparison. Jesus worked a tough crowd.

The character of the miracles he did form another clear-cut pattern marking the "fingerprints of Jesus" on history. The Jesus Seminar denies that Jesus did any spectacular miracles. But the even-more-skeptical historian Morton Smith argued that "all major strands of gospel material present Jesus as a miracle worker who attracted his followers by his miracles." Nor were miracles like those Jesus enacted common in the ancient world. Studying Buddhism, Taoism, and Hinduism, I found no genuine parallels.[12]

---

12   See David Marshall, *Jesus and the Religions of Man* (Seattle: Kuai Mu, 2000), 209–57.

Jesus did not do supernatural acts at random, or for convenience. His miracles always, or almost always, followed a specific pattern. Jesus' miracles were *realistic, purposeful, constructive, respectful,* and *pious,* meaning that they pointed people to God.

First, Jesus' works were set within *realistic* narratives. Read the story of Jesus healing the twelve-year-old girl in Mark 5. The derision of the neighbors; the despair of the parents; the practical, almost prosaic tenderness of Jesus; her age; the Aramaic words Jesus used; and other details clearly set the passage apart from sensational tales of legendary wonderworkers. This is obviously intended as a historical account. The same is true of most miracle accounts in the four Gospels.

Second, Gospel miracles are *purposeful.* They accomplish specific and practical goals: life from the dead, wine for a wedding, bread and fish for a hungry crowd, health for a blind or crippled man. They are not done for show, like the stone *lingams* (penises) produced by Hindu gurus, "holy" ash made from burnt cow dung, or clay pigeons coming to life in the apocryphal Gospels.

Third, the miracles of Jesus are uniformly *constructive* (apart from the symbolic withering of the fig tree). This sets them apart from "black magic," the Indian guru Yogananda who cursed his sister in a childish act of revenge, some miracles recorded of the Tibetan Buddhist hero Milarepa, or late tales about Jesus making his playmates die with a word then bringing them back to life.

Fourth, the miracles of Jesus *respect and enhance human dignity.* Jesus looks people in the eye and treats them as moral agents, not just as "patients." "What do you want me to do for you?" (Mark 10:36,51; Luke 18:41); "Who touched me?" (Mark 5:31; Luke 8:45); "Your sins are forgiven"; "Give her something to eat" (Mark 5:43; Luke 8:55). He calls even the sick to responsibility. He never overpowers a person unwilling to be healed, makes them bark like animals (as in some "revivals"), or sends people into a trance. In fact, the effect of healing is often to bring people into fuller possession of their faculties.

Fifth, Jesus' works are *pious.* They serve as "signs." They direct people, not to the shamanistic powers of the healer, but to faith in God. They do this, in part, by reflecting the nature of God. Jesus works miracles most often neither by simply praying (like Honi the circle drawer, Augustine, or the Muslim Jesus), nor by occult incantations. Rather, Jesus speaks authoritatively: "Be still!" (Mark 4:39); "Come out!" (John 11:43); "Get up!" (John 5:8).

The astonishing thing about the Gospels is not that sometimes Jesus is referred to as "Son of God" or "Messiah," or even that he forgives sins and works miracles (though these things are surprising enough). Even more astonishing is that these actions fit the picture the Gospels paint of a peasant from the Galilean hill country. At these subtle levels, his miracles echo, in compelling and recognizable humanity, the voice of God. Jesus' miracles often seem to echo, in fact, the creative power and simplicity of the divine, "Let there be light" (Gen 1:3).

Interestingly, the same characteristics that mark the miraculous works of Jesus were also typical of the attitude of early scientists: empirical realism, transformative and constructive purpose, a desire to enhance the state of humanity in this world, and piety towards God. As C. S. Lewis noted about Jesus' miracles:

Each miracle writes for us in small letters something that God has already written, or will write, in letters almost too large to be noticed, across the whole canvass of Nature. They focus at a particular point either God's actual, or His future, operations on the universe ... Not one of them is isolated or anomalous: each carries the signature of the God whom we know through conscience and from Nature. Their authenticity is attested by the *style*.[13]

---

13   C. S. Lewis, *Miracles* (New York: HarperCollins, 2001), 219.

–TEN–

THE RESURRECTION

EARL PALMER

Earl Palmer served as senior pastor at University Presbyterian Church in Seattle for some seventeen years, as well as at churches in Berkeley and Manila. He is the author of some eighteen books.

The death of Jesus is the most public event in holy history, unlike his birth, which was quiet, almost unnoticed. Christ's birth was hidden, with only a very small circle of visitors invited to be present as the historical witnesses; Luke and Matthew tell of two sets of witnesses: the middle-of-the-night shepherds and foreigners from outside of the borders of first-century Judea. These Magi and night-shift shepherds were there, not Herod or the preoccupied religious leaders of Jerusalem.

During the public ministry of Jesus, his fame had spread in both Galilee and Judea, but it crashed into catastrophe at the week like no other week. And when Friday came, it became a public Roman event, because death by crucifixion was by design totally public and secular. There was no restraint on that Friday in human history. God allowed the full terror of that public Friday to happen to his beloved Son. Three days later, on the day we call Easter, Christ's victory over death was made known in place and time and, like Christmas and Good Friday, the resurrection of Jesus is concrete, real, and factual. But like Christmas, Easter is quiet, restrained, almost private. One empty tomb is like every other empty tomb; if you have seen one, you have seen them all.

When we read the Gospel accounts we may be surprised by this restraint. Only a few people meet Jesus the risen Christ. None of the key civil, religious, or political leaders of Jerusalem are invited to witness the victory over death that is won by Jesus of Nazareth: not the house of King Herod, not the resident official of the Roman Empire, not the high priesthood's powerful Annas or his son-in-law Caiaphas, not the band of zealot insurrectionists, not the quirky and mystical Essenes at Qumran. The ones who do experience the victory are a small band of disciples, and they will begin in that very city the movement of faith that continues to live and grow, even now twenty centuries later. They became fathers and mothers in faith for all who believe in the trustworthiness and goodness of God the Father and his Son, Jesus Christ. Their names became a part of the resurrection legacy too: Mary Magdalene, John, Peter, the other women at the tomb looking for the body of Jesus, Thomas, two men on the road to Emmaus, Mary the mother of Jesus, James his brother, and one who later met Jesus on the road to Damascus, Saul of Tarsus.

There is a major question that every believer and inquirer must answer one way or another. Will I trust the witness of these quite ordinary followers, especially since their number does not include prominent first-century authority figures? There are three ways to question the meaning and trustworthiness of what the Gospel records tell about the third day. The first looks directly at the New Testament texts and narratives themselves. Peter tells about the resurrection of Jesus plainly in his first sermon from Acts 2. In that sermon he says of Jesus that "it was impossible for death to keep its hold on him" (Acts 2:24). This means that the death of Jesus on Friday was real. Jesus in fact died on Good Friday, therefore there was no rescue strategy at that most dangerous hour on Friday itself. What is also clear is that there was not a supernatural, mystical intervention on Friday so that Jesus would only appear to die but, because of his spiritual greatness, the humiliation of Roman death could not finally happen to him. If either were the case, his victory would involve the denial of Jesus' real death. Jesus at Good Friday would not be allowed that extreme identification with the whole of humanity since 100 percent of us in fact do actually die; in these views the transcendence of Jesus Christ is never endangered by a Roman governor. We know that the gnostic teachers in the second century did argue for this kind of mystical triumph. This invincibility is necessary for their theory about the nature of Jesus. They needed this kind of victory because the gnostic Jesus is a phantom Jesus who only appears to be physically human. In reality, his is superhuman, mystically human—therefore he cannot really suffer the humiliation of death.

But this is not the New Testament witness. On Friday we watch the actual death of Jesus. At the cross our Lord takes onto himself the three foes of humanity. Jesus disarms the power of evil in the cruelty of a brutal empire and triumphs over cosmic evil too. Satan the accuser, who opposes the will of God, has battled the Son of God at the mountain of defeat and humiliation. It is Jesus who disarms that scorn; he allows the worst danger that Satan can inflict to happen to himself, and by doing so defeats Satan at Mt. Calvary. Our sins are there too, and at the cross Jesus absorbs into himself human weakness and human wrath. He does what we cannot do. He is the Lamb fulfilling the Day of Atonement so that in Jesus Christ, the power of our rebellion, confusion, and harmful acts are forgiven and healed. But there is another foe of the human story, and that is death itself. At the cross Jesus takes upon himself our death and all death as the final boundary. In that final taking of the three foes—the power of every form of evil, the cumulative crisis of human sinfulness, and the death that boundaries all living things—Jesus is the Lamb who was slain. It is not as in a story or in an imaginary way, but concretely, within the record of history, "under Pontius Pilate" (Apostles' Creed). This means that Jesus identifies with us across the whole way of our life narrative and the narrative of every life, so that we can sing John Newton's song, "Amazing grace, how sweet the sound that saved a wretch like me."

I can sing it because it really happened on Friday. And then three days later, when no one expected anything more to happen, grace was stronger than ever before, and death could not hold Jesus Christ—the very Jesus with nail scars has conquered death. His victory, costly in the humiliation on Friday, is joyously validated on the morning of the first day of the next week. But two more questions remain: Can we trust the witnesses who affirm to us this new and radical event? And if the event happened, then what does it all mean for us today?

The first of these questions invites two modes of inquiry. The one is textual: what weight should be attributed to the New Testament records as we read the accounts there and then hear the songs of worship that tell of the resurrection through the ages. Secondly, we should also ask about the reliability and intellectual wholeness of the New Testament narrators themselves. Are they to be believed? Why should we trust them as witnesses?

First, the textual question asks if the narratives of Good Friday and Easter have textual integrity when taken together. Do they fit as parts of one whole document, or do they textually jar us so that Good Friday's account and Easter's account are not one fabric—but the second part is artificially attached to the first? If this is the case, then the straightforward rules of linguistic and textual criticism will point it up to the careful reader. We then could conclude that the joyous victory day narrative of Easter should be understood as a later attachment by the Christian church intended to cheer up believers and encourage more faith. But what do we find when we read the Gospel accounts? Textual studies of the four Gospels do not support such an interpretive model except for the one final section in Mark's Gospel (16:9–20).[1]

What we have is a whole narrative in each Gospel written in the same form and word choice pattern as the rest of the Gospel that precedes the surprise of Easter. Therefore, as we read these texts we need to decide how much confidence we will invest in the four Gospel writers. Do we trust their witness? And then later as we read the New Testament letters we must also ask, do we trust the secondary narrative witness of Paul, James, Peter, the writer of Hebrews, Jude, and John the Gospel writer who also writes letters and the book of Revelation?

Therefore, this second mode of inquiry becomes very important to the determination of the validity of these witnesses to the resurrection of Jesus Christ. How do we decide whether to trust the tellers of the story? This question is not so different from what we face when it is required that we evaluate the trustworthiness of a living contemporary who has a story to tell. We, as listeners, must weigh their words as they seek to persuade us with a narrative witness about an event or series of events that we did not ourselves physically see or observe. Our task is to find some measuring markers that will test for reliability. Some of these markers are factual accuracy markers. Are the streets actual streets? Are there other sources of record that attest to the essential factualness of the narrator's account? One of the key evaluative markers will be character tests of the integrity of the reporter. Is there a reason to question the intentions of the witness, or does his character and track record encourage us to trust his account?

---

1   Linguistic evidence here causes some interpreters to see this as an attachment by a different writer than the earlier part of Mark's Gospel.

There are also nontechnical but highly valuable criteria for evaluation that ask implication questions of a narrative. Garry Wills, the Pulitzer-Prize-winning historian who wrote *Lincoln at Gettysburg: The Words that Remade America*, has also written about his journey to Christian faith in his short book *What Jesus Meant*. He is convinced of the New Testament historical record of the resurrection of Christ, mainly through this vital but nontechnical way of testing truthfulness. He is profoundly impressed and convinced by implications that the New Testament believers in Christ conclude from the fact of Christ's death and resurrection. They primarily are motivated to love and reach out in love beyond their own safe inner circles even in the face of persecution. He also notes that one remarkable psychological proof of the resurrection of Christ is how the early church showed no interest whatsoever in the burial place of Jesus. This is not what would be normal in ancient or political movements. Only later generations and the tourist industry will become fascinated by the location of the empty tomb.

The most persuasive of all proofs of the faithfulness of the resurrection narratives is that the ethical and concrete moral hopefulness of the early believers does not sound or feel like a lifestyle and ministry that has its source in deception, such as would be the case if the disciples had stolen the body of Jesus and then created a myth of victory to tell each other.

The New Testament therefore wins our respect in each criterion of evaluation. The careful attention to detail is clear and in each of the texts. The quality of character that shows up in the preaching and writings of the New Testament believers is convincing. There is a genuineness marker throughout.

The resurrection of the body of Jesus Christ has profound theological implication at two vital crossroads of faith. First, it establishes that Jesus Christ, the living Lord, is not a phantom king in the spiritual vapor, what Karl Barth describes as the "Cloud-cuckooland."

> It is best not to apply the idea of invisibility to the Church; we are all inclined to slip away with that in the direction of a *civitas platonica* or some sort of Cloud-cuckooland, in which the Christians are united inwardly and invisibly, while the visible Church is devalued. In the Apostles' Creed it is not an invisible structure which is intended but a quite visible coming together, which originates with the twelve Apostles. The first congregation was a visible group, which caused a visible public uproar. If the Church has not this visibility, then it is not the Church.[2]

It is the actual Jesus who did fully identify with us in our humanity and who is the Lord we worship. As Jesus Christ is the One who won the real physical victory over death, so our lives as his disciples must be real and concrete too. C. S. Lewis portrays this actual concreteness as well as any writer I've read in his dramatic and even whimsical description of the full and complete and costly identification of Christ with us in his book *Miracles*:

> In the Christian story God descends to re-ascend. He comes down; down from the heights of absolute being into time and space, down into humanity; down further still, if embryologists are right, to recapitulate in the womb ancient and

---

2   Karl Barth, *Dogmatics in Outline* (New York: Harper & Brothers, 1959), 142.

pre-human phases of life; down to the very roots and sea-bed of the Nature He has created. But He goes down to come up again and bring the whole ruined world up with Him. One has the picture of a strong man stooping lower and lower to get himself underneath some great, complicated burden. He must stoop in order to lift, he must almost disappear under the load before he incredibly straightens his back and marches off with the whole mass swaying on his shoulders. Or one may think of a diver, first reducing himself to nakedness, then glancing in mid-air, then gone with a splash, vanishing, rushing down through green and warm water into black and cold water, down through increasing pressure into the death-like region of ooze and slime and old decay; then up again, back to colour and light, his lungs almost bursting, till suddenly he breaks surface again, holding in his hand the dripping, precious thing that he went down to recover. He and it are both coloured now that they have come up into the light: down below, where it lay colourless in the dark, he lost his colour too.[3]

The second theological implication is at the crossroads of determination and understanding of our identity and meaning as human beings. The creed is clear in the three articles: (1) "I believe in God, creator of heaven and earth," (2) "I believe in Jesus Christ his only Son … on the third day he rose again," and (3) "I believe in the Holy Spirit … the resurrection of the body." We hear the very good news about our forgiveness and also our resurrection in the creed's third article. That resurrection affirmation is about us. The meaning and worth of our complicated, physical selfhood is settled by God in the death of Christ in our behalf and in his victory in our behalf. This is why Saint Paul looks beyond our historical existence and our death, about which we all know and even fear. But in Romans 8 Paul sees that the whole created order has been boundaried by death (100 percent of us die). But then Paul writes we are boundaried "in hope" (Rom 8:20,21). This remarkable text is about the fulfillment, not the destruction, of the whole of creation. That hope is itself within the marvelous final setting of Romans 8, in which Paul affirms that nothing can separate us from the decision God has made to love us, "For I am convinced that neither death, nor life, nor angels, nor rulers, nor things present, nor things to come, nor powers, nor height, nor depth, nor anything else in all creation, will be able to separate us from the love of God in Jesus Christ our Lord" (Rom 8:38,39 NRSV).

Resurrection and the fulfilled promise makes the grand difference in the way we see and read our own lives and the way we relate to the world around us right now.

This chapter on resurrection is within a larger volume that is dedicated to the memory of two friends of mine who lived faithful lives of hope and healing to our generation: Paul Brand and Ralph Winter, the one a missionary strategist for Jesus Christ and the other a healer of bodies and souls of men and women. Both men lived as believers and witnesses to the reality of the resurrection of Jesus Christ.

---

3   C. S. Lewis, *Miracles* (New York: Simon & Schuster, 1996), 148.

–ELEVEN–
A CONVERSATION WITH RODNEY STARK

Rodney Stark is one of the world's most influential sociologists of religion. His rational choice theory is a standard model of how religions behave. His series on the rise and influence of Christianity marked, among other things, a bold yet empirically detailed defense of Western civilization in general, and the effect of Christianity in particular. Stark taught sociology at the University of Washington for thirty-two years, and is now co-director of the Institute for Studies of Religions at Baylor University. A scholar whom Ralph Winter often cited, Dr. Stark moved in the early twenty-first century from friendly agnosticism to positive Christian faith. He spoke with me from his home in New Mexico.
© 2012 David Marshall

I. WAS MARXISM A "RELIGION"?

David Marshall: **You define religion as "explanations of the meaning of existence based on supernatural assumptions and including statements about the nature of the supernatural."[1] Some people would define religion in what they might see as a more neutral way, as an "ultimate concern," as Paul Tillich put it.**

Rodney Stark: Paul Tillich didn't have a religion.

One thing I like about Tillich's definition is, you have a movement like Marxism-Leninism, which a lot of people say looks like a religion in many ways. Isn't it better to have a more neutral definition?

---

1   Rodney Stark, *One True God: Historical Consequences of Monotheism* (Princeton: Princeton University Press, 2001), 15. Stark offers similar definitions in *Acts of Faith* (2000) and *Discovering God* (2007).

To the contrary! I think confusing the two greatly hinders analysis. Let me explain why. I think you can say you have secular movements that have some of these characteristics, like high levels of commitment, true believership, and that sort of thing. But there's an enormous difference between systems of thought that openly are predicated on the existence of the supernatural and those that are purely worldly. For example, the purely worldly ones are subject to failing all the time! The supernatural ones don't need to.

Sociologically, in terms of how they operate in society, it seems that there are many similarities.

Well there are similarities, but I think that the important one is that, you know, why do utopias always fall apart? That is to say, the nonreligious ones.

It has been 150 years, and there are still some pretty radical Marxists out there.

Oh, no, no, no, no. Start a utopian community, OK? We're going to go out here and we're going to have this commune and we're going to, you know, whatever.

The problem is, they've got to succeed here and now in making the wonderful thing happen. And they can't. But if it isn't going to happen until the next life, then you can. So religious communes are vastly more durable. God knows whether there were any serious Communists in Russia at some point, except for ignorant people. They were mostly in Western universities. I can't imagine that the intellectual elites in Russia really were Communist after some point. Because it wasn't working, and everybody could see …

Isn't it your point when you talk about temple religions (in *Discovering God*) that the elite priests didn't really believe in it either?

They may not have. And for good reason! They had God right there in the building with them, instead of in heaven where he belongs!

I'm sure Stalin didn't bear much scrutiny up close, either …

No, I'm sure he didn't. But I think it's very important not to confuse the two. I mean, yes, there are enormous similarities. But I think the differences are absolutely critical. The ability to sanction morals and put the payoff in another life, I think, is vastly more durable and less likely to lead to tyranny.

II. RELIGION IN EUROPE

You talk a lot about toleration and conformism and how monopolies work. Do you see any overall trends in Europe right now?

Yeah, I think Europe is coming apart at the state church level, and we see finally, despite all the resistance, the breaking out of some competition.

In Western Europe?

I'm think about Scandinavia, and France, and Belgium, and Germany, and whatnot. It looks like the tide is shifting, that religion's picking up—I know that there's been a considerable rise in religiousness in Italy, for example.

Is that within the Catholic Church, or within Protestant denominations?

It's a lot of things. There's been quite a bit of competition for the tax withholding. And it's led to a heck of a lot of advertising every spring—you know, "Mark us down for your tax withholding." See, you have to pay a church tax, and you can pay it to anybody you want. Some big campaigns seem to have stimulated religious interest more generally. Church attendance is up a lot, especially among young people, and so is belief.

I'm doing a doctorate at the Oxford Centre for Mission Studies right now, so I have the privilege of spending a lot of time in Oxford. And I've been very impressed by how alive the church is there. They're all Anglican, but there's evangelical Anglican, there's charismatic Anglican, there's high church …

Yeah, well, they're starting to break up. They're starting to work at attracting followers. That's the thing that's missing! You've got state churches—the check comes, and I don't care. But I have to care—suddenly I have an empty church and no check!

That's sounds, I don't know …

Oh, it sounds terrible!

It sounds cynical, worldly …

No, but it's just human nature! My word! "I'm not motivated, I'm really pretty lazy."—"You ought to be motivated for God!" Yeah, right, [but] maybe you're not even attracting people like that into the clergy! In Germany, the union contract for clergy says that if fewer than eight people show up, you don't have to hold church! If I were over there, I'd make my services so dreadful I'd never get eight people! [*Laughs.*]

But if you're some little Baptist preacher sitting out there, [you] say, "If I don't increase attendance I'm not going to get a check!" It makes a difference! And I see nothing wrong—hell, the key to success, at least in [America] and I would suggest anywhere, is having a really vibrant religion!

The reason that the liberal churches have been slumping in this country for a hundred years is because when you get there, they don't hold church! I don't need to go to some Episcopal church to hear how terrible it is that there are people who don't like homosexuals, or that there are starving children in the world. The high churches have an advantage in that, at all levels across the spectrum, they do somewhat better than their somewhat similar low-church neighbors. Because the liturgy takes out of the priest's hands the ability to trash the service, if you will. I have a Catholic friend who put it really well. He said, "We just despise our parish pastor. We just don't listen to the homily. The rest of the time, he's got to say Mass." [*Laughs.*]

III. THEORY AND PRACTICE

Did you know historian Donald Treadgold at the University of Washington? He was a mentor of mine.

The problem with the UW is, it's an urban university and people live all over hell, including on the islands. There's just no social life. Consequently, I never really did get to know him—I never really got to know anybody.

He reminds me of you a bit, because he had a real passion not only for his work, but for its consequences in society. Of course, he was an old cold warrior.

Yeah, so am I.

How do you feel about how your books are used by people of Christian faith, or religious faith in general; by missionaries, for example. Some find your books very useful.

This is backing into it, but I think it'll make the point. I once ran a conference out on Orcas Island [in the San Juans, in northwest Washington State]. And the people who paid for it were the Moonies …

The Unification Church?

Yeah. They had nothing to do with who was invited or anything that went on. We just had a bunch of their graduate students show up in the audience. And somebody once assaulted me, in effect, and said, how dare I have done that, because what if they had learned something from our conference that helped them in their church life? And I said, "I'd be embarrassed if they hadn't." I didn't write my books to help missionaries, but I certainly would be delighted if they had been of any help.

But you recognize that some church leaders are, in fact, charlatans ...

Yeah, sure, but life isn't perfect. I mean, we just [got] a tax fraud as Secretary of the Treasury. What can you do about that? [*Laughs.*]

You've moved from agnosticism in the direction of a general Christianity, a generic or nonaffiliated Christianity over the years?

Yes. Somebody asked me once how I got back to religion, and I said, first of all, I was always a cultural Christian. Christendom meant something to me, so does Western civilization, and Western civilization is Christendom. Beyond that, I guess I wrote my way back.

So those books actually did have something to do with why ...

Sure. I've been exploring religion over the last fifty years or so, in a not purely sociological kind of way. And as I comprehended more, it became ... more and more plausible and likely, and here I am.

IV. MISSIONS, CULTURAL CAPITAL, AND THE RISE OF CHRISTIANITY, REVISITED

In *The Rise of Christianity* you wrote about how Christianity could be explained without the need for miracles. You followed the upward curve of the Mormon Church and concluded that maybe the Christian church did the same thing. Of course that doesn't necessarily mean that miracles didn't happen ...

No, of course not!

Have you changed in your thinking about that?

If miracles happened, they happened! What I'm saying is that no miracle was required. It was a pretty ordinary growth rate ...

People who sat down and did the arithmetic thought that it's pretty inconceivable that in the time that history provides, that you could have converted the empire. And what I was trying to do was put some discipline on those kinds of claims and point out that, actually, a very ordinary growth rate will do it, and you don't have to sit here postulating all these miracles. And, you know, somebody went into town and gave a sermon and five thousand people jumped up and said, "I'm for Jesus!" It didn't happen that way. At least if it did, that was a miracle, because in social science we have no knowledge of such phenomena.

When you have missionaries going into a tribe like the Dani in New Guinea or the Lahu in Burma, you do see some pretty phenomenal growth rates.

Sure you do, once you get a start. Those are really intense, highly integrated communities. And if you can get a wedge going, if you can get some people to convert, then I would expect, because of the intensity of the networks, for the faith to spread really rapidly.

One of the keys in many cases seems to have been what you talk about with the "preservation of religious capital," where people saw Christianity as a fulfillment of their highest ideals.

Yes! That works, for sure. Yeah, one of the things on this cultural capital that people really miss—we all see the cultural capital with Judaism. Jews can become Christians and throw away nothing. Add the New Testament; they don't have to throw away the Old Testament. OK, fine. But some of the things that are said about Christianity as attacks—it sounds very, very pagan—the virgin birth, the wise men, the star. [Such critics] don't notice the enormous cultural continuity that has for pagans, who are out there to be converted! And if we accept the whole notion that God speaks to people in a language they can understand, the whole Christ story happens that way in many respects—including the blood sacrifice of the crucifixion—precisely because it speaks so directly and with such great familiarity to this whole pagan world!

Justin Martyr picked up on the term "tutors to Christ" …

Justin Martyr says to some Roman, "I should tell you the story of Jesus because it's a story you're familiar with. It's like your story."

This is something that's greatly overlooked. The rationale, of course, is if Christianity is so plausible, the second people heard about it and thought about it, they said, "Yeah, right!" That's not the way life works.

V. ISLAM AND THE "DARK AGES"

Stark told me how he got into sociology after a short but successful career in journalism. I asked about reviews; Dr. Stark said most reviews have remained generous, even as he moved toward Christianity. He then noted that he is presently working on a book in which he defends the Crusades. I replied:

Oh, boy! I'm sure you'll get a negative review of that!

Sure I will. But the point is, I'm able to demonstrate, I think, that the so-called "famous Muslim or Arab culture" was in fact the culture of the *dhimmis*; that is to say, of the various Christians and Jews and whatnot they were sitting on. In the 1300s, when they started to kill all these people, their culture went away. Suddenly, in 1500 the Arabs are all so backwards. How did that happen? Well, they were always backward! I've got all kinds of material that shows that, throughout Arab lands, all the bureaucrats were Christians! Every once in a while, they'd kill them all, and they couldn't replace them, and they'd hire Christians back again.

They might bring back witch-hunting.

Yeah, well, I don't give a damn.

All the inventions that are credited to the Muslim civilization, you would say basically came from Jews and Christians?

The whole medical thing [was from] Nestorian Christians. No, it's pretty much a myth. There were some universities at that time. They were Nestorian! … At the Battle of Lepanto, which is 1571, the Muslim fleet is sunk. What's interesting is that the admirals on both sides were Christians. And the boats were built in Venice. They never had a navy.

This is the problem that Bernard Lewis talks about in *What Went Wrong***?**

My answer to Bernard Lewis really is, nothing went wrong. It was an illusion in the first place.

What went wrong was they converted and killed off all the Christians and Jews. And with the demise of the *dhimmis* [came] the demise of the delusion! When they built Baghdad, or the big mosque in Jerusalem, it was Byzantine architects.

But isn't that true of Christianity too? I mean, we borrowed Greek and Roman architecture.

Well, sure! But this is not borrowing, this is like having Greeks and Romans come back and build them for you …

I had to sit down and read all this stuff. [When I got] about to chapter 3 in this book on the Crusades, I had to face the [question]: How was it that these … "ignorant, savage Middle-Age [Crusaders]" could travel 2,500 miles, lose about 75 percent to 80 percent of their numbers on the way …

And still take Jerusalem.

And kick butt when they got to the other end! The fact is, they had much better weapons, and they had better armor, and better strategy, and they were more advanced! So how does that work? Gosh, maybe I'd better start looking back here. And you've got [the] thesis that Europe went down the drain because the Arabs took control of the Mediterranean.

You go back and look, and the Genoese and the Venetians and whatnot are raiding Arab coastal towns throughout the entire so-called Middle Ages. The Byzantines can land troops anywhere they want. Where is this control of the sea? And the answer is, it wasn't there!

Byzantium was in fact a corrupt nightmare. For the Arabs to run over part of it—not a big surprise. But then the first time they faced the Franks, bam! They really got kicked.

Even if the lifestyle of the people in Europe was better as you say, isn't it true that the Muslim world had huge libraries, while most people in Europe couldn't read or write?

Well, but isn't it interesting that Saladin—the famous, wonderful liberal— destroyed the biggest library in Islam, gave the books away. It's not at all clear and clean.

You could make a case for the Dark Ages just from the fact that there wasn't much reading and writing going on in Western Europe.

There was enough. No. I think the Dark Ages was a complete fraud. The fact that you may not be too familiar with the early Greeks, that you may not in fact write such good Latin, what's that got to do with the price of eggs? They were building dams and windmills and things that the Romans couldn't have imagined.

And they were much healthier, and much better fed. And I'm sorry, science was going forward. Science doesn't just suddenly jump out of the wall in the 1400s and 1500s. It was there in the 10, 11, 1200s. The university is a Dark Ages institution. And it was very sophisticated.

Spending some time in Oxford, walking around and looking at the history—a lot of it is legendary, you don't know exactly how it started—is a real education. I'm amazed that someone like Richard Dawkins has managed to be such an anti-Christian bigot in a place like that.

And an ignorant bigot. His attacks are third grade. I have a student who has written a wonderful book that you might like ... *The Plot to Kill God* by Paul Froese. It's about the seventy-some-year attempt in Russia to get rid of religion, and how after seventy years they got nowhere. He points out that one of the problems is the people who were planning the atheist curriculum were all guys like Richard Dawkins; they didn't know diddle about religion! They didn't have enough respect for it to think they needed to know anything. So they're always aiming these "killer arguments" that demonstrate the falsity of religion that half the peasants knew the answers to! [*Laughs.*]

PART IV.
CHRIST IN PHILOSOPHY AND SCIENCE

–TWELVE–

THE PRAYER THAT PRAYED ME

RANDAL RAUSER

Randal Rauser is associate professor of historical theology at Taylor Seminary in Edmonton, Canada. He has written several books including *The Swedish Atheist, The Scuba Diver, and Other Apologetics, Rabbit Trails,* and *Theology in Search of Foundations.* Randal lectures widely on topics of apologetics, worldview, and systematic theology, and blogs regularly at http://randalrauser.com. He lives in Edmonton, Canada, with his wife, daughter, and two yappy dogs.

I remember it like yesterday. As we were driving along in our blue Oldsmobile station wagon, my parents got into a conversation about the enmity between God and the devil. Usually when they took to discussing a dispute between two parties in my presence, they would revert to hushed tones, forcing me to resort to stealthy eavesdropping. But this was different: far from speaking in hushed voices, they were telling me *everything* about the God/devil feud. I strained against the seatbelt with rapturous interest in this cosmic gossip while suddenly feeling very grown up. "Wow," I thought to myself, "God and the devil *really* hate each other!" While I was intrigued, that didn't mean I was ready to take sides. I had always prided myself on being a peacemaker, and this seemed like the ideal occasion to test my skills. "Maybe I can be friends with *both*," I quipped hopefully. "And then I can make them be friends with each other!" With that I sat back in my seat triumphantly, basking in the afterglow of my diplomatic brilliance.

My satisfaction didn't last for long. Mom turned around to look squarely at me. (In retrospect, she may have been a bit worried that I might get my bell rung by a passing thunderbolt). She hastily informed me that my Neville Chamberlain solution was a nonstarter: "You *can't* make them friends," she said sternly. "You have to *choose*."

My five-year-old shoulders slumped in disappointment and I sat back in my seat dismayed. I didn't want *anyone* angry with me. Did I *really* have to choose?

Later I was sitting in the family room when I decided to heed my parents' advice and give up on the route of diplomacy. Needless to say, once I agreed to pick a side, it wasn't hard to decide which one to choose. If my parents were going with God, then it made good sense to follow their decision. Even so, I didn't want to pray right then and there. Somehow it didn't seem right to make that kind of solemn commitment with my brother flopped on the couch eating Pop-Tarts and watching *The Six-million Dollar Man* on TV. So I wandered out into the backyard in search of solitude to ratify this somber decision. After finding the perfect spot (a rock beside the ravine), I sat down and stumbled through the faltering prayer of a five-year-old:

"Dear God, please come into my heart. I want to follow you, not the devil. Amen."

What exactly was I praying?

"Dear God." What did I understand the word "God" to refer to? Looking back, I can't be sure what my five–year-old mind was envisioning, though I have little doubt it included a blushing dose of crass anthropomorphism. And I know what it *didn't* include. It didn't include a concept of the Trinity as one *ousia* in three *hypostases*. Nor did it include a conception of the divine attributes like aseity, simplicity, omnipotence and immutability. And it certainly didn't include any reference to the divine processions of filiation and spiration. I also know this: had my five-year-old theology been subjected to careful scrutiny by a theologian, it would have emerged looking desperately primitive, piecemeal and, if it had been assembled into a formal creedal statement, quite heretical. Not an auspicious beginning.

"Please come into my heart." I never stopped to reflect carefully on the meaning of the language of Jesus or God being *in* us until I hit my early twenties. Prior to that point, by default I held a quasi-literal understanding in which I saw God taking up some kind of spatially extended residency within my physical body. It was only later that I began to see this language as a metaphorical reference to relationship in spatial terms (think of Peter Frampton singing his ballad, "I'm in You," or Tony Bennett belting out his signature song, "I Left My Heart in San Francisco"). Needless to say, if my inchoate view at twenty was still hamstrung by crass literalism, my thinking fifteen years earlier was probably no clearer.

"I want to follow you." By this time in my life I'd seen several images of Christ hanging on the cross, but they were either cartoonish pictures like those that appear in coloring books or on Sunday school flannelgraphs, or the ethereal, pietistic images of Renaissance and Baroque art. Neither furnished me with the slightest comprehension of what it really meant to die on a cross. Nor did I realize that the core metaphor of following Christ involved an invitation for each one of us to climb up on our own crosses daily. What did it *mean* to follow God (or his Son, Jesus)? Looking back, I had no idea what I was saying. Years later I watched Mel Gibson's *The Passion of the Christ* in the theater. A man with more piety than brains sat next to me and planted his child of about five next to him. I pleaded with him, "Sir, this is an R-rated film. Your child should *not* be here." He just smiled placidly and for the next two hours subjected his terror-stricken, sobbing son to the horrific sight of a man beaten and crucified. How could the poor child possibly understand the bloody spectacle unfolding on the silver screen?

God, regeneration, discipleship: each one a concept that exceeds the grasp of a child by unimaginable orders of magnitude. However, it is one thing to declare that a great gap in understanding exists. It is another thing to contemplate in concrete terms just *how great* that gap really is.

An illustration I have used before may help here.[1]

When my daughter was six she asked me the size of the Milky Way galaxy. When I told her that it was 100,000 light years across, she took a moment to process my answer and then replied with this question: "Is that farther than from here to Colorado?" The question caught me off guard. I knew she wouldn't be able to grasp the distance of a light year (truth be known, I can't really grasp it). But I was surprised by how far off her point of reference actually was. Even so, I also saw that there was logic to her question. Without any conception of the distance "100,000 light years," she was fumbling for a comparable scale. And the greatest distance she could think of was the two-day drive our family makes annually to visit relatives in Colorado.

But even if it was a reasonable starting point, it was also an incredibly limited one. I felt at a loss how to explain the difference between photons flying through space at 300,000 kilometers per second for 100,000 years, and our car rolling down the highway at one hundred kilometers an hour for just two days.

There is no doubt that a child's grasp of the immensity of the galaxy is grossly limited. But there is also no doubt that this limited grasp pales in comparison to the challenge of understanding the God who called 100 billion galaxies into existence. While the universe is unimaginably vast, it is still finite, and so our ignorance of it, however vast, is likewise finite. But God is infinite, and thus our understanding of God, no matter how great it may be, always fails to grasp God by an order of infinity.

When you recognize that God is always infinitely beyond our understanding, it puts our best theological work into a humbler perspective. That certainly has been my experience. In the thirty-four years since I prayed that prayer, I have earned three theological degrees including a PhD in systematic theology. Over the last decade I have taught at a Christian college and a seminary. I have written several books and journal articles and preached and lectured on three continents. Yet as much as I have learned in the intervening decades, I still find myself standing shoulder to shoulder with that five-year-old gazing in wonder at a God who infinitely transcends my understanding.

A story about Thomas Aquinas illustrates this point. Thomas was in his fifties and had distinguished himself as one of the great intellects of Europe in his or any age before he went to church on the Feast of Saint Nicholas, December 6, 1273. But something profound happened to Thomas during the service. As best we can surmise, Thomas underwent some sort of mystical experience. Afterwards he returned to his quarters in a daze and described all his theological writings to his associate Reginald as "straw." A few days later Reginald came to Thomas to ask when he would begin his writing again. Thomas reiterated the point with greater force: "All that I have written seems to me like straw compared to what has been

---

1   I first told this story in Randal Rauser, *Finding God in the Shack: Conversations on an Unforgettable Weekend* (Colorado Springs: Paternoster, 2009), 21.

revealed to me."[2] Think about that. One momentary mystical encounter with the living Lord of the universe could lead one of the greatest theologians in history to fall silent.

Yet I do not think we should use this story to prop up an insipid anti-intellectualism. The lesson is *not* that there is no difference between the prayers of a five-year-old and the theology of a learned academic. The New Testament is clear on the obligation Christians have to seek an intellectually mature faith (e.g., 1 Cor 3:1–3; 2 Cor 10:5; Heb 5:14; 1 Pet 3:15). So the point is not that Thomas knew nothing more than a child, but rather that even with all he knew there was still an infinity he did not know. Thus we can say that the writings of Thomas are like straw next to the infinite God they purport to describe, even as we affirm them as an invaluable treasure trove of careful theological reflection for the church.

This yields a new perspective on the prayer of conversion. I now look at that simple child's prayer as akin to Lucy's wardrobe in *The Chronicles of Narnia*. The wardrobe was a humble piece of furniture, but it provided a portal to a world of unimaginable beauty and complexity. Similarly, the prayer itself was a humble, nondescript utterance, but it opened a door to a God of unimaginable beauty and complexity. And the same is true of my prayers today. Set against infinite majesty, they too are humble and nondescript. These days when I pray, "Dear God," my head floods with specialized knowledge from Scripture, theology, philosophy, and church history. But far from "taming the facts," I find that all this information draws me further into that divine mystery. In this regard I can sympathize with theologian Bernard Lonergan who wryly summarized trinitarian doctrine as follows: "The Trinity is a matter of five notions or properties, four relations, three persons, two processions, one substance or nature, and no understanding."[3] To be sure, I am better at avoiding rank heresy than the five-year-old me. I can now state my views with analytical precision, seasoned with biblical references and Latin and Greek terms, but when it comes to *understanding* what and who God is, an infinite horizon of mystery still remains. The same mystery extends to the rest of that prayer as well. My understanding of the plea for God to "come into my heart" so I may "follow" him may no longer be stuck in the absurd literalism of a child. But that is not to say I have anything more than the barest grasp on the theological dimensions of conversion, regeneration, and discipleship that my simple confession references.

But if we really are this limited in our understanding, then how do we manage to pray at all? If a great theologian like Thomas Aquinas could look at his greatest theological efforts as straw, then what is a child's conversion prayer? Mere dust? Indeed, when you think about it, you might even be tempted to think it is impossible for a child to formulate a theological confession sufficiently correct that it could be an effectual occasion for true regeneration. But surely this *can't* be right, for Jesus said, "Let the little children come to me, and do not hinder them, for the kingdom of heaven belongs to such as these" (Matt 19:14). It would seem that Jesus meets children where they are, as he meets all of us where we are. So how does that happen exactly? How can it be that a child so woefully ignorant of who God is that he would

---

2   Frederick Christian Bauerschmidt, *Holy Teaching: Introducing the* Summa Theologiae *of St. Thomas Aquinas* (Grand Rapids: Brazos, 2005), 20.

3   Gerald O'Collins, "The Holy Trinity: The State of the Questions," in *The Trinity: An Interdisciplinary Symposium on the Trinity*, ed. Stephen T. Davis, Daniel Kendall, and Gerald O'Collins (Oxford: Oxford University Press, 1999), 2.

seriously propose a devilish reconciliation could pray a theologically meaningful confession? How did the wardrobe ever provide a gateway to the mysteries beyond it? In the rest of this paper I would like to analyze my prayer from two complementary perspectives. First, I'll consider it as a visible linguistic sacrament rooted in what I as a theologian and philosopher call "prior knowledge of acquaintance." Second, I'll explain why our prayers to God always mean much more than we can ever imagine, whether we pray as an ignorant child or as the world's greatest theologian.

I KNOW THAT SUGAR IS SWEET AND I KNOW THAT MY REDEEMER LIVETH

My question is how a child's prayer can be correct enough to be heard. How was my confession more meaningful than the charming nonsense of Lewis Carroll's "Jabberwocky": "Twas brillig, and the slithy toves. Did gyre and gimble in the wabe"? We begin to address that question by noting that it is rooted in the assumption that our relationship with God, including our very ability to enter into relationship with him through a prayer of conversion, depends on the cognitive, doctrinal precision of the prayer prayed. According to this assumption, if my knowledge of certain doctrines is too weak, then the efficacy of the prayer must be undermined, since conversion to God and relationship with him requires the correct understanding and articulation of these doctrines.

This assumes that conversion and faith require propositional knowledge. In order to see if this is so, we need to unpack the concept of knowledge,[4] beginning with the concept of a proposition. A proposition is the semantic content of an assertion or an object of belief. For example, "God is three Persons" is a proposition which can be believed and, if true, can presumably be known as well. Thus propositional knowledge simply is *awareness of the truth of one's belief* as in "*I know that* 'God is three Persons.'" Needless to say, if we think of our relationship to God as rooted fundamentally in propositional knowledge, then we face a serious problem. What are the essential propositions that we must believe and confess in order to be saved? And that in turn leads us to a disturbing personal question: have *I* believed and confessed those propositions? Those are daunting questions at the best of times, but when the prayer in question is prayed by a five-year-old, they can seem hopeless.

Fortunately there is a way to avoid the skeptical fears that are introduced by making conversion dependent on the adequacy of our propositional knowledge of theology. That comes in recognizing that there is a type of knowledge more fundamental. I speak of acquaintance knowledge, and submit that it is *this* knowledge which serves as the ultimate ground for our prayer. An excellent example of acquaintance knowledge is found in Charles Darwin's autobiography where he writes, "My father used to quote an unanswerable argument, by which an old lady, a Mrs. Barlow, who suspected him of unorthodoxy, hoped to convert him:

---

4   For further discussion see Randal Rauser, *Theology in Search of Foundations* (Oxford: Oxford University Press, 2009), 65–69.

'Doctor, I know that sugar is sweet in my mouth, and I know that my Redeemer liveth.'"[5] In this passage Mrs. Barlow seems to be drawing a comparison between her knowledge that Jesus rose again and her knowledge of the taste of sugar. But what is the comparison exactly? Surely the point was not concerned with propositional knowledge: when Mrs. Barlow refers to her knowledge of sugar, she is not thinking about propositions describing the effect that edible crystalline carbohydrates have on human taste buds. She is thinking about her experience. And when she describes her knowledge of Christ, she likewise is thinking not of accumulated theological and historical statements about the Person, Jesus Christ, but rather the experience of Christ in her life. As Mrs. Barlow had *tasted* sugar, so she had *experienced* Jesus.

Let's unpack the relationship between propositional knowledge and acquaintance knowledge a bit more by considering a particular case. Imagine a scientist named Dr. Sweet who has focused his career on studying sugar and its chemical properties. Dr. Sweet has an immense amount of propositional knowledge about edible crystalline carbohydrates like sucrose and fructose. But imagine that while poor Dr. Sweet studies sugar endlessly, he was born without the ability to taste its sweetness. In that respect, despite all his vast propositional knowledge of sugar, he would lack the direct acquaintance knowledge of sugar that Mrs. Barlow possessed in virtue of *tasting* it. Just as Dr. Sweet's propositional knowledge of sugar is much greater than Mrs. Barlow's, so a theologian's propositional knowledge of God is much more extensive than that of a child. But then this works the other way too. Just as Mrs. Barlow could have an intimate acquaintance knowledge of sugar unavailable to Dr. Sweet, so a child can have an intimate acquaintance knowledge of God unavailable to a great theologian.

This point pertains not simply to children. Consider, for example, the case of Adam, a severely handicapped man who lived at L'Arche community in Toronto. Spirituality writer and priest Henri Nouwen became Adam's caregiver, feeding him, helping him go to the bathroom, changing his clothes. Although Adam had no ability to speak, Nouwen discovered in this quiet soul an individual who enjoyed profound acquaintance and knowledge of the living Lord of the universe. After Adam passed away, Nouwen was overcome with grief and offered the following tribute for this beloved friend:

> Here is the man who more than anyone connected me with my inner self, my community, and my God. Here is the man I was asked to care for, but who took me into his life and into his heart in such an incredibly deep way. Yes, I had cared for him during my first year at Daybreak and had come to love him so much, but he has been such an invaluable gift to me. Here is my counselor, my teacher, and my guide, who could never say a word to me but taught me more than any book, professor, or spiritual director. Here is Adam, my friend, my beloved friend, the most vulnerable person I have ever known and at the same time the most powerful.[6]

---

5   Ibid., 255.
6   Henri Nouwen, *Adam: God's Beloved* (Maryknoll, NY: Orbis, 1997), 101.

Adam did not even have the cognitive capacity of a five-year-old. And yet he enjoyed a profound acquaintance knowledge of God. Looking back I can now see that my prayer of conversion, with all its doctrinal ineptitude, was rooted in a knowledge of acquaintance not unlike Adam's (even if far less profound). And that means that the weight of my faith did not all rest on the dubious theological adequacy of the vague and garbled statements that tumbled out of my mouth. Rather, that prayer was rooted in the relationship I experienced with God through his Spirit. My prayer of conversion may have been important as a psychological realization of the grace God had been working in my life from the earliest moments of my existence, but from another perspective the real story was the grace operating behind the scenes. Theologian Thomas F. Torrance provides a powerful illustration of the divine role in the gifting of our faith:

> I sometimes recall what happened when my daughter was learning to walk. I took her by the hand to help her, and I can still feel her little fingers tightly clutching my hand. She was not relying on her feeble grasp of my hand, but on my strong grasp of her hand, and even my grasping of her grasping of my hand.[7]

The dilemma I faced was rooted in the fact that I viewed my prayer as my feeble hand attempting to grasp God's hand. Little did I know that in the Spirit-mediated knowledge of acquaintance that enveloped my simple prayer, God's hand was already firmly grasping mine.

Given the marginal difference between a child and a great theologian, if we think of propositional knowledge as the necessary gateway for salvation, then we are *all* potentially in trouble. Have we believed the right things? Have we refrained from believing the wrong things? But things are very different when we view the prayer of conversion and the life of faith as arising out of a prior graced knowledge of acquaintance. From that perspective our theological formulations from the prayer of conversion onwards change from being potential obstacles for faith to linguistic and conceptual sacraments of the grace that even now saves us. From this perspective few things are as beautifully and quietly sacramental as the hopelessly vague, breathtakingly naive, and theologically askew prayer of a child—a prayer which, when offered up to the Lord of the universe, can become a gateway to eternity.

THE INFINITELY WIDE MEANING OF A CHILD'S PRAYER

Now we turn from the foundation of acquaintance knowledge to consider the propositional content of prayer. When the nature of this content is understood more fully, it will be seen not as a potential threat to the adequacy of prayer but rather an extraordinary demonstration of it. We will see that the grace that conditions the life of faith extends into the propositions

---

7   Thomas F. Torrance, *Preaching Christ Today: The Gospel and Scientific Thinking* (Grand Rapids: Eerdmans, 1994), 32.

spoken as we consider how the semantic content (the meaning) behind the prayer prayed in faith is greater than the one praying can possibly imagine.

Let's begin by considering a significant moment in the Gospels when the mother of Zebedee's sons came up to Jesus and boldly asked that her two sons might sit at his right and left hand in his coming kingdom. Jesus memorably replied, "You don't know what you are asking." (Matt 20:22). When you think about it, it is surprising to charge somebody with not knowing what they are asking. You'd think that when we ask something, we surely *do* know what we're asking since, after all, we *asked* it! Of course there is a simple way to address this dilemma. Jesus did not literally say the woman didn't understand what she was saying, but rather that she didn't appreciate *the full implications or significance* of the request. She asked for *x* without realizing that *x* entailed *y* as well. In other words, our statements often carry more meaning than we realize. While this seems basically right, I think there is much more to be said here. This brings us to a position much discussed by philosophers in recent years called *semantic externalism*. I believe that spending some time understanding this concept can further illumine the nature of the prayer I prayed so many years ago.

Consider the concept of semantic externalism against the backdrop of a famous thought experiment by the philosopher Hilary Putnam. (Putnam's thought experiment may seem to imbibe of that fanciful irrelevancy that laymen often ascribe to philosophers, but as you'll see, it does make a good point—and is fun besides.) Putnam asks us to imagine that the year is 1750, a time before anyone on earth knew that water was H_2O. Putnam then asks us to imagine another earth as well, a so-called "twin earth," which is completely identical to ours in all respects (including all the citizens living on it). A man named Oscar lives on earth while his perfect twin ("Twin Oscar") lives on twin earth. There is only one substantial difference between the two worlds. While water on earth is H_2O, on twin earth it is another chemical compound which Putnam calls XYZ. But, and this is key, both H_2O and XYZ are *identical in all their sensory properties*. Since the external appearances are identical, Putnam points out that when Oscar and Twin Oscar think or refer to "water," they have the identical thought in terms of the internal semantic content. Despite this fact, Putnam avers that there clearly is a difference in their beliefs since when Oscar thinks "water" he thinks H_2O, while when Twin Oscar thinks "water" he thinks XYZ. In other words, despite the fact that their internal thoughts are identical, those thoughts differ in virtue of having different substances to which they refer.

Now this presents us with an interesting puzzle. Where do you locate the different meaning of those thoughts if not in the internal awareness that Oscar and Twin Oscar have of them? Putnam responds by arguing that we should locate this semantic difference in the wide content of their beliefs as rooted in the structure of the world. Simply in virtue of living in an environment where water is H_2O, Oscar's beliefs about water include the wide semantic content that it is H_2O, while Twin Oscar's beliefs about water include the wide semantic content that it is XYZ. In other words, semantic externalism is the view that, for at least some of our beliefs, there are two kinds of content: that which is internally available to us, and that which is external to our awareness. With a touch of hyperbole Putnam famously concluded, "Cut the pie any way you like, 'meanings' just ain't in the *head!*"[8]

Putnam's argument for semantic externalism is focused on our knowledge of natural kinds; that is, things which belong in a natural (as opposed to artificial) grouping like lions, planets or, in this case, water. But if semantic externalism is correct, and there is good evidence that it is, then many other beliefs we have may include content external to our awareness.[9] All sorts of truths could have external semantic content unavailable to the one holding the belief, and that surely includes beliefs about the infinite God. We begin by recognizing that Oscar's belief about water includes wide content external to his awareness, like the fact that water is a substance which, in its basic molecular form, consists of two hydrogen atoms covalently bonded with one oxygen atom. Once we've accepted this about water, it is hardly surprising that our beliefs about God also include content external to our present awareness. Consider, for example, Thomas' stunning confession upon seeing the risen Jesus: "My Lord and my God!" (John 20:28). It is impossible for us to know precisely what the narrow content of Thomas' confession was, because we cannot get into his head to know what he was internally aware of at that moment. But looking back from the hindsight of developed Christian doctrine, we have the benefit of information which certainly was external to Thomas' confession. For example, according to orthodox Christian theology, Jesus Christ is the second Person of the Trinity, eternally begotten of the Father. Thomas would not have known this, and thus it would have been external to his awareness in the same way that the fact that water is H_2O was external to Oscar's awareness. From this perspective you could say that for the last two millennia the church has been growing corporately into a greater understanding of the stunningly wide content of Thomas' confession.

In the same way that the church has been growing into the infinitely wide semantic horizons of Thomas' confession, so, in a much more modest way, I have been growing into the infinitely wide semantic horizons of that prayer I prayed more than thirty years ago: "Dear God, please come into my heart. I want to follow you, not the devil. Amen."

Those were a few simple words uttered by a child who was at the time just three years out of diapers. And yet those words, for all their faltering ineptitude, are not an obstacle to faith, but rather the door into it, a humble wardrobe from which opens up a horizon of infinitely broad semantic content. When one thinks about the implications of this picture, of simple statements grappling with infinity, it is no leap to call that prayer a linguistic sacrament of silent grace made audible.

In addition to being sacramental, this prayer may be properly viewed as iconic. At this point I turn again to the theologian Thomas F. Torrance, who offers another strikingly apposite illustration. He points out that in a Byzantine icon of Christ the lines of sight moving into the

8   Hilary Putnam, "The Meaning of 'Meaning,'" in *Language, Mind, and Knowledge*, Minnesota Studies in the Philosophy of Science, vol. 7, ed. Keith Gunderson (Minneapolis: University of Minnesota Press, 1975), 144.

9   For example, Tyler Burge, "Individualism and the Mental," in *Midwest Studies in Philosophy*, vol. 4, ed. Peter A. French, Theodore E. Uehling, and Howard K. Wettstein (Minneapolis: University of Minnesota Press, 1979), 73–121.

distance do not move to a point of convergence as you would expect. Rather, they diverge from one another, opening out into an infinite horizon. The theological lesson is clear:

> The Son of God become man could not be presented as one who had become so confined in the limits of the body that the universe was left empty of His government. He could not be represented, therefore, as captured by lines which when produced upwards met at some point in finite space, but only between lines which even when produced to infinity could never meet, for they reached out on either side into the absolute openness and eternity of the transcendent God.[10]

The simple, stumbling prayer of conversion is like that icon. It is rooted in a knowledge of acquaintance of the grace that goes before us. And as it is prayed, it opens up to an infinite horizon of semantic content in a way that is simultaneously awe-inspiring and humbling. The journey of faith and discipleship is, from this perspective, the journey into the infinite depths of the simplest of prayers to God which embodies an infinite range of semantic content.

A CONTEMPLATIVE CONCLUSION

This perspective has utterly transformed my understanding of the journey of faith. For years I thought of that prayer as a narrow point forced to bear the weight of salvation, like Atlas as a ninety-eight-pound weakling, holding the world on his puny shoulders. I now see things quite differently. That prayer was first rooted in an intimate knowledge of acquaintance of which I was only barely aware. And looking forward from that moment, I see that the prayer itself contained an astounding, broad semantic content that I have been gradually growing into over the last thirty-four years and which, Lord willing, I will continue to grow into for eternity. As the world quietly rolled on around me, in a brief and inconsequential moment I touched eternity. And now as I reflect on this marvelous reality, I come to the staggering conclusion that the prayer I prayed so long ago was in fact the prayer that prayed me.

Amen.

---

10   Thomas F. Torrance, *Space, Time and Incarnation* (New York: Oxford University Press, 1969), 18.

-THIRTEEN-

CHRISTIAN HISTORY OR SECULAR MYTHOLOGY?

ALLAN CHAPMAN

An Oxford University historian of science, Dr. Chapman studied and has now long taught at Wadham College, from which John Wilkins once gathered the group of young men that evolved into the Royal Society in the mid-seventeenth century. Chapman has written on key figures in the scientific revolution. He is fellow of the Royal Astronomical Society and presenter for the BBC series, *Gods in the Sky*.

© 2012 Allan Chapman

I never cease to be amazed, and sometimes amused, when I hear prominent atheistic scientists sounding off about science and Christianity. For there is a strange irony when one hears a person who, in the laboratory, is a meticulous and methodical researcher, descending into myth, urban folklore, and grotesque distortions of the historical record when they pontificate on religion. And literary scholars, who should know the difference between documented evidence and "received opinion," can be just as bad.

For does it not stand to reason that "the church" has always been an enemy of "progress" and freedom of thought? That the modern world only came into being when brave unbelievers stood up to the "blind dogmatism" of the Christian church? Is that not why the felicitous souls of the "Enlightenment" characterized Christendom between AD 500 and 1500 as a backward Middle (or "Dark") Age, between the glories of free-wheeling pagan antiquity and the sweetness, reason, and light of the worldly, freedom-loving eighteenth century?

It was the same church that so terrified poor Copernicus that he only dared publish his book about the earth rotating around the sun as he lay on his deathbed. Less timid "martyrs of science," such as Giordano Bruno and Galileo, had the courage to speak "the truth" and paid a terrible price at the hands of the Inquisition for doing so: bogus trials, torture, imprisonment, burnings, and martyrdom. Thank goodness for the "Enlightenment," which, in the tolerant and humane air of the eighteenth-century "Age of Reason," began an all-out assault on the dark forces of clerical superstition! Yet it would prove a long, hard fight, because even in the nineteenth century the church tried to suppress the infant science of geology and enforce the biblically derived creation date of 9:00 a.m. on October 21, 4004 BC. True scientists who were coming to think, by the early nineteenth century, that instead of being the descendants of sinful Adam and Eve, humanity evolved over vast aeons of time from simple, innocent monkeys, had to keep their heads down if they did not want to get into trouble.

Then in 1859 came the heroic Charles Darwin, bravely bestriding the world of superstition, like Richard Dawkins in a frock coat and stovepipe hat, openly declaring that men had evolved from monkeys. Reason finally triumphed in a world-changing, set-piece debate held in Oxford in June 1860, when that young champion of evolutionary science, Thomas Henry Huxley ("Darwin's bulldog"), verbally destroyed the aged, reactionary, ignorant, superstitious bishop of Oxford, "Soapy Sam" Wilberforce. Indeed, the metaphorical slaughter of the gibbering old bishop became a *cause célèbre* and a watershed. For before the relentless pounding of Huxley's scientific reasoning and oratorical skills, religion went into headlong retreat and secular science, including the infant sciences of sociology and psychology, began that forward march from darkness to light which makes the early twenty-first century so wonderful, so free, and so rational!

I have heard all these clichés about the conflict between science and religion (and a good few more besides) rehearsed to me many times over the years, by both scientists and arts people, including students and eminent professors on both sides of the Atlantic. Intelligent and honest people, moreover, swallow this urban mythology of science *versus* religion hook, line, and sinker, as gullibly as they believe a religious person swallows the "God myth." But where did these myths come from, and how did Christianity really influence science?

One has to concede that Western science's spectacular progress over the last four centuries, and especially over the last two, has been a significant factor in making religion appear vulnerable. I say "Western" science in particular, for say what we like about the natural philosophies of other cultures, it has been the science of Western Europe, and later North America, that has changed the world beyond recognition, both in terms of physical explanation and of applied science-based technology. For Western science *works*, and the experimental method has provided constant, verifiable explanations for all manner of phenomena once attributed to divine *fiat*, from the source of the winds to causes of disease, not to mention modern transport, the Internet, and other wonders of applied science.

Yet while the experimental method has shown us how nature works, and human intelligence has led us to use nature's mechanisms to transform the human condition, we are not one whit closer to understanding *why* nature is so wonderful than we were in AD 1300. The more deeply we probe into nature, the more ordered and wonderful it becomes. A common mathematical language can be used to describe pretty well everything, from the formation of galaxies to the way in which genes are activated. And even when we enter the seemingly topsy-turvy world of relativity and quantum physics, we still encounter mind-bogglingly beautiful and fascinating states of being for the human mind to wrestle with.

The truly amazing thing about the whole phenomenon of nature is that we can make sense of it—or at least make sense of it *provisionally*, until discoveries of new phenomena compel us to modify our explanations. For this, quite simply, is what the entire history of science has been about: new human perceptions of nature leading to fresh explanations. First there was Greek geometry in 600 BC, which is still very much with us today. Then there was Aristotle's idea of four eternal elements in permanent, chaotic relationship with each other, which explained life, light, energy, matter, and change, from 350 BC to around AD 1600. Then, four centuries ago, inspired by new instruments—such as accurate clocks, telescopes, magnetic devices, and barometers—we began to see nature as a great, wonderful machine. The Newtonian universe after 1687 was perceived as vast and ordered, with the motions of stars, sun, moon, and planets governed by the imponderable yet universal force of gravity. But a growing number of physical and mathematical problems with the Newtonian cosmos were emerging by 1910. Albert Einstein, Max Planck, and others then pointed to a new reality of bent and warped space and time, of atoms that were not solid, and of a physics that seemed more like something out of *Alice in Wonderland* than a workshop manual for building motor vehicles.

Yet at no time has this universe failed to make sense. The universe seems to possess an orderliness which is so profound and so wonderful that it is taking us centuries to plumb its depths, as we gradually adapt our imagination to new insights. Why should this be so?

Even more wonderful is why humanity is bothered. Why, if we are no more than superior apes, should we possess brains and intellects that compel us, instead of merely fighting for food and mates like our fellow animals, to ask "big questions" that can have no bearing whatsoever on our brute survival? What conceivable relevance can unravelling the big bang, or the DNA code, have to hoarding food or finding shelter? In addition to the big questions of science, why should we pathetic humanoids be driven to write poetry; record our cultural ancestries; construct vast buildings that bear no relationship to snug, dry caves; make music beyond mating grunts; and devise law codes and economies which are absurdly excessive when measured against the simple necessities of self-defence, hoarding chunks of meat, or exchanging apples for nuts? Why do those three-pound lumps of meat in our skulls which we call "brains" possess this awesome, dazzling potential for order, understanding, and imagination, and drive us relentlessly to search out what the Epicurean Roman poet Lucretius called "the nature of things"?

Perhaps most bizarre of all, what drives us to philosophize about an invisible Being or intellect, a creative agency that we construe as being so immeasurably greater than ourselves that we call it "God," and which we set above the heavens? Some people might regard me as pitiably naive for arguing thus, but I would humbly suggest that we act in this way because it is an authentic response to a greater truth. Yes, there really is a strange yet lawlike universe out there. Yes, our brains do give us a developing grasp of reality. Yes, there is not only a great plan, but also a Great Planner, who gave us minds which can, on a rudimentary level, key in to his mind, even glimpse parts of the great plan itself. Our gropings for an explanation we call "religion."

One reason, I would argue, why Western science grew up in the way that it did is because of monotheism. Polytheistic cultures tended to see the forces of nature as the playthings of competing deities, such as gods of wind, fire, disease, or good order. But when Jehovah first spoke to Abraham in the land of Ur of the Chaldees, perhaps around 2000 BC, a major shift in human understanding took place. And no matter how one chooses to interpret the Genesis story, probably put into the form we know today in the sixth century BC, over a thousand years after the events described, but clearly based on older sources, what cannot be denied is that the concept of a preexisting Creator God who made everything that exists from nothing was a profoundly radical departure from the ideas of other cultures of the time. There are no true equivalents in the ancient religious cultures of Babylon, Assyria, India, or China; though one might say that there was a brief glimpse in Egypt in the Aten (or Aton) cult of Pharaoh Akhenaten in 1360 BC, with its concept of a universal sun-father deity.

For what monotheism does is create the *potential* for an ordered, unitary, integrated creation, being the product of one single act of formation. Nature ceases to be a playground for autonomous activating spirits, but is seen to be not only logically at one with itself, but also with the beholding human mind, which is in turn part of that wider divine creation. With monotheism, therefore, *science*, as opposed to the mere recording of coincidental events, becomes possible, as nature becomes a thing that one can understand through logical processes rather than a chaotic domain of spirits that have to be placated to secure human advantages. And while the monotheistic Jews of the time of Solomon did not invent science—for that was not their priority—certain philosophical Greeks of ca. 500 BC were independently developing monotheistic ideas: philosophers such as Heracleitus and Anaxagoras, in their concepts of the *Logos* and the *Nous*: concepts of eternal perfection and intelligence that quite transcended the powers of squabbling deities of Mt. Olympus. Plato's doctrine of immutable Forms, and Aristotle's idea of an "Unmoved Mover," and perhaps most of all the eternal, perfect, and intellectually deducible realm of geometry and mathematics that inspired philosophical Greek intellects from Thales and Pythagoras onwards, all tended towards this idea of a greater, more rational, and transcendent Being or Agent.

When in the wake of Alexander's conquests these Greek ideas encountered the Creator-Father God of the Jews in Alexandria, Ephesus, and elsewhere, a fundamental change—not only in religious understanding but eventually also in understanding of the physical world— was ready to take place. I would argue that the full impact of this change manifested itself after the Creator became incarnate in Jesus Christ two thousand years ago. Nowhere is this parallelism between Greek and Jewish perceptions of the rational, loving, transcendent Creator God seen more clearly than in the opening sentences of Saint John's Gospel: "In the beginning was the *Logos* ..."

Indeed, the mystical philosopher Philo of Alexandria (ca. 20 BC–AD 50) saw the God who spoke to Moses on Sinai and the *Logos* as one and the same Being. Philo's influence on early Christian thinkers like Saint Clement, Origen, and Ambrose was significant. Saint Augustine also, around AD 400, wrestled with how a Christian came to terms with the intellectual truths of pagan Greek thought: surely a loving Creator God could not create truths that contradicted each other. An obvious example was how one reconciled the seemingly flat earth and tabernacle, or tentlike, sky implicit in the Old Testament with the spherical earth and heavens of Greek geometry. Surely the real point was that, both in Genesis and in geometry, one discerned the same all-wise and all-powerful Creator in action. That was the message: not a quibble between an ancient text and a later mathematical demonstration. Both were true in their respective contexts, because God spoke with one voice, although his creatures might possess minds with different kinds of understanding.

Writers and thinkers of the early Christian centuries, however, were not concerned with science *per se* (although deeply interested in Greek philosophy). This was not because they were antiscientific, as many atheists claim, but because they believed themselves to be living in the latter days, and regarded preparation for Christ's imminent Second Coming and Judgment as a more pressing matter. The preparation of one's soul to stand before God at the end of time was infinitely more important than studying natural phenomena. And was not the Creator-Savior-*Logos* going to make "a new heaven and a new Earth," as in Revelation 21:1, that would vastly transcend the stones, planets, and beasts of this old creation?

It would be incorrect, however, to say that Christianity killed off Greek science, for in many ways the great age of classical science (500–200 BC) was long past its creative peak by AD 30. While there was a flourishing of scientific achievement in the first and second centuries AD, with the natural history of Pliny, the astronomy of Ptolemy, and the physiology of Galen, the intellectual style and assumptions of these late pagan classical scientists were still in the tradition of what had gone before. Indeed, well before the time of Christ, classical antiquity's cutting edge had shifted from science to polite letters, law, constitutional theory and practice, politics, and philosophy (with the emphasis on what constitutes a good and civilized life). Far from killing off classical intellectual culture (apart from pagan religion), one might say that Christianity was in harmony with these later styles. The collation of Old and New Testament texts and empire-wide organization of the church, Christian study of how ephemeral and eternal worlds relate, and the ultimate classical expression of "civic virtue" in Saint Augustine's *City of God* (AD 426) represented an elegant flourishing of the classical intellect in its most refined, mature, and visionary form.

Calendrical astronomy was perhaps the science most actively cultivated by early Christian churchmen, and this in turn involved not only observation and recordkeeping but also a lot of Greek geometry. This same geometry, from the eighth century onwards, also influenced the rapidly expanding culture of the new Islamic world, as Greek writers such as Ptolemy were translated into Arabic. For Islam, like Judaism and Christianity, needed an accurate calendar if its prayers, fasts, and feasts were to be observed at the correct times. But when the sciences began to thrive in a dynamic and creative way in medieval Europe in the late twelfth century, it was largely in the context of those new and burgeoning institutions of higher education, the universities. Europe's universities were fascinating institutions, often established under the patronage of a bishop and training young men for Holy Orders, yet famously libertarian, reveling not only in profound study, but also in daring argument, debate, and intellectual challenge.

Let us now examine the myths about science and Christianity mentioned above, which atheists and secularists trump to show the backwardness and repression of the church.

To begin with, is it true that the medieval church suppressed scientific understanding under the dead weight of Bible-based dogma?

It would be incorrect to conflate medieval Christianity with strict biblical literalism. A rigid literalism, sometimes called "fundamentalism," is in many ways a twentieth-century phenomenon. Often associated with the 1611 King James Authorized Version of the Bible, it grew up largely as a reaction to Darwinian evolution and German "Higher Criticism" and has a very different spirit from the often speculative and critical yet deeply devout traditions which informed the Universities of Paris, Oxford, and Bologna—institutions that built on the late classical traditions of Christian scholarship.

Consider first what was taught in the great *studia generalia* of medieval Europe. The arts degree curriculum fell into two major divisions: the *Quadrivium* (Four), consisting of astronomy, geometry, arithmetic, and music; and the *Trivium* (or Three), comprising grammar, rhetoric, and logic. Astronomy was based on the geocentric cosmology of Ptolemy. A popular student primer in the subject was John de Sacrobosco's *De Sphaera Mundi* (*On the Sphere of the World*) after ca. 1240, which contained ideas drawn from Hipparchus, Aristotle, Ptolemy, and other Greek scientific writers. Geometry and arithmetic taught the student the eternal truths of divine mathematics—very Platonic—while music was not so much a performance subject as study of the resonances that existed between the spheres of heaven and the proportionate harmony that God had built into the cosmos. Natural philosophy, based on the *Physics* of Aristotle, was also taught. Everything hinged on the idea that the earth was a sphere, as were the orbits of the planets; the popular myth of the medieval flat earth was largely invented during and after the so-called "Enlightenment," in an attempt to denigrate the Middle Ages.

The *Trivium's* three components were likewise based on the essential rationality of the God-Man-Creation relationship. Without grammar one could not have ordered language, and without rhetoric one could not develop the ordered power of speech that enabled one to persuade and argue, rather than merely fighting like brutes. Logic was the crowning glory of mankind, giving us ordered understanding and an ability to glimpse the Divine Mind.

Both individually and taken together, the seven arts or sciences proclaimed the primacy of *reason* in intellectual life. In addition to these essentially undergraduate studies, Europe's great universities rapidly developed higher or postgraduate faculties, and awarded doctorates in divinity, civil laws, and medicine. These doctorates were given only after many years of study, at the end of which the candidate had to submit himself to be grilled, or cross-examined, *viva voce* (in living voice), when he had to defend a thesis or argument. Doctors of divinity could be examined upon their knowledge of the church fathers, biblical interpretation, or philosophical theology. Civil lawyers were grilled not just in law but in ideas and sources of justice, Greek and Roman writers, and the differences between divine, natural, and human law. Physicians would have to display an organized knowledge of classical medical authors, sometimes including those in Arabic translation.

Far from being about blind dogma and obedience to authority, the whole educational system of medieval Europe was about argument, criticism, defence, and rationality. What separated men from the beasts were the divine gifts of language and reason, giving us access to the very mind and word of God. In addition to "textbook" science, from the twelfth century Europe saw a burgeoning of published research into a variety of other sciences, such as optics, magnetism, chemistry, clinical medicine, speculative cosmology, dynamics, and both applied and theoretical mechanics. Scholars debated the possibility of life on other worlds, whether it was more "economical" for God to turn the earth on its axis in twenty-four hours than to turn the vast cosmos around a stationary earth, and whether an infinitely powerful Creator God could have made an infinite universe if he had so chosen. And beyond academia, medieval Europe also saw the invention of great labour-saving machines, such as the windmill and water-powered saws; the rise of navigational cartography; the arts of printing and paper manufacture; and the development of remarkable mechanisms such as large musical organs, firearms, and elaborate geared clocks that not only told the time but simulated the celestial motions, rang bells, and activated automata. It was medieval Europeans, too, who invented credit banking, modern accountancy techniques, capitalist economics, international trading companies like the Hanseatic League, charitable organizations, and the beginnings of practical democracy. For the governing councils of Venice, Florence, London, and other great merchant cities, along with the governing fellowship bodies of Oxford and Cambridge colleges and London's legal Inns of Court, were all self-electing and self-regulating corporations operating independently under only the common law, the king, and God.

Contrary to received mythology, no one got punished or executed for any of this. Indeed, some of the most *avant-garde* speculative thinkers of the medieval centuries died in their beds with mitres or even cardinal's hats upon their heads, such as Archbishop Thomas Bradwardine, Bishop Nicole d'Oresme, or Cardinal Nicholas of Cusa (Kues).

WHAT ABOUT COPERNICUS, BRUNO, GALILEO, AND THE "ASTRONOMICAL REVOLUTION"?

Contrary to the myth that Copernicus lived in fear of the church, and for that reason delayed publication of *De Revolutionibus* (1543) until he was on his deathbed, his ideas about the *possibility* of the earth rotating around the sun had been freely discussed in scientific circles for thirty years before his *magnum opus* was published. Indeed, heliocentric ideas had been explored in his *Commentariolus* (a substantial manuscript circulated around 1507). Two men had for years urged him to publish: Georg Joachim Rhaeticus and Andreas Osiander, Protestant scholars in Luther's own University of Wittenburg. (All the evidence suggests that Copernicus, the Roman Catholic canon of Frombork Cathedral in Poland, was in open, friendly correspondence with German Lutherans.) Moreover, one plain fact scuppers the myth that Copernicus had, out of fear, withheld publication until he was preparing to draw his last breath: his Lutheran protégé Rhaeticus published announcement of the heliocentric theory in his thirty-eight-page pamphlet *Narratio Prima* (Gdańsk, 1540, followed by a second edition in 1541). Nor was Copernicus clearly in terminal decline by

1541; as a distinguished medical doctor (MD, Padua, ca. 1503), in that same year he was well enough to provide a medical consultation to a close friend of Prince Albert of Prussia, and apparently saved the man's life—even as his heliocentric theory did the rounds of Europe via Rhaeticus' *Narratio!*

It was his other Lutheran disciple, Osiander, who effectively saw the book through the press—in Nuremberg—and who wrote the famous "Preface" presenting the heliocentric theory as a mathematical "model" rather than as a necessary description of physical reality. Why should Osiander write so guardedly in a book that was dedicated to His Holiness Pope Paul III?

Skeptical mythology explains this reticence as arising from fear of authority, because Copernicus' theory contradicted Scripture. In fact, it mainly contradicted the authority of Aristotle's *Physics*—the standard university physics text in 1500 in Europe—though it is also true that Psalm 104:5 stated, "He laid the foundation of the earth: that it should not move at any time" (paraphrased).

But Copernicus knew that his theory also flew in the face of common-sense experience. For did not the world *feel* fixed? Otherwise, surely we would be thrown off into space, and falling objects would fly upwards into the sky rather than downwards? Common sense leads us to believe that it is the heavens that rotate, not the earth. Furthermore, a spinning world, in a preinertia physics, would be constantly buffeted by easterly gales. Nor did zodiac constellations 180° apart get bigger and smaller in an annual cycle, as they should have done according to other medieval assumptions. Scholars assumed that all the stars were the same distance from the earth, being attached inside a crystalline sphere, with us at the centre. But if the sun were at the centre and the earth rotated around it, then individual zodiac constellations should get bigger and smaller as we approached and receded from them. If you walk around a chair placed in the centre of a room, the door in one wall will appear to get bigger as you approach it, and the window in the opposite wall gets smaller, and *vice versa*, so long as you keep circling the chair. Copernicus knew that the constellations *should* do the same if the earth moved. Yet they stayed exactly the same angular size. What Copernicus did not know was that the stars are so vastly remote that this "stellar parallax" caused by the moving earth was so tiny that it would remain undetected until 1838.

Planets were another matter. In effect, the only real advantage of the Copernican system was that an earth that revolved around the sun better explained the retrograde, or backwards and forwards, motions of Mars, Jupiter, and Saturn than did the old earth-centered system. Rotating around the sun in 365¼ days, while Mars rotates in 2 years, Jupiter in 12 years, and Saturn in 29½ years, creates the illusion that we are constantly catching up, overtaking, then falling behind these slower-moving planets. What is more, the apparent retrograde looping of the outer planets seems to occur in multiples of the terrestrial year, thereby suggesting that the earth just might be causing the effect.

Yet when Copernicus' *De Revolutionibus* was published, no one was arrested or punished, and a second edition came out without a stir in 1566. The church, it seemed, was not especially bothered. Indeed it was not, for during the medieval centuries church authorities had made no effort whatsoever to interfere with scientific ideas. Nor, indeed, did the church make any move against Copernicus' *De Revolutionibus* until seventy-three years later, when Galileo's abrasive advocacy of heliocentricism forced the censure of 1616, which will be discussed below. What *did* make the church take action was directly challenging Christian belief: publicly denying the Incarnation, the Resurrection, and the work of Jesus as Savior. But physics were deemed innocent.

So why was the Copernican scientist Giordano Bruno burnt alive in Rome in 1600? The tale is a stock favorite myth of how the Catholic Church persecuted science. To understand what really occurred, one must look at the bigger picture—studiously ignored by the persecutionists. In addition to being a Copernican, Bruno was a man with a dangerously exotic background for a sixteenth-century Italian. He was, in sequence: a lapsed Dominican friar, Protestant sympathizer, cryptopagan, denier of Christ's divinity and of the pope's spiritual jurisdiction, and—on his travels in Germany, France, and England—a conspicuous troublemaker. In addition, drawing primarily on Greek pagan mysticism, he believed that the sun lay at the heart of creation. His mocking invective had insulted Catholics, Protestants, and Oxford University men among others; and by the time he was arrested he was what might be called a "Grade A" heretic, double-starred!

Such a catalogue of misdemeanours would have sent anyone to the stake in 1600, irrespective of what one believed rotated around what in the solar system. This was not an age of "intellectual freedom," and if one so plainly denied the Christian faith, one got burned. It was simply how that society worked. So to see Bruno as a "martyr of science" is a patent misrepresentation. Not much comfort to Bruno, I agree, and not much credit to the Renaissance church, but those were the rules of the game in 1600. Powerful men can be vengeful in all ages—even church dignitaries, for such is the consequence of original sin.

Bruno and Galileo shared little but their Italian nationality. At no stage in his career was Galileo's status as an orthodox Catholic Christian ever in doubt. His crime, trial, and condemnation had more to do with a clash of powerful personalities: Galileo's failure to stick by the 1616 injunction that he could not teach as *true* what could not be demonstrated; his perceived abuse of an old friendship with Pope Urban VIII; his often offensive and haughty "superstar" manner, which made him many enemies; and the Byzantine world of Renaissance Italian court politics, especially that of the Vatican.

Until his midforties, Galileo was a frustrated, relatively obscure Paduan University mathematics professor. Galileo's original telescopic discoveries, published in *Siderius Nuncius* (*The Starry Messenger*) in March 1610, won the admiration of cardinals and senior churchmen, as well as of European royalty and the thinking classes of Europe. What he found through his telescope propelled him, at the age of forty-six, into instant Europe-wide intellectual celebrity. He reveled in it, resigning his teaching job to become court mathematician to the Grand Duke of Tuscany, Florence. Buoyed by this success, and by his acrimoniously contested discovery of sunspots—which he used to argue for the Copernican theory and vilify the Aristotelians—Galileo moved into a scientific collision course with leading men in the Jesuit Order.

By 1616 Galileo had begun an open assault upon geocentric cosmology, the orthodox Aristotelianism of the Italian universities, and the Jesuit explanation of sunspots, which was that the spots were not actually on the sun's surface (this would contradict the classical *pagan* dogma of a pure and flawless sun) but were little planetoids rotating around it, seen as line-of-sight specks. The spots really were on the sun, but Galileo's love of contemptuous language for those who disagreed with him upset many, as did his attacks on men who, independently and in good faith, also claimed to have seen the spots first, such as the German Johannes Fabricius. In 1616 Galileo was told by Cardinal Robert Bellarmine—himself a great Renaissance scholar—that he must not teach the Copernican theory. Or at least he was not to teach it as anything more than philosophical conjecture, for in fact no physical *proofs* (as opposed to geometrical analogies) or demonstrations of the earth's rotation or orbital motion were yet available.

In 1615, however, Galileo published his *Letter to the Grand Duchess Christina*, his patron's mother Christine de Medici, destined to become one of the key texts in scientific and Christian understanding. Some of Galileo's arguments went back to Saint Augustine. The book makes abundantly clear Galileo's respect for the Christian faith and its compatibility with science and the intellect. Had not God written two books—one the *Word* (the Bible) and the other his *Works* (nature)? Could God write two books that contradicted one another? Definitely not! Science, Scripture, and reason formed a divine unity. On the other hand, we should not use the Bible to ascertain specific details of science. Galileo cited Cardinal Boronius' dictum that the Bible teaches us *how to go to heaven*, not *how the heavens go*! That we could fathom for ourselves, using the logic that God had built into his creation. Scripture, in short, could not be read as a physics textbook. This process of progressive discovery would come to be styled by Galileo's devout German Protestant contemporary, Johannes Kepler, as "thinking God's thoughts after him."

So why was Galileo tried for heresy by the Roman Inquisition in 1633? It had to do with his friendship with Cardinal Matteo Barbarini, who in 1623 became Pope Urban VIII. Galileo hoped, now that his patron was on the throne of Saint Peter, that he might get a free hand to advance Copernicanism and have the prohibition of 1616 revoked. But in spite of Galileo's easy access to His Holiness and their discussions, Urban would not budge. Galileo seems to have felt pretty optimistic, however, that when he wrote his overtly pro-Copernican *Dialogue on the Two Chief Systems of the World* (1632), nothing would be said. He was allocated friendly censors, Father Niccolo Riccardi and Father Raffaello Visconti, who seemed to know little about astronomy and were easily persuaded by Galileo and his Medici supporters to give an uncritical authorization for the book's publication. Yet the tone and style of the *Dialogue* were so pro-Copernican, and Galileo displayed such an urge to denigrate those who still advocated the fixed earth, that Urban became outraged, as did the Jesuits.

This, I would argue, was the real cause of Galileo's trial and condemnation: not a conflict between free scientific research and the Bible so much as a perceived abuse of patronage by a not entirely humble prince of the church. Once Galileo was on the slide, he did not lack enemies to hasten his fall. For the Vatican, like the entourages surrounding the king of France or King Charles I of England, constituted a royal court. Once a former favorite had begun to "fall," no one dared risk their own careers by trying to save him.

Yet "heresy" was not a simple offence, and heresies came in a variety of grades, in much the same way as murder and parking offences are both classed as "crimes" in British law. Giordano Bruno's heresy, with his implicit denial of the divinity of Christ, came in the top and most heinous bracket. Galileo's heresy, by contrast, being one of disobedience (breaking the anti-Copernican prohibition of 1616), came closer to the parking-ticket variety. For in fact Galileo could no more demonstrate the actual, physical motion of the earth in 1633 than he could in 1610; he could only put forward arguments from analogy and geometry, laced with a good bit of mockery directed against his opponents.

Oddly, when the papal *nuncio* arrived in Spain and told the Spaniards that they must also condemn Galileo, the Inquisition refused! Not because the Spanish Inquisition had any love of Galileo or Copernicus, but because they resented the Vatican meddling in Spanish domestic politics, following a flaming row which Pope Urban had recently had with the Spanish diplomat Cardinal Borgia. For the Roman Catholic Church was *not* the international, monolithic, heavy hand of popular secularist legend. Indeed, the French, Spanish, and German cardinals and bishops not infrequently took the rulings of their Roman brethren with a pinch of salt!

The culturally pivotal "martyrdom of Galileo" only really acquired its present-day status in the eighteenth century, when deists, unitarians, atheists, secularists, and other declared enemies of revealed religion transmogrified Galileo the orthodox Catholic anti-Aristotelian "bruiser" into a harmless, timid old man whose courageous stand for "scientific truth" was his undoing. It was also the so-called "Enlightenment" that did the knife job on the Middle Ages, turning one of the great flowerings in the history of world civilization into the terrifying "Dark Ages" of legend, and the stuff for bizarre romantic novels and mad Hollywood blockbusters.

In some ways, though, one can excuse the *philosophes* of the Enlightenment for their often rabid anti-Christianity. The contemporary French church publicly epitomized social injustice, as bishops lived like princes, and a feudal peasantry often starved. Things were even worse in Spain, where the Inquisition was still active and ran a secret police service; while in Austria, Southern Germany, and Italy, prince-bishops, cardinals, and great churchmen lived lives that were a million miles removed from the self-giving love of Jesus Christ. Yes, they might patronize architects, artists, poets, and musicians like Mozart, but where was the apostolic simplicity and the selfless service to the poor and the outcast of the Gospels?

These *philosophes* warmly admired the autonomy they found in Great Britain—almost total freedom of expression; religious tolerance; equality before the law; an independent judiciary; no secret trials; a free Parliament; and a constitutional monarchy with limited powers; along with a large, rich, independent middle class; and levels of economic liberty and prosperity unknown elsewhere in Europe.

(Britain also had a state church that warmly supported scientific research—many leading scientists were in Holy Orders, in either the Anglican or legally tolerated dissenting churches— and took intellectual freedom for granted, though the *philosophes* rarely mentioned that.)

Hence a wide range of these *philosophes*—most notably Voltaire, Rousseau, and Diderot— came to develop a model for the human condition in which, broadly speaking, freedom was equated with secularism, science, and "reason," and revealed religion and "the church" with backwardness, oppression, and bondage.

Yet even when one weighs in the many sins of the Roman Catholic Church, one is still faced with an abundance of scientific discovery that came out of Catholic countries, not to mention Protestant ones like Holland, Germany, Scandinavia, and Scotland. It was in Bologna, deep within the Papal States, that Marcello Malphigi used the microscope in 1661 to discover those capillary vessels which confirmed Harvey's theory of blood circulation. For over one hundred years, Spanish Jesuit scientists undertook a whole range of researches in Central and Southern America (their instruments are still preserved in Madrid). Other European Jesuits reequipped and ran the Imperial Observatory in Peking. (While the Jesuit convert, Xu Guangqi, reformed Chinese agriculture, and the Ming dynasty used Jesuit cannon to fight off Manchu invaders!) The French Académie des Sciences became, like the Royal Society of London, one of the great scientific bodies of Europe. French, Spanish, English, and other astronomers were cooperating globally by the 1760s to observe eclipses, Venus transits, and other important celestial phenomena. In the 1730s and 1740s, the astronomers of the French Académie had made geophysical observations in France, Lapland, and Peru which demonstrated that, in accordance with Newton's laws, the earth was an oblate, or orange-shaped, spheroid; while the Hungarian Jesuit Maximillian Hell led an expedition to the north polar circle to observe the 1769 transit of Venus. Nor am I aware of any Catholic scientists being punished for any of this work, be it in astronomy (where the Copernican theory was pretty well taken as read by 1720), physiology, or geophysics. With the trial of Galileo the church realized that it had made a tactical mistake, and was keen not to make another.

So where was the church that persecuted science when Jesuits were using telescopes to demonstrate sunspots to the emperor of China, and lay professors in Bologna were making discoveries with microscopes? The myth of Enlightenment "liberation" falls apart as soon as secularist legends are faced with real, hard, scientific and historical *fact*. We must, moreover, be careful not to confuse the church with those secular governments of Europe, such as France or Naples, effectively autocratic police states with an overprivileged aristocracy, where there was no free speech or free press, and where *political* dissidents were severely punished. It was political oppression that gave rise to "rights of man" movements, and not the church *per se*; although the presence of rich, worldly bishops and cardinals hurt the church by connecting it with well-known social injustice.

Elsewhere I have described the Enlightenment as an "élite talking shop," big on grand ideas and lacking in results.[1] Soon after the French Revolution broke in 1789, when France became "liberated" from the church and "*Liberté, Égalité, Fraternité*" was proclaimed and the goddess "Reason" worshiped, the Revolution rapidly degenerated into a blood-soaked secular (or pagan) inferno. When later revolutions in Russia and China proclaimed Communist liberation, the same descent into oppression, torture, secret police, and totalitarian intolerance of everything outside the brutal secular ideology was repeated on an industrial scale! Post-1789 experience showed that officially godless states can be even more barbarous than corrupt Christian ones. "Reason" is a neutral intellectual tool and can also be used to

---

1   Allan Chapman, letter to the editor, *Oxford Magazine*, Noughth Week, Hilary Term 2011.

justify the bully in his murderous zeal. And without God and no concept of judgment in the next world, the only limiting factor in the potential cruelty and oppression is naked physical power and magnitude of ego possessed by the current top thug.

When one looks at *real* humanitarian improvements from about 1720 to 1830, one finds that an overwhelming majority came from evangelical Christians. Consider the empowering force of eighteenth-century Methodism, when milkmaids and tin miners found a new voice and dignity; the abolition of the slave trade; the removal of cruel punishments from the British Statute Book; prison reform; and the protection of women and children working in factories. In the 1860s the Salvation Army and other charities reached out to help those at the bottom of society. Not only was the secular "Enlightenment ideal" shown to be no more than hot air, but it was activists motivated by the Christian gospel who really began to make the world a better place, in the practical sense, during the "Age of Reason."

While one may not think of Christian social reform as especially scientific in its inspiration, one should remember that the secular movement which came to be seen as an "Age of Enlightenment" or "Age of Reason" was heavily influenced by borrowed scientific and even reductionist thinking. For the mechanical philosophy of Descartes, the geometrical psychology of Thomas Hobbes, the "iron laws" of Newtonian gravitation, John Locke's ideas of the human mind, and other scientific models—by no means antireligious in themselves—were all seen as feeding into what would become the accepted ways of thinking of the eighteenth-century intellectual: from naturalistic theories of moral sentiment to the deterministic laws of economic supply and demand; from Rousseau's natural innocents, "liberated" from the oppression of original sin and living at one with "Nature," to romantic notions of free emotional expression. How did all of this scientifically inspired free thinking turn out in practice?

In 1791, when slaves on the French Caribbean island of Saint Domingo (Haiti) heard of the "Liberté" being proclaimed in France, they revolted against their taskmasters. But far from confirming the slaves' freedom, the revolutionary government in Paris sent out soldiers to brutally put down the rebellion, and failed to bring the freedom-hungry slaves to heel. So much for "*Liberté, Égalité, Fraternité*" outside the snug world of the élite intellectual salon! And attempts by the French Revolution to impose its ideological model of "Liberté" on French-occupied European countries made the Spanish Inquisition look humane by comparison.

English evangelicals, however, had at the same time acquired land in Sierra Leone, West Africa, to establish a new colony for the repatriation of liberated slaves, its capital appropriately named "Freetown." In accordance with its gospel inspiration, ex-slaves, local African people, and white settlers were all equal before the law: the first attempt to found an egalitarian society for black and white people. Sadly, the colony eventually failed in its wider aims because of human corruption, but as a hands-on Christian ideal it was streets ahead of anything that came out of the "Age of Reason."

Perhaps closer in spirit to English thinking, however, and influential upon both English science and charity was Sir Francis Bacon's dictum, "It is an excellent thing to speak with the tongues of men and angels, but because if it be severed from charity, and not referred to the good of men and mankind, it hath rather a sounding and unworthy glory than a meriting and substantial virtue."[2] In short, grand ideas, unless backed up by generous actions, are worth no more than the paper they are written on!

What about the Church of England's attempts to suppress the infant sciences of geology and evolutionary science between 1800 and 1860—until the supposedly world-changing "Oxford Debate," when Thomas Henry Huxley threw the obstructionist church into headlong retreat?

This nexus of fairy tales has become so firmly rooted in popular imagination that it is not easy to know where to start. Perhaps I should first point out that it was Anglican clergymen who first advanced the science of stratigraphic geology. The Rev. Canon Professor Dr. William Buckland of Christ Church, Oxford, and the Rev. Professor Dr. Adam Sedgwick of Trinity College, Cambridge (and prebend—or ecclesiastical dignitary—of Norwich Cathedral), between them exerted an influence over British geology between 1810 and 1860 which it is impossible to quantify. Both were brilliant, charismatic teachers; pioneers of fossil anatomy who were inspired in turn by the original fossil researches of the Swiss-French comparative anatomist Georges Cuvier, a devout Protestant, along with other field geologists.

During the five decades or so that Buckland and Sedgwick were active teachers, over a thousand young men must have attended their popular classes in Oxford or Cambridge. These young men were destined, in adult life, to take leadership roles in their communities. Many became clergymen; others barristers, doctors, Members of Parliament, senior civil servants, colonial administrators, magistrates, and country gentlemen. All would have known their Bibles and classical authors too; yet all would have heard during their student days about a vastly ancient "pre-Adamite" or "antediluvian" globe, the extinct fossil remains of which could be dug out of rocks and, perhaps, compared with the bones of modern-day fish or reptiles. Oxford and Cambridge were not the only British universities where geology was taught, but Buckland and Sedgwick ran the largest geology classes. They ended up generating a vast geologically literate body of men who would in turn influence their own spheres of life. Their very presence in British society makes a mockery of the belief that when Darwin published *The Origin of Species* in 1859, reason suddenly broke through, and new ideas of an ancient earth, extinct species, and successive prehuman life-forms rocked the nation, as everyone found that their simple, literal adherence to a six-day creation was all wrong!

By 1840, fossil collecting had become a clerical passion: hordes of clergymen were members of the Geological Society of London. Most lay geologists fell somewhere on a spectrum between active Christians and dutiful churchgoers. In fact, active unbelievers were conspicuously thin on the ground, for did not geology, like the other sciences, proclaim the designing providence of God?

Buckland, Sedgwick, and their fellows, while accepting that the present disposition of the earth as regards oceans, continents, and species might date from the garden of Eden in around 4004 BC, nonetheless saw that God had made the planets, cosmos, and long-extinct animal forms hundreds of thousands or even millions of years before he made Adam and Eve. Were not the strata breaks in the rocks, which separated one mass of species types from another, visible remnants of the great "catastrophes" that had punctuated terrestrial history, as

---

2   Francis Bacon, "The Proficiency and Advancement of Learning," *Francis Bacon: A Selection of His Works*, ed. Sidney Warhaft (New York: Macmillan, 1997), 203.

providence wiped out a "lower" form of creature—such as primitive fish—to replace it with a "higher" one, such as lizards? Articulated giant reptilian skeletons were already on exhibition in museums, and pictures of the fleshed-out beasts were routinely published in books by 1840. It was the Anglican anatomist Sir Richard Owen who gave these extinct forms the collective name they are known by today: *dinosaurs* (Greek: *deinos*, terrifying; *saura/sauros*, lizard). Indeed, far from trying to forbid geology, even nondigging clergymen warmly encouraged its study, for it demonstrated God's awesome and providential majesty through vast aeons of time, as he gradually prepared the earth for that being he would make in his own image.

So what really happened in Oxford on June 30, 1860 when, according to secularist legend, evolution was advanced against the old, out-of-touch, reactionary Bishop Samuel Wilberforce? In fact, historical research has shown the myth to be largely a twentieth-century construction, built upon fragments contained in the letters of Charles Darwin's friends, and a "flash in the pan" of the most transient kind.

In June and early July 1860 the British Association for the Advancement of Science was holding its annual jamboree of science in Oxford. Bishop Wilberforce gave a highly entertaining speech (thereby lightening the atmosphere after the catcall-inducing drone of the American atheist professor John W. Draper) to seven hundred or so people. So buoyed by his oratory had Wilberforce and his audience become that, in full *ad libitum*, he asked the evolutionist Thomas H. Huxley whether it was from his grandmother's or grandfather's side that he was descended from the apes. It seems the audience was so amused that scarcely anyone could hear the bishop's apology, for "he did not want to hurt the professor's feelings." After all, it was bad manners for one gentleman to imply that another gentleman's grandmother was a monkey! Huxley responded by attacking Wilberforce, yet in a voice as yet so unaccustomed to noisy meetings that he could scarcely be heard. Joseph D. Hooker, who later claimed to have "smashed" the bishop, is only tangentially mentioned in the twentieth-century "official" constructions of the event intended to posthumously lionize Huxley.

Then as now, it was the media that decided what was a big event, and the virtual absence of the debate in national newspapers gives one a sense of how transient the exchange was. But the local paper, *Jackson's Oxford Journal*, July 7, 1860, in a few lines, gives us our best insight into what really occurred. The *Jackson's* reporter makes it clear that the bishop's criticism of Darwin's recent *Origin of Species* was on entirely *scientific* grounds. Nothing at all was said about religion. The *Origin* was regarded as "unphilosophical" (or unscientific) by Wilberforce because *no one had ever witnessed one species turn into another*. Hardly the Bible-punching antiscientific rant of legend!

Who was Bishop "Soapy Sam" Wilberforce? He was a radically different personage from the stock character of evolutionary folklore. In 1860 Bishop Sam, the son of William Wilberforce, the revered slave-trade abolitionist, was only fifty-five years old. He held a first-class honors degree in mathematics from Oriel College, Oxford. He had been a full fellow of the Royal Society for fifteen years. His training as a young man, however, had veered more towards the physical and mathematical sciences than to what were now emerging as the biological. But under no conceivable circumstances was Sam of Oxford a scientific ignoramus or reactionary. And as an Anglican bishop he was, theologically speaking, a High Churchman, familiar with contemporary German biblical criticism and in no way an ancestor of modern fundamentalism.

Almost certainly, what packed the seven-hundred-strong crowd into a venue designed for less than half that number were Sam's legendary powers as a public performer. He was renowned as a wit and *raconteur*, and for his self-deprecating sense of humour. "Soapy," in Victorian usage, could also mean "smooth" or socially accomplished, and he was wont to acknowledge his "Soapy Sam" nickname by saying that, although he was often in hot water (through the many controversies of church and state in which he became embroiled), he always emerged with clean hands! It was even said of him on one occasion that, if the Church of England were ever disestablished and lost all its endowments, Sam was such a popular figure that he would never lack for dinner tables at which to eat—and, no doubt, to spellbind the assembled company!

But what about Thomas H. Huxley, his opponent? Mythologists of the so-called "Great Debate" tend to project the powerful "bishop-eating" evolutionary orator of 1885 back into the much-less-assured thirty-five-year-old Huxley of 1860. As great an orator as Huxley would become, however, he seemed to lack the easy charm and likeableness of Sam, for the earnest, agnostic evolutionist was more of a natural puritan. On the other hand, agnostic though he was, Huxley recognized the major role played by the Christian faith in forming Western civilization. He had clerical friends and made it clear to official commissions investigating the need to educate the working classes that the Bible and the history of Christendom should be taught in schools. For not even Huxley was a secularist in the sense in which we know it today. (For that matter, Darwin himself, as an English country gentleman and magistrate, was liberal in his financial support of his local parish church—Saint Mary's, Down, Kent—as well as contributing to the Christian mission in Tierra del Fuego, seeing Christianity, theological niceties apart, as a civilizing force in the world.)

So the present debate is not only about science and Christianity; it is also about mythology and urban legend on the one hand, *versus* documented historical research on the other. When advocates of secularism claim to stand for demonstrable truth in the face of "superstition," they should be told in no uncertain terms that they must first of all put their own house in order before they start asserting truth claims. And it is my suspicion that, if they are told this loud and clear, and if the fairy-tale status of many secular notions of Christian intellectual and scientific history is finally driven home, then the science and faith debate may enter a healthier and more realistic phase.

–FOURTEEN–

FAITH SEEKING EXOPLANETS

GUILLERMO GONZALEZ

Guillermo Gonzalez made key discoveries about planets that circle other stars, while at the University of Washington and then Iowa State University. The author of *The Privileged Planet* and a fellow of the Discovery Institute, Dr. Gonzalez was subject to a campaign of criticism while at Iowa State having to do with his espousal of intelligent design. He was, in the end, denied tenure at Iowa State, for reasons that are debated, including in the movie *Expelled*, and in online criticisms of the movie. I asked Dr. Gonzalez to talk about how he became interested in astronomy, how the study of stars and planets relates to faith in God.

© 2012 Guillermo Gonzalez

I was born in Cuba, but I have no memories of that country. My family fled Cuba as refugees in 1967, when I was only three. Some of my earliest positive memories involve observing the night sky from our home in Miami. I received my first telescope as a Christmas present when I was six or seven. Although it was tiny, the views of the moon and bright planets (Venus, Jupiter, Saturn) it afforded were awe inspiring. I especially enjoyed seeing the craters on the moon and the rings around Saturn. Watching the Apollo moon landings and Star Trek on TV strengthened my interest in other worlds. Over the years, as I acquired larger telescopes, I observed a greater variety of objects and began learning how to photograph celestial objects. At age fifteen I bought an eight-inch Newtonian reflecting telescope, and a few years later my father helped me build a roll-off roof observatory in our backyard to house it. Despite all I've accomplished since, in my heart I still feel like that boy in Miami looking up at the stars in wonder.

From the first time I can remember looking up at the night sky, I have had a deep sense that some mind was "behind the curtain." This idea has motivated me to observe and study the universe. I came to believe in God at an early age, not from hearing a sermon but from the silent witness of the starry realm. Apart from a year in a Catholic school in the second grade, I did not have any religious training. However, by the time I later heard and understood the gospel in my early teens, I was receptive to its message.

My experience is not unique. I've met many Christian amateur and professional astronomers who, like me, fell in love with astronomy at an early age and became more religious as a result. Historians of science report that many great astronomers and other scientists of the past five centuries have been motivated to study nature in order to learn about its Creator. It is not surprising then that Boyle, Copernicus, Kepler, and Newton were fond of Psalm 19:1: "The heavens declare the glory of God."

I went on to obtain a PhD in astronomy from the University of Washington, specializing in quantitative stellar spectroscopy, study of stellar spectra with the goal of determining their physical properties. At first my research focused on determining the chemical composition of stars that were nearing the end of their lives. Measurement of the chemical abundances of carbon, nitrogen, and carbon, in particular, in the spectra of red giant stars, for example, gives us clues as to the nucleosynthesis and mixing process that have taken place in their interiors. Within a few years I had also begun to study stars similar to the sun, which would eventually become the main focus of my research.

In 1995 I visited India to do research with other astronomers. I timed the trip to coincide with the total eclipse of the sun on October 24. I had observed several partial solar eclipses and lunar eclipses, but that was to be my first opportunity to observe a total solar eclipse. The day of the eclipse, the weather was perfect. I took photos of the eclipse and made meteorological measurements with my computer; other astronomers in the compound took a variety of measurements, primarily in an effort to solve lingering mysteries about the solar corona. Several groups had visited the site weeks before to set up concrete platforms and piers to hold telescopes of various sorts. A couple of the setups resembled what I had seen in old photographs of solar eclipse expeditions from a century ago. The experience was just as awe-inspiring and beautiful as I had come to expect from my readings about historical solar eclipses.

It struck me that even though the astronomers understood what was happening in far greater technical detail than local Indian viewers, both had similar emotional reactions. Onlookers surrounding our compound spontaneously applauded and cheered during key points in the eclipse, especially at the end of the total phase, during the second "diamond ring." And even for professional scientists, mystery remains at a deeper level. For instance, why do the moon and sun appear the same size in our skies? This is a question I considered for a few years after returning from India.

While in India, I listened to BBC radio on my shortwave to keep abreast of the news abroad. One evening I heard that astronomers had announced at a conference in Italy the discovery of a planet orbiting a sunlike star, 51 Pegasi. I was skeptical. There had been several announcements of planets around other stars in prior decades that had turned out to be false. What's more, this planet was found to have a very tight orbit (an orbital period of about four days!) around its host star. Soon, however, it was confirmed by another group of astronomers in Berkeley.

Upon returning home, I planned on obtaining a high-resolution spectrum of the new planet's host star at McDonald Observatory in West Texas on my next observing run in December 1995. At the time, I was doing postdoctoral studies at the University of Texas at Austin and observing at McDonald once every five or six weeks. In the first few months of 1996 I observed a few more exoplanet host stars that had recently been announced. I published my results in March 1997, noting that the stars hosting planets tend to be more "metal rich" (astronomers describe elements heavier than helium as metals) than stars without planets. I have since confirmed this initial finding with additional observations, as have other research groups around the world.

The study of exoplanets, or planets that circle other stars, has since become a rapidly growing new field in astronomy. Some 550 candidate exoplanets have been discovered so far using ground-based telescopes, and another 1,235 candidates have been discovered with the space-based Kepler telescope by early 2011. Already evident with the first exoplanet discovery, the new planets tend to have properties very different from those in our solar system. Some, like 51 Pegasi, orbit extremely close to their host stars, now called "hot Jupiters." Most others have highly elliptical orbits. Planets in our solar system, on the other hand, are characterized by large circular orbits.

My discovery concerning the link between metals and planets has important implications for our understanding of how planets form and, more generally, for the possibility of life on other planets. The latest data imply that exoplanet host stars tend to be more metal rich because planets are more likely to form around stars with more metals. It was this discovery that later led me to propose the Galactic Habitable Zone (GHZ) concept. A GHZ is the region within a spiral galaxy like ours in which environmental conditions maximize the probability for complex earthlike life. The fact is, the Milky Way Galaxy varies in different properties from place to place, so we can't expect other regions of our galaxy to be exactly the same as in our own neighborhood.

One might object that earth may not offer the only set of conditions needed for life. Maybe, but the peculiar chemistries of carbon and water make substitutes unlikely. Even if some simple form of life based on an alternative chemistry exists in an exotic environment, it will probably be restricted to a simple form. Also, the constraints for complex life in space are far more restrictive than for simple life, and it is complex life that most people are really interested in. It is hard to prove that earth is *the optimal* planet for life, but to date no one has come up with a more habitable planet, real or theoretical. Even Mars apparently is not sufficiently earthlike to host life of the simplest kind.

The metal abundance of the interstellar matter that stars form from is one property that varies with location in the galaxy and affects the formation of planets and their character. In particular, the Milky Way is known to have a radial metallicity gradient. In other words, the abundance of metals varies with distance from the galactic center. Stars near the galactic center tend to have more metals than those close to its edge. Thus, the character of planetary systems depends on where they form in the galaxy. There are several other such trends across the Milky Way that also help define the boundaries of the GHZ. These include the distribution of supernovas and gamma ray bursts, outbursts from the vicinity of giant black holes that are present at the center of galaxies, and galactic tides that pull on comets believed to circle most stars at a distance (such as the Oort cloud around our sun), like the moon pulls on our oceans to cause terrestrial tides.

Taken together, these large-scale trends result in a GHZ that is shaped like a ring with fuzzy boundaries around the center of the galaxy. The GHZ begins as a narrow ring and grows in diameter and width over time. My idea of the GHZ was first introduced in print by my colleagues Donald Brownlee and Peter Ward at the University of Washington in their popular book *Rare Earth: Why Complex Life Is Uncommon in the Universe*. The idea grew out of a number of hallway conversations we had while I was a postdoc at the UW. The following year we published a popular article in *Scientific American* and in a technical paper in the planetary journal *Icarus*, which Carl Sagan once edited. The GHZ concept continues to be a unifying concept in astrobiology for discussions of habitability on the galactic scale.

The GHZ superficially resembles the Circumstellar Habitable Zone (CHZ), a region around a star in which a rocky planet must remain so that liquid water can flow on its surface. The CHZ concept has been discussed by astronomers at least since the 1950s and has served as a primary unifying concept in astrobiology. I knew about the CHZ before viewing the solar eclipse in 1995, and it occurred to me the next year that our existence is intimately connected with our ability to observe total solar eclipses.

First, the requirement that Earth must be within a CHZ for us to exist constrains the size that the sun must appear in our sky. In addition, a good case can be made that the sun is the best type of star where life can establish itself on an orbiting planet. Stars more massive than the sun have shorter lifetimes, while smaller stars have less stable energy output. Second, a large nearby moon makes a terrestrial planet more habitable. For example, the moon causes strong tides on Earth; this helps to mix mineral nutrients from the continents to the oceans, is one of the driving forces of the deep ocean circulation, and stabilizes the tilt of Earth's rotation axis. Our moon not only makes Earth more habitable than it would be otherwise, it also makes it more likely that we can observe total solar eclipses. What's more, solar eclipses have figured prominently in science. Solar eclipses provide the best opportunities to observe the sun's corona, and they provided the first major tests of general relativity. In these ways our existence on Earth is intimately linked with scientific advance.

This isn't the only case in which the conditions needed for life are related to the conditions needed for observation. Jay Richards and I detail several more examples in *The Privileged Planet: How Our Place in the Cosmos Is Designed for Discovery*. We suggest that the universe may not only be designed for life, but that a variety of fortunate characteristics seem to have been set in place to allow sentient beings to explore and understand it.

What does all this have to do with God? The connections are subtle and intricate. First, we made a case in *The Privileged Planet* for the design of the universe. It may be possible to rule some kinds of designers out, but the astronomical evidence does not precisely specify the identity of the designer. Design of the universe is certainly compatible with the biblical God and in some ways supports what the Bible says about him. Second, Psalm 19:1 tells us that we can discern evidence of God in nature, but it doesn't say specifically what kind of evidence will reveal him or even if that evidence will be amenable to scientific investigation.

I did already believe in the God of the Bible before making these discoveries, but they no more require a belief in God to accept than does anything else science reveals.

My Christian beliefs did make me open to considering possible evidence for design and purpose in nature via scientific methods. Like many of the Christian astronomers who have preceded me, I have been motivated by the message of Psalm 19:1. I think this is an important advantage that we theistic scientists have over our nontheistic (and some theistic) colleagues. The nontheistic scientist already "knows" that nature is not designed or, even if it is, that there is no objective scientific way to discover that design. While the theistic scientist believes in a designed cosmos, he is open to both options regarding its scientific detectability.

The problem for scientists who have closed their minds to the design option, as philosopher of science Del Ratzsch put it, is that "the universe is not obliged to conform to our expectations." There are many examples in the history of science that show that the nature of physical phenomena often take the scientific world by great surprise, such as Kepler's discovery that the planets orbit in an ellipse rather than a circle, special relativity, general relativity, the quantum realm, and biological "nanomachines" found within cells.

I do not, however, argue for design from the many instances of what I call "local fine tuning." These include the CHZ, GHZ, and various planetary parameters that must fall within a narrow range for life to exist somewhere in the universe. I am not convinced that we know the probabilities of these astrophysical factors obtaining in one place well enough to completely exclude unguided natural processes as the best explanation for Earth's habitability. And I don't think that the question of extraterrestrial life is of paramount importance. Whether or not we are alone in the universe is theologically ambiguous; historically, Christians have been on both sides of this question. The tendency among popular science writers, however, is to view the discovery of life beyond Earth as a blow to religious beliefs. This popular error is often justified by the discredited and misnamed Copernican Principle. I say this because Copernicus would not, I think, agree to it if he were alive today; he actually believed the Earth to be privileged. Also, removing Earth from the center of the universe does not imply that its metaphysical status need be diminished.

When conjoined with the several well-established examples of how the universe as a whole is "fine-tuned," such as the mass of fundamental particles, the strength of fundamental forces, and cosmological initial conditions, the total fine-tuning required for life shows that we live in a highly improbable universe. Even this evidence is not sufficient for some. When confronted with the evidence for fine-tuning, some scientists refer to one of the many species of multiverse theories. It is impossible to disprove the existence of other universes, so this will always remain an option to explain fine-tuning. To be sure, there are some theoretical motivations for believing in multiverses from inflationary cosmology and quantum mechanics. However, appeal to other unseen universes does not explain the type of evidence for design we present in *The Privileged Planet*. In a sense, we live in a highly extravagant universe. We don't *need* to see solar eclipses, the stars, or distant galaxies to exist. The universe we inhabit is extravagantly observable and knowable. We argue that the number of possible universes that are habitable but unfriendly to scientific discovery far outnumbers the number of universes like ours.

When *The Privileged Planet* was published in 2004, I expected criticism from some quarters, and I thought I was ready for it. While intelligent design (ID) is highly controversial in the biological sciences, historically, cosmologists and physicists have been much friendlier to the idea. I had received a grant from the Templeton Foundation to write the book, and the University of Washington and Iowa State University officially sanctioned my work by agreeing to handle the disbursement of the funds while I was their employee. The Templeton review committee included eminent cosmologists Max Tegmark and John Barrow, philosopher Michael Ruse, and physical chemist Peter Atkins. Finally, the prominent scientists Owen Gingerich and Simon Conway Morris endorsed the book. I give all these details only to show that I had considerable "cover" for publishing my controversial arguments.

But none of that helped. A firestorm of controversy erupted in the summer of 2005, first at the Smithsonian and soon thereafter at Iowa State University, where I was an assistant professor in the physics and astronomy department. First, skeptics organized a nationwide campaign to have the Smithsonian cancel their showing of the *Privileged Planet* documentary, because, they argued, a government institution should not be promoting a religious point of view. At Iowa State professors feared that having an ID proponent in a science department there would be tantamount to bringing religion into the science classroom. In every instance, the most vocal opponents were self-professed atheists. All this culminated in the university denying me tenure. Investigations by the Discovery Institute and the *Des Moines Register* of previously secret emails during my appeal process in 2007–2008 revealed that my colleagues in the department did not want an ID proponent in their midst. The emails also made it clear that they considered ID to be religious. What they failed to understand is that ID has religious implications, like the big bang and Darwinian theories, but it is not based on any religious premises. I probably could have pursued a lawsuit on religious discrimination grounds, but I did not want to be subjected to the same kinds of abuse biologist Michael Behe, a well-known proponent of intelligent design, experienced at the Dover trial and afterwards.

The forces allied against me put out some misinformation about my case that was widely disseminated (and can still be found on various Internet sites) and might be good to correct. It is said I was not denied tenure at Iowa State for my ID views but for failing to meet the necessary academic requirements for tenure. First, I supposedly had failed to bring in enough grant money. However, the physics and astronomy department's tenure requirements documentation does not say a word about bringing in grant money as a requirement for tenure. While this is a requirement at some universities, it was not one at Iowa State when I came up for tenure review.

Second, it is said I didn't have any PhD students and only one MS student who didn't finish during my six-year probationary period. This is not correct. I was the main advisor to Chris Laws of the University of Washington on his PhD. I supervised him long distance, and I also traveled twice to Seattle to meet with him and discuss his progress. I was also on Rory Barnes' PhD committee. Both completed their PhD requirements in the 2004–2005 period.

Third, there are several smoking guns regarding the actual reasons I was denied tenure. Perhaps the most damning one is a statement made by the department chair, Eli Rosenberg, in my tenure dossier folder (accessible to voting members of the department) that my ID views disqualified me from serving as a science educator. Finally, Charles Kerton, who had been hired as an observational astronomer (as I was) at Iowa State two years following my hire, was awarded tenure on schedule. He supervised one PhD student to completion of his degree requirements, but his publication record was far weaker than mine. I am pleased that Charles received tenure—he deserved it. Clearly, however, very different standards were employed by those voting on his tenure compared to mine.

These experiences were painful. Some years have now passed, and the wounds have been healed by the great Healer. I learned many lessons from my experiences in Iowa. I learned that one must be willing to take risks in advancing ideas. The history of science confirms that it is often the lone scientist going against the consensus of his day who produces the greatest advances. I close with a poem ascribed to Sir Francis Drake, the great British sea captain who helped explore our own globe:

Disturb us, Lord, when
We are too well pleased with ourselves,
When our dreams have come true
Because we have dreamed too little,
When we arrived safely
Because we sailed too close to the shore.
Disturb us, Lord, when
With the abundance of things we possess
We have lost our thirst
For the waters of life;
Having fallen in love with life,
We have ceased to dream of eternity
And in our efforts to build a new earth,
We have allowed our vision
Of the new Heaven to dim.
Disturb us, Lord, to dare more boldly,
To venture on wider seas
Where storms will show your mastery;
Where losing sight of land,
We shall find the stars.

-FIFTEEN-

THE SUPERB DESIGN

DON N. PAGE

Don Nelson Page completed a PhD in physics and astronomy in 1976 at Caltech, under the supervision of Kip Thorne and Stephen Hawking. He was a postdoc under Hawking at the University of Cambridge until taking a physics faculty position at Penn State University in 1979. He moved in 1990 to the University of Alberta, where he does research in black holes and cosmology. Don married Catherine Anne Hotke in 1986. They have five children, including two adopted from Haiti.

I am honored to be asked to contribute an essay in memory of Paul Brand and Ralph Winter. I regret that I never had the privilege of personally knowing Paul Brand, but I did have many encounters with Ralph Winter when I was a graduate student at Caltech (from 1971 to 1976) and a member of Lake Avenue Congregational Church in Pasadena. I was impressed with hearing Ralph emphasize the goal of bringing the gospel to the unreached people groups of the world. I also recall that Ralph gave an inspiring series of lectures on the history of Christianity at Caltech. I remember even better Ralph's daughter Becky, a beautiful and devoted Christian with whom I served on the council of the Caltech Christian Fellowship. I think I admired her more than any other young woman I knew before I met my wife-to-be Cathy, though I realized that my calling in physics would not fit with Becky's strong calling to world missions.

I grew up in small villages in Alaska, where my parents, Nelson and Zena Page, were elementary school teachers. Since there were no stores selling fresh meat in the villages, we had to fish or hunt for our own—I caught many salmon and trout, and I bagged a moose, bear, caribou, and Dall sheep with a rifle on hunting trips with my father and brother. I also often went bowhunting by myself, but the only game I ever got that way was one willow ptarmigan, a grouse with feathered feet that turns white in winter and is the state bird of Alaska.

My parents were Christians and taught me and my younger brother Lindell about God and His Son Jesus Christ. Many of the village people were devoted Christians, but the church services were in the Yup'ik Eskimo language that we did not understand, so we rarely attended church. However, my Uncle Weslie Payne, a Baptist pastor in a small town in Missouri as his father John Payne (my maternal grandfather) had been before him, used to send us Sunday School material that we would study at home. We also appreciated listening to Christian radio stations in Nome and North Pole, Alaska. And of course the beautiful scenery of Alaska tended to inspire belief in a Creator. I was taught that I needed to make my own decision to follow God, and around age twelve I made a public decision to accept Jesus Christ as my personal Savior at my Uncle Weslie's church on a visit there, as did my brother. I knew that I needed my sins forgiven, such as fighting with my brother or being disrespectful to my parents, though I was not a particularly rebellious child.

One Saturday morning, though, while out hunting on skis, I did climb a 600-meter mountain near our home without telling anyone, which could have been somewhat dangerous in the winter, should I have broken an ankle where no one would have expected to look for me. Since the people of our home village of Manokotak did not seem to have a name for this peak, afterwards I submitted the name Gnarled Mountain to the US Board on Geographic Names. It is now officially so named and can also be found on Google Earth, with the Geographic Names Information System report noting, "Gnarled Mountain has many twisted ridges on the (west) side giving it a gnarled appearance."[1] I felt a certain sense of satisfaction in being able to name a mountain with a mass that I estimate to be on the order of a billion tons, more than the mass of all the humans on earth today.

I was homeschooled for most of my elementary education, except for grade 5, in the village of Emmonak, the only year I had classmates before college. I did grades 6–8 in the new two-room school in Manokotak, a village of about 150, where we lived from 1959 to 1966 and where my parents taught as the first college-trained teachers. So initially none of the students there were above the fourth-grade level. With no high school in the village, I took high school courses by correspondence from the University of Nebraska extension division. I then went to William Jewell College, a small Baptist liberal arts college in Liberty, Missouri, where my parents and maternal grandfather had gone and which was near the homes of four of my aunts. As a freshman thousands of miles from home (then Beaver, Alaska, on the Yukon River near the Arctic Circle), I rededicated my life to Christ at a Billy Graham crusade in nearby Kansas City in the autumn of 1967.

It was too expensive to fly home for Christmas, aside from the danger of getting stuck in the village with no connecting roads if the weather turned too cold for airplanes to fly. Indeed during my senior year, on January 23, 1971, the record low for the United States, -80 Fahrenheit or -62 Celsius, was set at Prospect Creek only 95 miles west of our home in Beaver.[2] I found out later that no airplanes flew into Beaver for several weeks, and my father

---

1   http://geonames.usgs.gov/pls/gnispublic/f?p=gnispq:3:::NO::P3_FID:1866435.
2   My father also wrote that in their thermometer, which had markings that only went down to -60 Fahrenheit, the alcohol level contracted down into the bulb so that it appeared that the bulb itself was only 2/3 full, though I suspect that last observation was an optical illusion from the refraction of the glass. I do regret that there were no official thermometers in Beaver that winter, as an even colder record

had to cancel school for a few days when the schoolroom could not be warmed up enough for the children to be able to remove their mitts and write. He once went to get a mop to mop up some water that had spilled, but the mop was frozen to the floor and pulled up some tiles when he lifted it. He said he shouldn't have bothered, as the spilled water had frozen to the floor by the time he got back to it.

My academic interests had been mathematics and some physics, but it turned out that at William Jewell College, the Physics Department was the stronger (with the head, Wallace Hilton, later winning the Oersted Medal in 1978, the most prestigious award of the American Association of Physics Teachers). Professor Hilton took me under his wing and, to my embarrassment, called me "Dr. Page" as his way of motivating me to continue my education. I had the opportunity to do independent study and research with lasers and make some holograms (which with a one-milliwatt laser required exposure times of several minutes, late at night when the building was empty to minimize vibrations, on a crude isolation bench I had constructed). I mainly learned that I was less adept doing experiments than theory, so when I went to the California Institute of Technology in Pasadena in 1971, I chose to work in theoretical gravitational physics with Kip Thorne.

Saul Teukolsky, a year ahead of me as Kip's graduate student, had just shown how to solve the equations for electromagnetic and gravitational perturbations of rotating black holes. He had found that certain waves get amplified to become stronger after they pass by black holes. I thought what this might mean in quantum theory. It took me an embarrassingly long time to realize that it was what is called stimulated emission, the basic process that occurs in a laser that also amplifies light. I then realized that there should also be what is called spontaneous emission even if no waves were coming in. (This would be analogous to light emitted from a laser with no incoming light.) The spontaneous emission from a rotating black hole would extract the rotational energy of the black hole itself.

I brought Richard Feynman over to our group one afternoon, and he agreed that my observation was correct, but later that same afternoon I read that Alexie Starobinsky and Yakov Zel'dovich in Russia had already noted that fact. I was crestfallen, not realizing that actually I was at the right place at the right time to make the much greater discovery that even nonrotating black holes emit. But the right way to do the calculation did not occur to me.

After Stephen Hawking heard of our investigations and the Russians' earlier work, on a trip to Moscow he talked to them about it. He liked their result but did not like the way they derived it, so he set out to do it himself. Much to Stephen's surprise, he found that even nonrotating black holes emit what has come to be known as the famous Hawking radiation.

After Hawking's paper came out in 1974 with the basic equations for black hole radiation, I did computer calculations of the precise rates of this Hawking emission for my PhD thesis. I discovered that if a black hole started with a mass of about a half a billion tons (somewhat more than the mass of all living human beings today, and somewhat less than the mass

<hr>

for the U.S. might have been set there, perhaps beating the 1947 Canadian record low of -81 Fahrenheit or -63 Celsius at Snag in the Yukon Province. Now with global warming, there is probably little chance of the U.S. ever beating the Canadian record.

of Gnarled Mountain), it would decay away within the present age of the universe (now measured to be about 13.7 billion years).

Stephen Hawking visited Caltech for the 1974–1975 academic year as a Sherman Fairchild Visiting Scholar, so I had an opportunity to get to know him. It took several days for me to learn to understand his voice that was weakened by amyotrophic lateral sclerosis (also called Lou Gehrig's disease in the USA and motor neurone disease in the UK). Besides finishing up my papers on the rates of Hawking radiation, I also wrote a paper with Stephen on gamma-ray emission by primordial black holes. Kip kindly suggested that I list Stephen as my co-advisor, so at least unofficially I had both Kip Thorne and Stephen Hawking as PhD supervisors.

When I was applying for postdoctoral positions, Stephen informed me that since his assistant Gary Gibbons had been invited to Munich for a year, it freed up money for Stephen to support me as his postdoctoral assistant. In the end I obtained support to work with Stephen for three years in Cambridge (1976–1979), while living in his home to help him get up, get dressed, get breakfast, and get into the Department of Applied Mathematics and Theoretical Physics in the morning. Often at breakfast I would share what I had been reading in the Bible that morning, such as Jesus' parable about the man who hired people to work in his field, starting at different times of the day, and then paid them all the same at the end. Stephen responded, "The trade unions would not like that story, would they?"

In 1979 I became an assistant professor at Penn State University, becoming full professor effective July 1, 1986. The night before, I slept on the floor of my crowded office with my new bride Cathy. We had gotten married two days earlier in London, Ontario, where she had just completed her medical residency. We then drove in separate cars (with signs saying "Just" and "Married") with her belongings to Pennsylvania and stored the items in my office on June 30th. It was too late to go looking for a hotel room, since we were leaving the next morning for conferences in Europe in the summer, to be followed by my sabbatical year at the University of Texas and at Caltech.

After our biological children were born (Andrew, 1987; John, 1989; and Anna, 1995), in 2000 we adopted Ziliana (then 2) and Marie (then 6) from Haiti, so we have a full family and have enjoyed many adventures. We have been back to Haiti many times to bring supplies and set up a medical clinic and a playground at the orphanage from which we adopted Marie. With some other friends, we founded the Haiti Children's Benefit Foundation, recently changing its name to Community Health International Learning & Development (CHILD), since we are now also involved in India, which several of us visited for the first time this February. My wife, who is much more practical than I, has spearheaded this humanitarian effort, collecting large amounts of medical and other equipment. But my academic schedule has allowed me to go along on most of these mission trips and also help with paperwork.

Besides assisting my wife in reaching out to the poor and medically needy, I have been deeply interested in the theoretical relations between my science and philosophical and theological aspects of Christianity. I personally take the main evidence for the truth of Christianity to be the historical records of the life, remarkable teachings, cruel death on a cross, and unexpected resurrection of Jesus of Nazareth. I have recently appreciated reading the masterful three volumes written so far by the renowned New Testament historian N. T.

Wright on *Christian Origins and the Question of God*. The third volume, *The Resurrection of the Son of God*, lays out strong evidence for the historicity of the resurrection, which is key to confirming Jesus' claim to be the Son of God. It seems clear to me from the historical records that Jesus' apostles claimed to have seen the risen Jesus, and the fact that most of them were eventually put to death for preaching this claim strongly suggests to me that they knew it to be true.

I believe that the specific revelation in the Bible of Jesus' life, teachings, death, and resurrection show us the deep love that God has for each of us, as well as the love that He wants us to show to others. The general revelation of God in nature shows us more of God's orderliness and faithfulness to all of creation, but perhaps less of His specific personal love to each one of us. Nevertheless, it is an important part of God's revelation to us, and I wish to understand what both the specific and general revelations of God tell us. One way I like to express the relationship is the following:

> Science reveals the intelligibility of the universe;
> The Bible reveals the Intelligence behind the universe.

On the whole, I have found little direct challenge to my faith in the science I have learned, though one issue that arose out of the doomsday argument of Brandon Carter and John Leslie that I have wrestled with for a long time was my discovery of what I called the "afterlife awareness" problem. I discuss the problem in a paper called "Scientific and Philosophical Challenges to Theism," and came to a tentative peace about it.[3] An issue that has troubled some Christians is the multiverse explanation for the observed fine tuning of the constants of physics, but I do not see a theological problem with that and have written a paper called "Does God So Love the Multiverse?"[4]

I have often said that nothing I have learned in science has challenged my faith so much as the problem of evil, which confronts everyone and which has been discussed at least as far back as the Book of Job in the Bible. For me the problem of evil is perhaps somewhat exacerbated by the fact that I do not believe in human free will in what is called the incompatibilist sense, meaning free will that is incompatible with determinism.

Free will in the contrary compatibilist sense means the freedom to act according to one's wishes and decisions, which I believe does exist. I would agree with Arthur Schopenhauer that "Man can do what he wills, but he cannot will what he wills."[5]

Here if I speak of "free will" without an explicit modifier, I mean it in the libertarian or incompatibilist sense, the ability to make choices that are not fully determined by causes outside the person, such as God. However, I do not wish to contradict beliefs or doctrines of the existence of free will, since if it is interpreted in the compatibilist sense, I have no opposition to that idea.

---

3   http://arxiv.org/abs/arXiv:0801.0247.
4   http://arxiv.org/abs/arXiv:0801.0246.
5   Arthur Schopenhauer, "On the Freedom of the Will" (1839).

If libertarian human free will were to exist, one might say that the ultimate responsibility for the actions of a person would lie in the free-will choices of that person, perhaps absolving God of the ultimate responsibility for the evil the person were to commit. However, there still might be the question of why God would permit a person to carry out an evil libertarian free will choice that hurts others. As Steven Weinberg notes, "It seems a bit unfair to my relatives to be murdered in order to provide an opportunity for free will for Germans, but even putting that aside, how does free will account for cancer? Is it an opportunity of free will for tumors?"[6]

On the other hand, if free will does not exist, then one might say that the ultimate responsibility for a person's actions would lie in the ultimate determining cause or causes outside the person, that is, God, if God is indeed the ultimate cause. This might seem to heighten the problem of reconciling evil with the idea of a perfectly good God.

Lest people think that they would be absolved of responsibility for their actions in a world without free will, I should hasten to say that I believe that the person would still have responsibility in the sense of respond-ability—the ability to respond to moral demands placed on him or her, even if the response is completely determined by external causes (which include those moral demands). Therefore, he or she can be held accountable for not obeying those demands. I do not believe that a lack of free will means that one can be justified in expecting not to be punished for one's evil deeds, or that society does not have the right to carry out such punishment. Indeed, such punishment can be viewed as a good cause for improving society and the welfare of its individuals.

In Romans 9:19–21, the Apostle Paul essentially says someone may ask how God can blame us if He determines our actions. Paul does not take this opportunity to deny determinism by God and say that we have free will, but rather he defends God's right to do what He chooses. I think this passage shows that God can hold us responsible even if it is His will that determines what we do.

Part of my skepticism about free will comes from my belief that the simplest theories of physics consistent with our observations are deterministic, though this is controversial. For example, quantum theory is often considered to be indeterministic. Some interpretations of quantum theory give probabilities of possible events, but then which event actually happens is a matter of chance and is not determined by the theory. (The random choice of which event actually occurs is called the collapse of the quantum state or wave function.) Some eminent Christian physicists, such as George Ellis and John Polkinghorne, do believe, in rather different ways, in both quantum indeterminacy and free will and think they may be related. Polkinghorne explained to me that he "accepts the indeterministic interpretation of quantum theory and sees it and other intrinsic unpredictabilities present in nature, such as chaos theory, as affording opportunity for metascientific interpretation as signs of a degree of causal openness allowing one to take physics seriously and also to believe in the existence of free agency, either human or providential."

However, there are several different interpretations of quantum theory. One that appears simplest to me and which seems to have become adopted among a majority, though not by all, of my theoretical cosmology colleagues (but perhaps only among a minority of all physicists) is the so-called Everett "many worlds" view. This model postulates that all possible outcomes that quantum theory predicts as possible really do occur, so that the totality of outcomes evolve deterministically, with no random collapse of the quantum state. It is true that one cannot predict uniquely which individual outcome will occur (since there is not just one). So each particular outcome may seem random, but if indeed all outcomes occur, the totality is not random but instead is uniquely determined by the initial quantum state and its evolution. Of course, this does not mean that it is determined apart from God, but rather in a theistic view one might postulate that God creates and determines the entire quantum state and its evolution.

For me an even more convincing reason for not believing that humans have free will is that I personally think the simplest belief, and the simplest interpretation of the Bible (such as Romans 9:19–21), is that God completely creates, causes, and determines everything other than Himself from nothing outside Himself. (By everything, I am excluding logically necessary truths like theorems of mathematics that I believe can be neither created nor destroyed. Here I also exclude God from "everything.") The meaning of creation from nothing (other than God) that makes most sense to me is that what God creates, He completely causes and completely determines, though many theists disagree with me.

I see at least these two mutually exclusive possibilities for the world:

1. God creates and fully determines everything.

2. There occur free-will choices not determined by God.

Most theists appear to believe the second possibility, but to me the first possibility seems simpler and more in accord with what I see the Bible says. Thus it seems to me that the simplest biblical view of God is that He completely creates, causes, and determines everything from nothing outside Himself. That is, I believe that all causal chains ultimately go back to God.

My hyper-Calvinist view, of course, makes God responsible for all that occurs within the universe, the evil as well as the good. So how can I possibly reconcile this with my view that God is perfectly good?

This problem of how to reconcile evil with an all-good God is something I believe my study of science has helped me with. I have come to a speculative hypothesis that has enabled me to see no conflict between the evil we experience and a God who is all-good, all-knowing, and all-powerful. My view is somewhat analogous to more traditional views in some ways, but the particular emphases I have developed are perhaps rather different from those of most people. It is rather at the opposite end of the spectrum from Ralph Winter's speculations about evil and perhaps more similar to the tough-minded views of Paul Brand, though mine are more extreme.

Since there are many speculations on the problem of evil, if others are content with their own understanding of the issues, I do not wish to upset them (unless they are apathetic about fighting evil, which I do not condone). However, if others have had some of the same questions I have had about evil and some of the same doubts about traditional explanations, I would like at least to suggest a new way of thinking. I do not claim that my speculations are correct or that they definitely follow from the Bible or any privileged revelation from God, but they might be helpful for some readers. I have been blessed by seeing the views of others on the problem of evil, even when I disagree, so I hope that my radical speculations may at least stimulate some readers' thinking. I should also make it clear that I am not writing as a representative of any community, such as my family, church, or university.

I essentially follow the viewpoint of the great seventeenth century mathematician and philosopher, Gottfried Leibniz, in his book *Theodicy*, that this is the best possible world. The idea is that it is the whole that is the best possible, and not necessarily each part in isolation. One can see creation as a tapestry, and our view of nearby threads does not show the entire pattern that God creates. One might wonder why God does not make each individual part the best possible, but this might not be logically compatible with optimizing the whole. The good of the whole and of a given part may logically compete. Even God is not immune from logical necessity, so in order to create the best, He may need to have some of the individual parts not appear best if they were viewed in isolation.

Of course, so far this is nothing new. A common theodicy, or explanation for the existence of evil, invokes free will. It is argued that it is more valuable for free will to exist than for evil to be absent, though I sympathize with those like Weinberg who disagree. I agree that there probably must be a trade-off between competing goods, even though I find the idea of libertarian free will implausible. Therefore, the free-will theodicy does not satisfy me intellectually. It also does not satisfy me morally in that I do not see that the value of free will would justify the evils that supposedly arose from it.

Another idea is that the existence of evil and suffering is necessary for soul building or character development, which may also implicitly be taken as a good competing with the good of no evil and suffering. For me, the trouble with this theodicy is that I do not see why evil and suffering are really necessary for soul building. I certainly understand that within the actual universe God has created, suffering and confronting evil often contribute positively to soul building, but even if soul building were of high value, I do not see why God would not have created an alternative universe in which souls could be built with excellent character without any evil or suffering.

My idea of what God values derives from what I see Him doing almost all the time, which is creating and sustaining a universe according to elegant and orderly laws of physics. I am not denying the existence of miracles that may violate what we normally take to be the laws of physics, as I think the resurrection of Jesus Christ did, but it seems that such violations are rare. Most of the time God acts according to laws that we have partially come to understand.

I speculate that since God acts so much of the time according to laws of physics, He must really value using them. I am not saying that they are external constraints on what He can do, since I believe that God is the author of the laws themselves and chooses to use them in creating the best possible universe. So far as I can tell, the laws of physics are not logically necessary truths like theorems of mathematics, but rather are contingent facts about our universe. To me the laws of physics seem somewhat similar to the Wisdom poetically personified in Proverbs as working alongside God in creation, though I do not think this personification should be taken literally.

Of course, God uses the laws of physics to accomplish other purposes, such as the creation of humans, whom I believe God also greatly values, but I do not think we humans are the be-all and end-all of creation. To give a blunt illustration, when a human steps off a cliff, God values both the life of the human and the law of gravity, but most of the time it is the law of gravity that He maintains rather than the life of the human.

Do I believe God does this because he is cruel to the human and desires his destruction? No, but I do believe that God places a higher value on the law of gravity.

Should we say that God is unjustly selfish for preferring His law of gravity to the life of a human? No, I would deny that also. But to express my views on this, I need to explain what I mean by value and say what I mean in speculating that this world is the best possible. (By world in this case, I mean the entirety of all that exists: our universe, God, and whatever else God may have created, and not just our universe.)

I take the value that is maximized to be the intrinsic value of conscious or sentient experiences. A painting may have instrumental value in eliciting positive feelings in a viewer, but I take the intrinsic value to be the pleasure or happiness or joy (or whatever positive word one might use) of the sentient experience of the viewer. Assuming that the painting itself has no conscious awareness, I do not ascribe to it any intrinsic value. Similarly, the laws of physics are presumably not sentient, but I do believe that they have great instrumental value in leading to pleasure in God's awareness.

So what I mean by intrinsic value excludes entities without consciousness (which can only have instrumental value). However, I do not assume that entities with consciousness have only intrinsic value, the value of their own conscious experiences. Humans can be highly instrumental in leading to intrinsic value in the happiness of the conscious experiences of others. Indeed, usually when we speak of a good person, we are not speaking of the intrinsic value of his or her own sentient experiences, but of the way his or her actions lead others to have positive conscious experiences. We do not say Hitler was a good man even if he experienced happy thoughts while dancing a jig during World War II. The suffering he caused is sufficient reason to label him as evil, despite what his own experiences may have been.

But when I consider the total goodness of the world, I mean intrinsic value—pleasure minus suffering, happiness minus sadness, joy minus agony—of all conscious experiences that occur. I am supposing that in our actual world, this total goodness (including the intrinsic value of God's conscious awareness as well as in those of His creatures) is the greatest that is logically possible.

Now if there were no God who is a Person (at least in the sense of having conscious experiences), and if our universe (perhaps a multiverse) were the only entity with any conscious experiences within it, then it would seem that such a world could be better if all the conscious experiences in our universe were happy. This might not be consistent with the actual laws of our universe, but surely it is logically possible and could be the case if the laws were suitably different from what they actually are. Therefore, under the assumption of no personal God, our observations would seem to be incompatible with the hypothesis that the world is the best possible. (Of course, atheists rarely do make the hypothesis that the world is the best possible, though even Richard Dawkins has said, "The world and the universe is an extremely beautiful place, and the more we understand about it the more beautiful does it appear."[7] Despite my appreciation as a physicist for the beautiful laws of physics, I myself would prefer to give up these laws whenever necessary to prevent cancer, or earthquakes in places like our beloved Haiti.)

On the other hand, if there is an all-knowing God who is completely aware of the entire universe He creates and fully appreciates the mathematical beauty of the laws of physics that He uses in creation, this omniscient conscious awareness could have enormous value and help make the entire world, including God and His own sentient experiences, the best possible world. Cancer and earthquakes may be logical consequences of these laws of physics. God Himself may grieve over the evils that are a consequence of the laws of physics that give Him even much greater joy, but there may be this inevitable trade-off.

Note that I am not saying that God is constrained by the laws of physics in the sense that they are any external limitation on His happiness. But if He had chosen to eliminate the evil, the laws of physics that He would have had to use to do that would have been different from what they actually are. Quite possibly they would have had to be less elegant and beautiful to Him than the actual laws He did choose, and such less-orderly laws may well have made Him much less happy, so that the total value of the world could well have been reduced.

One might complain that the choices God make appear selfish, placing His happiness above that of His creatures. But if God's choice really did maximize the total happiness of the world, then I see it as justified. Who are we to complain when God does what He pleases, especially if what He does actually maximizes the total intrinsic value of the world?

What I think is wrong about most human selfishness, including much of what I see in myself, is that it places a higher value on one's own happiness than on that of others. Far too often we act to increase our happiness by a certain amount, whereas if we had acted differently, other people's happiness could have increased many-fold. For example, if those of us who are financially well-off in developed nations contributed even just ten percent of our income to help those less well-off in poorer nations, our personal happiness might go down by a tiny fraction, but I strongly suspect it would go up by a much larger fraction for those helped. I am not saying that it is wrong to enjoy happy experiences and to seek to increase them, so long as doing that does not cause a greater decrease in happiness in others.

Therefore, if it is indeed true, as I postulate, that God gets tremendous satisfaction from the elegant laws of physics that He creates, it would not be right to expect Him to give that up for a much smaller happiness that might be afforded His creatures if they were spared from evils like cancer and earthquakes. God has created this universe to lead to much human

---

7   "Interview with Richard Dawkins," by Sheena McDonald, *The Vision Thing*, August 15, 1994, http:// richarddawkins.net/articles/92-interview-with-richard-dawkins.

joy, and I suspect that He has indeed sacrificed much personal happiness to achieve that. In particular, I believe that Jesus greatly reduced the happiness He otherwise would have had in Heaven by coming to earth as a human and enduring the suffering and shame He did, especially when He was unjustly executed on the Cross. But I think it would be unfair for us to expect God to give up more happiness than we would gain by some action of His, such as perhaps changing His laws of physics to prevent cancer and earthquakes.

Even if one believed in human free will as the cause for other evils, much of this discussion would apply to so-called natural evils. So I think that readers who do not see problems reconciling free will with creation from nothing might still consider my speculations as to why God seems to follow the same laws of physics most of the time.

However, for those who do not find creaturely free will plausible, I would suggest that these speculations might explain human evil as well. If our actions are determined by God, this may inevitably lead to evils produced by humans (but with the ultimate determination going back to God).

I am not saying that we are forced to do evil purely because of our genes, since genes are only a small part of the causal chain. There is far more information in what might be called nurture rather than in nature, though genes help form recurring traits, such as personality. For example, the tone of my writing may partially reflect genetic influences on my personality traits that persist, but the content of what I write is much more influenced by what I have learned.

In the Everett "many worlds" version of quantum theory, a person is continually branching into many copies (each copy in a different Everett "world," which should not be confused with the entire world of all that exists). Even with exactly the same genes and previous experiences (the same "nature" and "nurture"), the outcomes in the different Everett "worlds" will be different. In ours Hitler was an evil monster. But I suspect that in most Everett "worlds" with the same early "nature" and "nurture" for Hitler, he was not nearly so evil. (Of course, there is the flip side: in most Everett "worlds," Mother Teresa also did not turn out so good as she did in ours.)

I believe that it is a consequence of the laws of physics that when a person is faced with a moral choice, in some Everett "worlds" in which that choice is made, an evil choice is made, one that reduces the total happiness of the conscious beings in that Everett "world." There will also be Everett "worlds" in which a good choice is made, which increases total happiness. (One might postulate that Jesus was an exception, choosing to incarnate Himself with no quantum amplitude to make any evil choices.)

If God had chosen to use sufficiently different laws of physics (perhaps even to the extent of collapsing the quantum state appropriately as needed), I think He could have eliminated not only all natural evil, but also all human evil. However, that might actually have decreased the total happiness of the entire world by reducing His own happiness greatly at using less elegant laws of physics.

Of course, there might also be other reasons as well for why God values the way He actually runs the world. Often justice is viewed as a reason God acts and sometimes reduces individual human happiness through punishment. However, I tend to see justice as a way to maximize total happiness, such as preventing thieves from gaining a small degree of happiness by stealing from victims whose happiness is typically reduced by a much greater degree by their loss of goods. So it is hard for me to see justice as an independent reason for God's choices, but it is conceivable that God Himself gets satisfaction from some sense of justice that does not merely have the goal of maximizing happiness within the universe He has created.

Even if my speculative hypothesis can give an intellectual explanation for how the existence of an all-good, all-knowing, and all-powerful God can be consistent with the existence of evil, I do not wish to imply that we should passively sit back and accept the continuation of the evil we observe. I believe that God has created this universe so that we can join with Him in working to reduce evil and suffering. I do not think we can take pride in what I regard as the myth that we of our independent free will choose to do good and fight evil. But I do believe that by God's grace, part of the way He determines our actions is by His call to join Him in the creation of happiness and joy. Even when following this call may lead to a reduction of one's own happiness, a true personal sacrifice, we should follow that call to give an even greater increase in the happiness of others. I believe that it is the existence of this call by God, and the extreme example of carrying it out by His Son Jesus, that helps make this world the best possible.

In conclusion, I do not claim to have found the only, or even the main, reason why God has created a universe in which there is evil and suffering. But as a physicist with a dim sense of the enormous elegance and beauty of the laws of physics, it seems plausible to me that God may value this elegance (which we only partially grasp by virtue of having been created in the image of God) to such an extent that His faithfully employing the same orderly laws over and over really does maximize the goodness of the total world, despite the local evils and sufferings that result.

My speculation is that this is the best possible world, and that one aspect that helps make it the best is God's appreciation for elegant laws of physics. This speculation is of course highly tentative, uncertain, and controversial. There are many open issues in this conjectural theodicy, such as what the value of a world is, why elegant laws of physics might have value to God, whether there even is a best possible world, etc. But as a tentative working hypothesis, I believe God has created the universe as a Superb Design, and that His creation is literally for the best.

–SIXTEEN–
THE TREES OF LIFE

BEN MCFARLAND

Ben McFarland teaches biochemistry at Seattle Pacific University.
He earned his PhD at the University of Washington, where he researched
biomolecular structure and design. Ben is an enthusiastic teacher with wide-ranging
interests: he has also taught "Science Alive" for children at a Seattle public library,
led technical seminars on protein design, and taught New Testament scholarship at
Bethany Community Church.

I came to Oxford looking for trees, but where were they? It wasn't just jet lag and hay fever; the town seemed somehow inside out. Streets were lined with tall, beige stone walls looming over paved roads. Even on a bright summer day, it felt like walking down a corridor in an office building, with famous spires poking up here and there, and no green in sight. But paying the porter at Magdalene College, I passed into stone tunnels and found my way into Addison's Walk and the trees I particularly wanted to find.

Something happened here on September 19, 1931: C. S. Lewis and J. R. R. Tolkien were walking with their friend Hugo Dyson on this path. Lewis made a choice, the culmination of a gradual reversal, which he would later write about in his autobiography, *Surprised by Joy*, and Tolkien would reference in his poem "Mythopoeia." I wanted to breathe in the sensations of that night. Maybe the trees had absorbed what those two great authors had said about facts old and new, stories and truth, ideas that have come to deeply influence how I now see God's creation.

Addison's Walk is quiet and secluded, a broad, level path running along the River Cherwell. The path seems dominated by the living presence of trees, which run up to the path in a tangle of trunks, boles, and boughs. They seem almost to require herding. At times they arch over the path as if you are walking the aisle of a long, green chapel. Even on a dark night the trees would loom as a silent but palpable presence in the conversation. Tolkien thus begins "Mythopoeia": "You look at trees, and label them just so."

That night Tolkien convinced his friend that the story of the death and resurrection of God is the root of our mythopoetic stories and longings.

Paul Brand wrote of walking through an even lusher green cathedral with his grandchildren: the Hoh Rain Forest in Washington state. Brand described a row of trees with a straight gap running through their trunks, where a nurse log had nurtured the young saplings before it decayed and disappeared. Brand wrote, "When we die we not only leave seed, but we also leave an effect on the soil in which future children grow and future spiritual seed will be nourished."[1] At the end of Brand's life, he looked toward future generations who would seek understanding through faith. To him, the church also grows, like a forest.

As a student of the Bible and biology, I believe God likes trees. The righteous man is compared to a tree in Psalm 1. Scripture often speaks of a tree of life. Jesus describes the church as a mighty tree in which the nations nest, that grows from a little mustard seed.

But many trees seem hidden to casual observers, like those trees in Magdalene College. You have to look for them. After looking hard at proteins, I think I've seen relationships between different proteins that branch and grow like trees do. So I feel my own research on ancient proteins to be somewhere between Brand's study of medicine and life, and with how Tolkien saw words and stories. In all three cases, life is revealed as the branching of a great tree.

Branches are often tangled. Breeze and play of light can render their shapes confusing or menacing. Aside from its role in Genesis, the term "tree of life" also names perhaps the most common biological diagram used to describe evolution, which originated with Darwin.[2] So which tree of life "wins"?

My answer a few decades ago would have been "Darwin loses, obviously." In middle school I planned a science-fair project in which I intended to mathematically prove that evolution could not have happened. Turns out my idea didn't work, so I analyzed swamp muck instead. One of the reasons I became a scientist was to gain tools that would allow me to look closely at the world, in order to answer the question posed by these "competing" trees of life. I have arrived at an answer, at least provisionally—but I would like to begin to explain it by first describing what Brand and Tolkien found.

At first glance Tolkien and Brand don't seem to have much in common. Tolkien was a Catholic don, Brand an evangelical missionary doctor. Tolkien was a scholar of language who, though born in South Africa, lived most of his life in England. Brand trotted the globe, teaching doctors around the world how to rebuild hands and feet ravaged by leprosy and other infirmities, while his writing helped many readers see the world anew. Tolkien scribbled out a fictional world between classes, an imaginary home for the languages he also invented in his spare time. Brand was outspoken about his faith; Tolkien was more reticent in his most popular writing, to the point that some of his casual readers continue to be surprised to find that he held a deep, abiding, lifelong faith. (See, for example, chapter 10!)

---

1   Paul Brand, "Rich and Fertile Soil" in *God's Good Earth* (RBC Ministries, 2000), 21–25. Available online at http://web001.rbc.org/pdf/discovery-series/gods-good-earth.pdf.
2   A 2011 article in *PLoS Biology* (doi:10.1371/journal.pbio.1001096) points out that Darwin did not specifically call the pattern of relationship among species a "tree of life," but it has gained that label over the years.

Yet the two men shared more in common than their fondness for trees. Both were British. Both were indelibly shaped by world wars. Each stood before Queen Elizabeth II and received the metal eight-pointed star representing the award of Commander of the Order of the British Empire (Brand in 1961, Tolkien in 1972). More fundamentally, each was a committed Christian academic whose work exemplified "faith seeking understanding."

PAUL BRAND AND MICRO-MICROSCOPIC TREES

In the first chapter of his first book, *Fearfully and Wonderfully Made*, Paul Brand wrote about looking at a drop of pond water under a microscope. Unearthly, undulating amoebae swam through that drop, grasping one another with pseudopods and tumbling in microscopic currents. In the rest of the book, Brand and his coauthor, Philip Yancey, took readers on a tour of the microscopic world and explained how it influences physical and spiritual health.

My research as a biochemist begins at a smaller level still. An amoeba is half a millimeter across. If you and your microscope could be shrunk to the size of the amoeba (and if the unruly amoeba could be talked into holding still from its constant squirming, and if the properties of light could change so your microscope would still work), a menagerie of minuscule bacteria would appear before your eyes.[3] I study the proteins that make those bacteria move, eat, and live, which are yet more miniscule.

These tiny bacteria appear in more coherent forms than amoebae. Don't get me wrong, they're still blobs, but they are more like blobbish spheres, or kidney beans, or rods. A brown, plush, almond-shaped toy blob that represents the *E.coli* bacterium gazes at me from my office bookshelf, a gift from a student who was not content to give his teacher an apple. The bacterium that causes the leprosy studied by Paul Brand looks like a waxy rod. The bacterium that causes cholera, *V.cholera*, looks like a kidney bean with a tail. *V.cholera* is so small that it can live and reproduce inside an amoeba. Small as they are, these bacteria are the invisible cause of much disease and suffering for us larger creatures.

Microbiologists study the microbes, and we "micro-microbiologists" use X-rays and special types of MRIs to study microbial proteins, to learn how they cause disease, what they do. Sometimes it's just as important to know what microbes and proteins don't or can't do. For example, Brand deduced that the damage in leprosy is caused, not by the bacterium producing toxins or destroying cells directly, but indirectly, after the bacterium infects nerve cells and numbs the pain signals they send. The damage is caused when numbed flesh is torn by unfelt but dangerous objects—knives, flames, rats nibbling on one's fingers at night. The symptoms of leprosy are caused, then, not by the bacterium being there, but by pain signals *not* being there. Because the bacterium is buried in the nerves and not spread throughout

---

3   See also Genetic Science Learning Center, "Cell Size and Scale," University of Utah, 2008, http://learn.genetics.utah.edu/content/begin/cells/scale/.

the damaged areas, it is difficult to transmit from one person to another, and leprosy is not that infectious, especially after the initial phase.

Brand described how, when he was a boy in rural India where his parents were missionaries, lepers came to the family home. His mother kept the children at a distance and made them scrub themselves afterwards, just in case the infection had spread. After Brand discovered how difficult it is to transmit leprosy, he could treat the infected with less fear of contracting the disease himself. Understanding the root of the problem helped him know how to heal it.

Knowing root causes is powerful. Years ago I taught a biochemistry class about how scientists investigate the root cause of a cholera epidemic in 1850s London, by figuring out that cholera was waterborne and tracing its source to a contaminated pump. Now that the microorganism has been identified and extensive sewage systems built, cholera has mostly become a disease of the past. I didn't teach them this story for its practical value, because I assumed none of my students would ever be threatened by cholera—but I was wrong.

A student named Luke was in that class. After graduation he traveled with an international health care team to the Dominican Republic. On January 12, 2010, a 7.0 magnitude earthquake leveled Port-au-Prince in Haiti. Luke was sent across the border to provide care and help with disaster management. The damage was beyond comprehension. Water sources mingled with waste in a city of broken buildings and shattered pipes, creating prime conditions for the spread of cholera.

Water infected by cholera can be clear and pure, but Luke knew it held dangerous agents. Tiny, invisible cholera microbes brew batches of cholera toxin. Cholera toxin is a protein, not a small molecule like a drug, but a macromolecule, made of tens of thousands of atoms. It's still very small on our scale, but in chemical terms it is big and complex, and this is its Achilles' heel.

Cholera toxin has two parts, and it looks like an Apollo moon lander with five feet instead of four. When it infects a cell, the five "feet" of the lander stick to the sugary strands that coat the cell. Then the "head" of the lander can detach (just like in the Apollo missions), but instead of flying up and away, this "head" dives down and works its way into the cell. The toxin deploys several amazing chemical tricks to trick the security systems of the cell and sneaks through the cell, eventually finding its target—an important protein called G-protein S-alpha, which is one of the central "on" switches for the cell.

When the cell senses a signal like adrenaline, the message is passed to G-protein S-alpha and then on to adenylyl cyclase, which then makes hundreds or even thousands of tiny molecules that flood the cell with the signal to "get to work." Adenylyl cyclase proteins are like switchboards for the cell, or to put it in twenty-first-century terms, central servers.

Now, if it's important to turn the G-protein S-alpha "on" at the right time, it's also important to turn it "off" at the right time. Cholera toxin floats up next to S-alpha, like a normal protein, but hiding a secret ability. The toxin quickly grabs a neighboring molecule and glues it in, essentially flipping the switch "on" and breaking off the handle. Both S-alpha and adenylyl cyclase are now stuck ringing their bells and forcing the rest of the cell to stay buzzing with ceaseless, useless activity, which causes it to spew out ions and water at a debilitating rate. Worse still, because it is an enzyme, cholera toxin is not used up in the reaction but can move along to sabotage another S-alpha.

Cholera toxin is a protein with many tricks, but it is still a protein. This means it is big on the micro-microscale, so big that it is basically a solid, not a liquid or gas. So it can swim, but it cannot fly. This is why it spreads through contaminated water, but you don't have to worry about catching it from a sneeze or mist; it's simply too heavy, weighted down with its chemical arsenal. Remembering this, Luke knew that as long as he was careful to drink only clean water, he could treat the afflicted and collect data on the epidemic in distant mountains, immune to the disease. As I write this, Luke is back stateside and is planning to work up the data for a master's thesis to understand what worked and what didn't in communicating the rules for avoiding cholera to the people of Haiti.

Cholera holds other secrets in its genome as well. The DNA of all organisms contains long strings of information written in genetic words with an alphabet of four letters: A, C, G, and T. We can translate these words and read how *V.cholera* makes its protein toxin. We can even make a map of which bacteria are distant relatives, which are cousins and which are siblings. We can sketch a family tree in which the individual cholera samples are leaves, and work out what branches connect sample A to sample B. From branches, we can also find the root, the great-grandparent of all the bacteria. Thus we find an invisible tree of genes, a branching map of how the disease progresses.

So while Luke was climbing the mountains to research the spread of cholera, other scientists were collecting samples and mapping the relationships of the bugs' DNA to find out where the epidemic started. The process is similar to how literary scholars analyze texts to find which manuscript was original. Analyzing living texts of DNA, the scientists found that the original "manuscript" came from a point that coincided with a camp of United Nations peacekeepers. For the Haitians, this compounded tragedy with politically charged irony: this epidemic originated with an international group that came to help after the earthquake. Biochemical archaeology answered questions about the origin of the outbreak, but the political consequences remain tangled.

We can do this genetic archaeology with any organism. A DNA molecule is optimized for making copies of itself. Manipulating this trait with a few tricks, biologists make DNA copy itself in a tube and have now read the letters of DNA for an ever-increasing list of organisms. On a worldwide scale, we have found patterns of relationship that are like the patterns found with cholera, more complex but just as clear. We find leaves, branches, even roots, from the DNA manuscripts. And the human consequences of what we find are again often tangled and troubling.

Not surprisingly, we find that creatures sharing obvious biological characteristics also tend to share obvious biochemical characteristics. Two microbes that look similar under a microscope have DNA genes that read about the same. This applies to humans and similar animals, like chimpanzees and gorillas. As Brand recognized in *Fearfully and Wonderfully Made*, "All living matter is basically alike; a single atom differentiates animal blood from plant chlorophyll."[4] Biochemical similarities are vast, and they are true not only for structure

---

4   Paul Brand and Philip Yancey, *Fearfully and Wonderfully Made* (Grand Rapids: Zondervan, 1980), 57. Actually, in this case, Brand may be exaggerating the similarity, but that's a question of degree rather than kind.

of the genes but also their order and arrangement together along the long ribbon of DNA, called "synteny." (To get a little ahead of myself, Tolkien might point out that this beautiful word comes from the Greek for "together" plus "ribbon.") Similarities are also apparent in the order and arrangement of broken-down genes that litter the DNA manuscript like so many working drafts. Biochemical similarities among the world's creatures are as undeniable as are the social differences between man and beast.

Our continuity with the animal kingdom on the biochemical level is useful. I can study a protein from a monkey, a mouse, even a bacterium, and figure out how the corresponding human protein works. In fact, I became a biochemist so I could build proteins in the lab for healing. My senior year in college, a simple image kept grabbing at me: Jesus healing in the Gospel of Luke. I saw this as a vocation, but I knew I was not the person to enter medical school. As this picture kept recurring, it finally dawned on me that I could follow the path of healing in an unconventional way, by entering grad school in chemistry to pursue wholeness and health at the micro-microlevel. Now I use bacteria in the lab to grow proteins to find out how human diseases work, or how the defense shields of the immune system are built. Even a harmful machine like cholera toxin has a sprawling, complex architecture that is unlike anything that exists on the macroscale. It is a wonder and a privilege to explore this remarkable miniature world.

But what I found at this level has some troubling implications. If I look at the micro-microlevel and see a clockwork universe with mere gradations of letters between us and the animal world, is there any room for purpose or meaning in that jumble of atoms? We may ask, like King David, "What is man that thou art mindful of him?" (Ps 8:4 KJV).

One used to get philosophical vertigo by zooming out and looking at the unfathomable expanses of the universe; as Blaise Pascal wrote, "The eternal silence of these infinite spaces frightens me."[5] Now you can get just as dizzy zooming down to the tiniest scales. Just as earlier centuries struggled with the revelation that the universe is huge, we struggle with the revelation that the universe is biochemically the same from human to animal, that our connections to the rest of life run deep at the micro-microlevel and are so gradual that they cannot be easily explained away as functional requirements. This deep and intricate web of similarity suggests a natural, organic mechanism of creation.

When Brand wrote, DNA sequencing was still an infant technology, and the scale of the similarity between any two species of genes was not yet evident. Today that similarity is freely available to anyone with an Internet connection.[6] The wonder that Brand articulated so well must be balanced with the broad view of overall patterns that we find through DNA archaeology.

How should we understand this genetic tree of life written in letters of DNA? Another unseen tree helps me understand this as a Christian. It is a tree made with words, found in the theories of J. R. R. Tolkien.

---

5   Blaise Pascal, *Pascal's Pensées* 206 (New York: E.P. Dutton & Co, 1958).
6   Through databases like NCBI BLAST (compare a few genes in your spare time!). I invite you to learn how by tuning into my biochemistry lectures on iTunes U.

J. R. R. TOLKIEN: FROM WORD-TREES TO WORLDS

It may seem peculiar to ask a *Beowulf* scholar for help with a biochemical problem—but I see a deep connection. Tolkien studied Old English literature, which meant translating and comparing texts to reconstruct lost original manuscripts. This is similar to what scientists do with the biochemical "texts" made of DNA words. Like Brand and biochemists, Tolkien was good at making invisible things visible: hobbits, and words as well. One day while grading papers, a sentence occurred to the professor: "In a hole in the ground there lived a hobbit." *The Hobbit* involved, in large part, Tolkien writing a story to figure out what a hobbit was and entertaining his children. Another time he read an ancient text that mentioned "ents" without explaining what exactly they were. Tolkien figured out what an ent was by making one up and integrating it into Middle Earth. (Turns out Tolkien invented a walking, talking tree that sounded like his friend Jack Lewis pontificating in the Eagle and Child pub.) Tolkien's imaginary world was inspired and sustained not by geography or characters, but by an invented language. He told stories that fit the shape of his languages. For Tolkien, words came first, full of meaning, and creation followed from the word.[7]

Tolkien was a philologist, which means he organized words and languages into trees of relatedness. Tolkien was fascinated by the tree of words, and sought to trace the origin of words and recover their lost meanings. His first job after World War I was writing definitions for the "W" volume of the *Oxford English Dictionary*, including word origins. He would trace the origin of both a text and its words, comparing copies and sketching trees that show the family relations of words to one another.

Tolkien loved trees made of wood, and also those made of words and texts. *The Silmarillion* is so dense with family trees that it's difficult for many modern readers to penetrate. In his seminal essay, "On Fairy Stories," Tolkien wrote, "I feel strongly, the fascination of the desire to unravel the intricately knotted and ramified history of the branches on the Tree of Tales. It is closely connected with the philologists' study of the tangled skein of Language, of which I know some small pieces."[8]

Word-loving professors ("philologists") seek rules about how words change as they branch from each other. One famous philologist is Jacob Grimm, who didn't just collect Germanic fairy tales with his famous brother Wilhelm, but also developed one of the first laws of philology. Grimm's law established a rule for how sounds change from language to language, defining a mechanism for how languages branch out. Tolkien found joy in watching languages change over time according to relatively simple rules like Grimm's law.

---

7   Often when someone is criticizing Tolkien for deficiencies in his story or world, they misunderstand his intent because they have skipped the philology and poetry in his novels. To Tolkien, those were actually the most important parts.

8   J. R. R. Tolkien, *On Fairy Stories*, found online at http://brainstorm-services.com/wcu-2004/fairystories-tolkien.pdf.

Tolkien believed that there was an original language that held deep meaning in each word from which our current languages splintered and specialized.[9]

What inspires me about how Tolkien worked is what is not there, or in Arthur Conan Doyle's terms, the dog that did not bark. Tolkien was a philologist and a Christian, and his love of words led him to create a world that was suffused with faith beneath the surface. His love of words reveals itself in the languages and mythology of Middle Earth. But Tolkien never used the biblical story of word origins specifically to explain words. If there was a difficult word or a gap in explanation, Tolkien would mull it over, he would build his own explanation, he would argue (and he loved to argue), he would invent a world to help him understand it, but he would not suggest that God caused a word to change.

Simple laws and creative inventions of myths, of hobbits and ents, those were the tools Tolkien used to explain the origins of language.

It's not that Tolkien neglected the biblical story of origins, but that it ran deeper than mere mechanism. Tolkien had the idea of an old, deep language like the root of a tree of words spanning the world. It was like Adam naming the animals, after which language was splintered at the Tower of Babel. He alluded to Babel in a 1945 letter to his son to decry the "utter folly of these lunatic physicists … calmly plotting the destruction of the world," and then concluding, "We're in God's hands. But He does not look kindly on Babel-builders."[10] Genesis was foundational to Tolkien, and he used it to describe, judge, understand, and inspire his own "subcreation," but he did not use it as an explanatory mechanism. He found truth on many levels of Genesis, but not as philology.

In no way did Tolkien's interpretation of Genesis constitute a retreat from taking the text seriously or some sort of subconscious conformity to the academic pressure of the ivory tower. Don't forget, this is the man who convinced C. S. Lewis of the truth of the gospel story. He lived and breathed ancient texts, even translating the book of Jonah for the Jerusalem Bible. He was a literary groundbreaker whose writing inspired the entire Fantasy section in your local Barnes and Noble. If anyone knew how to take a text seriously, and how to think independently, it was J. R. R. Tolkien.

And so I am not ashamed to read DNA much as Tolkien read Old English. I delight in the family trees, word-trees, text-trees, and mythic tree-shepherds in Tolkien's work. I also delight in the biochemical trees connecting organism to organism through the DNA words hidden inside each cell. Tolkien didn't assume that gaps between branches should be filled in by divine action, but by rigorous comparison and intellectual creativity. More precisely, it may be that divine creative action works through mechanisms like Grimm's Law in philology, or natural selection in biochemistry. Tolkien had no need to invoke Babel in philology; likewise, I see no need to invoke intelligent design in biochemistry. In both cases the trees are still beautiful. Perhaps they are more beautiful because they are intact.

9　For more on how this perspective led to the mythology of Middle Earth, I highly recommend Verlyn Flieger, *Splintered Light* (Kent, OH: Kent State University Press, 2002).

10　"From a letter to Christopher Tolkien, 9 August 1945," in *The Letters of J.R.R. Tolkien* ed. Humphrey Carpenter (Boston: Houghton Mifflin, 1995, 2000), 116.

TRACING THE FAMILY TREE OF ENZYMES

I like the idea of tracing the tree of life back to its roots. Before the discovery of DNA, no one had any idea that there were actual words in the heart of life, words branching from each other in a complex tree of relatedness. One branch of biochemistry compares DNA words for specific enzymes to find the original "enzyme-root" that appeared before the others. Some call this original DNA word the "urzyme," the prefix *ur-* meaning "original."[11] This family tree of enzymes, with urzymes at the root, is the third invisible tree in this chapter. I am planning experiments to investigate this tree in the future, and looking at it now, I find it just as beautiful as the others. Let me give you one example to show you what kind of surprises may be found in the roots of this tree.

Tracing back to find an urzyme provokes much academic heat as well as light, the facts sometimes being as foggy as, say, the hazy medieval origins of Tolkien's beloved *Beowulf*. But it seems probable that urzymes were not "picky eaters" in terms of what chemicals they would work on. Apparently they took on all comers, binding many different types of chemicals with, as biochemists put it, broad specificities.

One urzyme described in a 2011 paper is the original form of the enzyme called thioredoxin, which uses sulfur atoms to move electrons from chemical to chemical. A team of scientists made seven possible urzymes of thioredoxin and then subjected them to a gauntlet of tests. They proved resistant to heat and acid and showed signs of broad specificities, as was expected of the original enzyme forms.

What surprised the scientists was what they found when they looked deeper, into *how* the urzymes move electrons around. Modern thioredoxins move electrons with an elaborate, sophisticated mechanism. The scientists expected that ancient thioredoxins would be cruder in some way, but found they have *the same complex mechanism*. It's as if you met a caveman who spoke perfect English with the diction and tone of Lawrence Olivier. In other words, these ancestral enzymes (at least) were not sloppy or haphazard, but as skilled as modern enzymes in how they do their chemistry. To return to our semantic analogy, these ancient biowords were just as powerful but had broader "meanings."[12]

Tolkien believed that original words carried powerful, broad, and lost meanings that have now become specialized and specific. One famous example is the word *Logos* from John 1:1: "In the beginning was the Word (*Logos*)." *Logos* didn't just mean "word" two thousand years ago, but also carried the connotation of "speech," "reason," "organizing principle," and "cosmic harmony."

When I taught John 1 in Sunday school recently, I was puzzled how to explain this. Why would one word have so many meanings to its original audience? Why it would take so long

---

11   The more common term is "reconstructed" or even "resurrected" enzymes, but I prefer "urzyme" because it is simpler and does not contain a theological error!

12   Let me reiterate that this is just one provocative example so far, and we need many more examples for other urzymes to see how general this conclusion is.

for us "enlightened" folk to say the same thing today? Tolkien would say it's because that older word is closer to its root and carries more meaning, and since then the meaning has splintered. I wonder if the urzymes are like this too, powerful old DNA words that over time specialized into more specific meanings.

In a broad sense, this is a positive example of how Tolkien's philosophy can help a present-day biochemist. But Middle Earth has its orcs, dragons, Dark Riders, and Balrogs, too. If we can talk about the mechanism of the tree of life that connects our enzymes to the original urzymes, have we displaced a personal God with random and capricious forces?

Brand and Tolkien's writings remind me that, however fabulous and intricate the mechanism, I must never focus on or worship the "all-powerful mechanism." I cannot limit God *a priori* to creation by natural selection and randomness if I believe he reversed death in the middle of history! But I can look closely at the evidence of what he did and how he worked. The overwhelming links among the DNA words deep within life, observed over more than a decade of study, lead me to conclude that God allowed life to branch and evolve. I think he like trees, because he put them inside his creations. If he "steps in," he does so with a clear reason and clear results; I see that in the historical texts reporting the first Easter and in the continuing work of the Spirit, but I just don't see it in the DNA texts recording the creation of life.

I think that certain rules for the mechanisms we find (whether in biochemistry or philology) may be driven by randomness, but even that randomness is not formless. It has a particular shape like a bell, for instance. If randomness is structured, it is at some level tamed, and it does not lack meaning. This dialectic between wild and tame in the "randomness" of creation reminds me of Leviathan in Job 41:4–5, "Will it make an arrangement with you for you to take it as your slave for life? Can you make a pet of it like a bird?" Yet the implicit message is that even the great and terrible Leviathan was created too.

There is darkness in nature that simply makes no sense to us. But there is also goodness and wonder, in how a hand is put together, in how a baby grows, in each breath you take. Darwin himself vacillated between these two poles, though he is often selectively quoted to mute one side or the other, as pointed out in an excellent talk by Denis Lamoureaux.[13]

So let's trace this question of meaning back to its ultimate root. Even if the origin of life were shown to be driven by a mechanism, it would depend on the chemical reactivities set up at the beginning of the universe, which are not random. They are arranged in the ordered rows and columns of the periodic table of the elements familiar to chemists everywhere. (In fact, the periodic table can take the form of a three-dimensional tree![14]) Even a random origin of life could therefore have a level of meaning given by chemistry. As Denis Alexander put it in *Creation and Evolution*: "These are God's chemicals and God's molecules that we are talking about."[15] In texts as old as the book of Job, it is clear that God is sovereign over everything, from the largest Leviathan to the smallest molecule.

---

13 Denis Lamoureux, "Darwinian Theological Insights: Toward an Intellectually Fulfilled Theism" (lecture, annual meeting of the American Scientific Affiliation, Washington, DC, August 1, 2010); the audio is available for free on iTunes.

14 The ElemenTree, designed by Fernando Dufour.

15 Denis Alexander, *Creation or Evolution: Do We Have to Choose?* (Oxford: Monarch, 2008), 349.

MAKING THE INVISIBLE VISIBLE

I've given several examples of how scholarship makes the invisible visible: Brand's work on the causes and transmission of leprosy; the study of disease proteins, DNA words, and urzymes; Tolkien's study of words, and of course hobbits. At each level, making the invisible visible is an act of what in "archaic" Sunday school language we called "seeking wisdom." Job was a prototypical seeker for wisdom in the midst of darkness. He spoke of delving into the roots of the earth with words that resonate with a chemist: "From the earth itself comes food, but underneath is molten fire, whose stones are the source of sapphire, and the place of particle gold." Job then concluded, "The fear of the Lord—that is wisdom, and to turn from evil is understanding."[16]

I heard that phrase a lot before I really heard it and fully recognized its original meaning. "Fear" is what I feel in the dark, an internal emotion, but it did not mean that for ancient Hebrew authors. As James Kugel explained of a similar passage, "'Fear' here (as so often with biblical emotions) really stands for external expression … of an internal state. The 'fear of God' is fundamentally the awareness of God's existence and power, the awareness that, ultimately, the human is not supreme."[17] Fear, then, can mean an external posture of respect, rather than a simple quaking in your boots. The original word is more powerful and avoids some of the problems I project with my twenty-first-century vocabulary.

The ancient word "wisdom" also had more connotations beyond bumper-sticker proverbs to science itself: "Wisdom's insights included the very rules by which the world was governed, both the natural world and human society … The word wisdom thus designated, among other things, the set of plans with which God had created and continued to run the world," stated Kugel. "In modern times, we think of the world's rules as autonomous: there just is something called gravity or the first law of thermodynamics. But in the biblical world of God's presence, it was God who established the rules."[18]

I think to read the Bible faithfully we must understand that the words had these multiple meanings, and adopt the perspective that the rules and words established at the origin of the universe are manifestations of the faithfulness of the Creator of all. Some words took the form of DNA. Some words were spoken from human to human to describe the world, others to tell stories, and really there's no absolute demarcation between the two. Or to put it better, "In the beginning was the *Logos*, and the *Logos* was with God, and the *Logos* was God." Into this skein of words and descriptions, at the nexus of history, stepped the Creator himself, the living *Logos*, whose word appeared cut short—until it wasn't.

Words splinter over time, becoming more specific and more widespread. As Brand and Tolkien showed, we can recover some lost meanings through a grand story that unites these words and shows how they relate. Brand did it through stories of human biology as organized by the Creator, and how we should live in light of that. Tolkien did it through

---

16   Job 28 translation and following quote in James L. Kugel, *The Great Poems of the Bible: A Reader's Companion with New Translations* (New York: Simon and Schuster, 2008), 105–6.
17   Ibid., 256.
18   Ibid., 108.

stories of a world and language that he made up, stories of creation and fragmentation built on the foundation of his belief in the same Creator that Brand talked about. Both Brand and Tolkien are part of the body of Christ, in whom all these gifts come together, continuing to this day. Both men's works shine with wonder, and both reflect the colors that came together at Christmas, Good Friday, and Easter.

Now the story that began at creation continues to this day in the church—for Brand, the physical body of Christ, and for Tolkien, the continuation of God's story. There are as many ways to make the invisible visible as there are believers at the foot of the cross. As Brand and Yancey wrote in *Fearfully and Wonderfully Made*, "Christ chose each member to make a unique contribution to his Body."[19] Together God is continuing to bring what was broken back together.

If we turn to Revelation 22, the end of God's book where all things are brought together at last, we see that the tree of life has returned in the temple city come down to earth. The tree gives twelve crops of fruit on both sides of the river. I used to imagine this as one huge tree with the river flowing through it somehow, a somewhat clunky image, but now I think it fits the text better to envision an orchard of trees lining the river and fed by its waters. This would mean there are multiple trees of life there, fed by one source from one God and one Lamb. If this is so, it would mean in my life there is room for two trees of life from one source.

We aren't told much about the twelve crops or what the tree looks like (wait and see!), but we know its leaves are "for the healing of the nations" (Rev 22:2). Brand and Tolkien's lives conformed to that purpose, bringing both physical and spiritual healing. Their words aid in the healing of nations. I've seen this myself, as their words nurtured my growth by leaving patterns to follow, like that nurse log in the Olympic rain forest.

When I see a tree of any kind, I see diverse objects brought together in one living creation. I'm grateful to Brand and Tolkien for showing me how that fits into a life of looking carefully and honestly at the world around us. They taught me to look, and to keep looking, for the trees that remain beyond the wall.

---

19   Brand and Yancey, *Fearfully and Wonderfully*, 52.

–SEVENTEEN–

A CONVERSATION WITH ALVIN PLANTINGA

One of most influential philosophers of religion writing today, Alvin Plantinga is the Emeritus John A. O'Brien Professor of Philosophy at the University of Notre Dame, and the inaugural holder of the Jellema Chair in Philosophy at Calvin College. He has written widely-discussed works in philosophy of religion, epistemology, and Christian apologetics. Plantinga is the author of *God and Other Minds; The Nature of Necessity; Warranted Christian Belief*, and recently, *Where the Conflict Really Lies: Science, Religion, and Naturalism*. He has delivered the Gifford Lectures three times. Dr. Plantinga is also a dedicated rock climber.

© 2012 David Marshall

I. CLIMBING

David Marshall: **As a child, Saint Anselm imagined the courts of heaven were located in the Alps around his hometown of Aosta in northern Italy. Anselm later wrote of a being "than whom nothing greater can be conceived." You're also a mountain climber—is God easier to find above the treeline?**

Alvin Plantinga: Well, I think, yes. The Psalms are full of references: "Unto the hills I lift up my eyes." Many people have found the mountains—and not only the mountains, but also crashing waves on the seashore, and many other natural phenomena—put one in mind of God. The same for viewing the stars, let's say, from the mountains at an altitude of ten thousand feet. The stars are ablaze—they blaze with the glory of God.

Anselm also spoke famously of "faith seeking understanding," as the slogan is usually translated. You criticize natural theologians for failing to recognize that faith in God is "properly basic," a perception that often precedes rational

arguments per se. It seems that the order was pretty much the same for Anselm—faith came first, and seeking came afterwards.

I think that's the way Anselm was thinking about it. When he speaks of faith seeking understanding, he means something like, "You've got this faith. And now you try to understand it more deeply by seeing how it is related to other things you believe, how all the various parts of the faith fit in with each other, what kinds of objections were raised to it, and what the right response to those objections are." I think that's how he understands faith seeking understanding. And that seems to me to be a very good way.

Biographically, he also began with faith.

Yes, right. I don't necessarily criticize natural theologians. I mean, natural theology is a perfectly sensible enterprise. All I say is, it's not necessary for rational or proper belief in God.

You argue that a person might have no specific evidence for believing in God, yet still be warranted in doing so. Why do you say that?

Well, there are lots of beliefs that we don't have evidence for, at least evidence in the sense of arguments, or evidence in the sense of other beliefs that furnish evidence for them. I mean, beliefs such as that there's been a past, or that there are other people. You can't really give a good argument for the conclusion that there are other people, but it's perfectly obvious that there are, and perfectly proper to believe that there are. And the same goes with the past. So it's just not the case that for all beliefs one has to have evidence from other beliefs for those beliefs to be acceptable or rational or reasonable. And I think that's the same way it is with belief in God. My thought is, God has created us in such a way that we've got a natural tendency to believe in God without necessarily believing on the basis of arguments or evidence. And when we do believe in God in that way, that's perfectly sensible. So no further evidences of an argumentative sort are really required.

With friends like Nicholas Wolterstorff, you have developed a view of faith and reason that you credit, in some form, to John Calvin, and that you believe can help Christians better understand the mysterious relationship between the two. Are apologists who argue to faith from what used to be called "Protestant Christian evidences" making any kind of mistake by doing so?

No, I don't think so. I think there are lots of good arguments for God. I've got a paper called "Two Dozen or So Good Theistic Arguments."[1] So I think there are lots of pretty good evidences. I do think, though, that none of these

---

1   Available at www.calvin.edu/academic/philosophy/virtual_library/articles/plantinga_alvin/two_dozen_or_so_theistic_arguments.pdf.

can take you all the way to serious Christian belief that the second Person of the Trinity really did become incarnate and live, died, and rose again for our benefit. That is the heart of the Christian gospel, and I don't think there are very powerful arguments of that natural theology sort for that. For that, one has to rely on something quite different.

Aristotle spoke of the "old, wise and skillful" in a community, and argued that aside from scientific evidence, it's also reasonable to believe some things based on the testimony of credible people. Isn't it dangerous, though, to accept hand-me-down beliefs?

But of course most of what we believe we do believe on the basis of testimony. Or maybe I shouldn't say most—an enormous amount. That I live in Michigan, I believe on the basis of testimony. That there was a Peloponnesian War, I believe on the basis of testimony. Thomas Reid once said, "If I never believed what anyone else ever told me, I would still be a changeling, I would still know no more than a baby." I mean, how much can you know just by yourself, without any testimony? Very little. You can know that you've got a pain in your left knee, let's say.

I think that was Aristotle's point, that that's the whole basis of civilization.

It's not even possible to conduct your intellectual life without relying on what other people tell you.

It's always funny when you hear skepticism about human testimony from scientists who in their own work rely very heavily on what other people say.

Well of course they do! How else can they conduct their work? I mean, they read journals, and the journals contain testimony of other people, which naturally enough they accept.

Should it cause Christians a loss of confidence to find that a disproportionate number of the "old, bright, and skillful" (as Dan Dennett might put it), who teach in our universities, are atheists?

Well, I think that's unfortunate. I certainly don't like that. But that doesn't necessarily shake my own beliefs in the great things of the gospel, as Jonathan Edwards calls them. I mean, if there were some powerful arguments these people provided for thinking that Christian belief is mistaken, that would be another thing. But there aren't. And the mere fact that there are lots of atheists in universities, by itself, doesn't give me that much pause.

It's interesting to speculate as to why that's the case. Why are there, say, in the United States, a higher proportion of atheists in universities than there are

among the population? I don't know what the answer is. But it would be kind
of interesting to know what it was.

II. GOD AND MAN

**You write of a "sense of divinity," a sort of innate intuition about or knowledge
of God that comes to us in certain moments, say, while hiking between Mount
Baker and Mount Shuksan (in the North Cascade mountains). Many atheists
would reply that this is some sort of evolutionary glitch in our mental hardware,
or perhaps a misfiring of our "intentional agency detectors," meant to alert us to
panthers in the African grass or thunderstorms in the mountains. Why should
we suppose that religious intuition is grounded in something real that is above
nature?**

They speak of a "hyperactive agency detection device." Dan Dennett tries to
use that as a means of debunking religious belief, saying it comes from this
"hyperactive agency detection device" that produces lots of false positives. It
leads us to think that in fact there are agents when in fact there aren't any—
faces in the clouds, or whatever. And the thought is, it's really a good thing that
it produces a lot of false positives. I mean, in our evolutionary history, it was
much better to receive a false positive than a false negative. A false negative,
and you're likely to end up as lunch.

Well, OK, maybe that's true. But this "hyperactive agency detection device"
is also, apparently—so they think—an explanation for our belief in other
people. They don't say, therefore our belief in other people must be doubtful
or something wrong with it because it's produced by this device that produces
lots of false positives. The fact that a belief is produced by such a device so far
doesn't tell us a whole lot. I mean, sometimes what it produces are not false
positives but true beliefs that have warrant, as [in] respect to belief in other
minds. The same thing, I say, goes for belief in God.

**Andrew Lang and Wilhelm Schmidt developed the idea (already present in Saint
Paul, Augustine, and Matteo Ricci) that a high God similar to that described in
the Bible is worshiped, or at least recognized, in hundreds of cultures around
the world. Would you see such discoveries as evidence for your hypothesis?**

I think it's evidence for the thought that John Calvin has that there is a sense
of divinity, *sensus divinitatis*—I think that's the phrase he uses—that God has
created us with. This sense of divinity [isn't sufficient] for full-blown Christian
belief, by any means. But there is such a sense among people generally. I think
this is pretty well confirmed by scientific studies in religion nowadays. So,
yeah, I think that does confirm Calvin's beliefs.

What would you say about a culture, say, the Tibetan culture, that has no very strong concept of God?

I wouldn't know what to say about that. I'd first have to know more about the culture, and just how it proceeds, and the like. No doubt there will be cultures in which the *sensus divinitatis* is more in evidence than in others. The way in which people are brought up, for example, could in some sense squelch the *sensus divinitatis*. Other ways of being brought up could encourage it. So why that culture would be, as you suggest that it is, I don't really know. I'd have to look into it.

It's interesting to read the Stoics, because it seems in theory they believed that God was remote and could not be prayed to. But in practice, people like Cleanthes and Epictetus seemed to find comfort in praying to God. Even what Richard Dawkins has to say about nature at times, it seems he is almost ready to drop to his knees in wonder before creation.

That's quite right. But he doesn't want to drop to his knees. For one reason or another, he's extremely opposed to doing that sort of thing, and he thinks no one should do it.

So is this the confusion that the Apostle Paul talks about in Romans 1–2, where Paul talks about not giving glory to God, and instead worshiping the created thing?

Well I guess I'd have to say that it is. Paul says people suppress the truth in unbelief—I think that does, in fact, happen. I think many people—I don't know how many people, but some people, anyway—don't like the idea of there being such a person as God, and they're resistant to it. So they sort of squelch or put down or suppress their natural impulse to think there is such a person as God.

C. S. Lewis said that God "whispers to us in our pleasures, speaks to us in our conscience, but shouts in our pains."[2] Can one see nature itself as a kind of semiotic code through which the Creator talks to humanity?

I'm not sure I see a connection between the last part of your question and what C. S. Lewis says there. But Christians, reformed Christians in particular, have talked about two books of revelation, you know. On the one hand, there is Scripture. But on the other hand, there is nature, which also tells us things about God, speaks of God to us. And if you think of nature that way, then you can think of it as a kind of code if you like, that somehow produces in us various appropriate occasions for sensing that God is great or that God loves us or that God can help—or maybe that God disapproves of some conditions, and so on.

2   C. S. Lewis, *The Problem of Pain* (London: Collins-Fontana, 1940), 81.

What do you think of the objection that God doesn't speak to us clearly enough through nature, or speaks in an ambiguous way?

Well, I think there's something to that! At least it might be that the reason we don't clearly hear God lies in us, rather than in what God actually does. We are blinded, as I think it's Anselm said, by the smoke of our wrongdoing. And if it weren't for sin, we might have the same complete and certain belief in God as we have in there being other people, for example. I guess I'm inclined to think that's the way it is. In a way, you might say it isn't that God's revelation isn't very clear to us, but that it's obscured by the smoke of our wrongdoing.

Why doesn't God revise then, given that we've fallen into wrongdoing? Why doesn't he make himself much more evident to everybody than he is? I don't know the answer to that. I've often myself wished that God would give me a stronger sense of his presence, and his glory, and beauty, and the like. It comes to some of us, Jonathan Edwards for example, with enormous force; to others of us once in a while, and without such enormous force. And those who fall into the latter category might well wish they were in the former.

III. THE USES OF PHILOSOPHY

Jokes and philosophical exercises both often involve setting logical traps, then blundering into them with eyes wide open. You seem to have a lot of fun in your writing. Is that a prerequisite for a good philosopher, to have a sense of humor?

I'm not sure it's a prerequisite, but I think it makes the whole thing more interesting. I'm trying to think of philosophers who I don't think had a sense of humor. I guess Aquinas would be like that. Maybe Aquinas had a sense of humor, I just don't know.

At least G. K. Chesterton got a lot of fun out of him anyway.

Yes, but in reading his writings, a sense of humor doesn't really come through very much. But maybe that's just [his] stylized way of writing philosophy. But I think a sense of humor is a real asset. For one thing, if you're writing on a heavy, hard topic, and you're just pounding away one hard thought after another, with no relief, that's going to really tire people out. And they're going to stop reading after a while. If you can let a little comic relief show through, then people can sit back for a minute and relax for a little bit, before they go on to try to fathom the next bit.

Compared to particle physics or archaeology, philosophy seems solitary, something one can still do alone in your study with a pile of books. But in your writing I get the sense of a community—that you're having a conversation

not only with people who disagree with you, but also with friends and contemporaries as well as people from the past.

I think that's how philosophy actually does work. I don't think there are very many philosophers who just sit by themselves and study and think. Descartes is reputed to have done that, but whether he actually did that or not, I'm not at all sure. He was brought up in a Jesuit school, he undoubtedly heard—of course he heard, he had a philosophical education—and then he went and sat in his room. But shortly after he did that, he sent his writing around to his friends, so they all criticized it, you know, and he responded to their criticisms. That's how philosophy goes. It's a matter of discussion, a matter of conversation, a matter of give and take. It isn't properly done, or maybe it can't be done, by one person in solitary splendor. It might be cooperative in a different way, from physics let's say. But it still is very much cooperative.

C. S. Lewis said that good philosophy is required, if for no other reason, because bad philosophy needs to be answered.[3] You seem to take the duty of a Christian philosopher towards ordinary believers very seriously ...

The older I get, the more I have thought this. Christian philosophers have to think of themselves as part of the Christian community. And that requires various things. For example, it requires answering the various kinds of arguments that non-Christians bring against Christian belief, which can otherwise be disturbing. And it's the job of the Christian philosopher to do this. They're the ones most equipped in the Christian community to do that. Another part of their job would be detecting various cultural currents that might, on further inspection, be incompatible with Christian belief, or misleading to Christians. I think that's a very important part of what Christian philosophers ought to do.

I remember reading in *City of God* a list of "hot topics" that Augustine said were debated in his day. It struck me that the same topics that I argue with my atheist and New Age friends are all on that list. Can philosophy really resolve questions, or is it like Sisyphus pushing his rock up the hill? In what sense does the Great Conversation of philosophy progress, or are these questions completely perennial and come up with each new generation?

Well, I think that they're more perennial. These discussions have gone on for a very long time, and no doubt will continue to go on. I don't know if this is like Sisyphus, it's more like a great conversation that extends over the ages.

Dennett's *Philosophical Lexicon* gives the following definition: "Alvinize, verb. To stimulate protracted discussion by making a bizarre claim. 'His contention

---

3   C. S. Lewis, "Learning in War-Time" in *The Weight of Glory and Other Addresses* (Orlando: Macmillan, 1980), 28.

that natural evil is due to Satanic agency alvizined his listeners."' One gathers that you find some of the arguments made by Dennett and other New Atheists "alvinizing," as well.

[*Laughs.*] Well, I don't know. I guess I wouldn't say I'm exactly "alvinized" by them—well I don't know how he's thinking. He's thinking of "encouraging extended discussion by making a bizarre suggestion." I don't think any of the arguments of the New Atheism are very strong. They're just very loud. When you compare them with the old atheists—say, Bertrand Russell and John Mackie—I would say their arguments are much less impressive. But they are delivered at a much higher decibel level, with lots of insults thrown in. That's what's unusual about them.

Dennett seems a little less liable to insults than Dawkins …

Yes, [less than] Dawkins or Hitchens—Dennett is somewhat more subtle, but he does some of the same sorts of things. He will often just tell stories, and sort of silly stories, rather than offer an actual argument. So in response to the suggestion that Christian belief is compatible with current science, he'll say, but yeah, sure, so is Santa Claus, and go on to compare Santa Clausism or Supermanism with Christian belief.

In your debate, which I found very entertaining, you wryly refer to the fact that Superman would "only" be about eighty years of age by now. That brought to my mind that you have a few things in common with Superman. You're both from the Midwest, you both recognize a duty to protect the weak, you both like to ascend vertically …

[*Laughs.*] And we're both about eighty.

Paul says, "Knowledge puffs up" (1 Cor 8:1), and warns us against "vain philosophy." How can a Christian thinker avoid these dangers?

He's talking about fables and genealogies. I think he's thinking of some of the stuff that comes from Greek culture. And I think the job of the Christian philosopher is to evaluate what one's current culture tells us on some topics that have relevance to Christian belief. So in one way I'm not sure a Christian philosopher has got a problem as such there. In another way, maybe a Christian philosopher, like any Christian intellectual, does. Saint Paul says, "Knowledge puffs up"—I think there's truth to that. Intellectuals often think of themselves as a cut above the ordinary. And with respect to some things, they are. But being a cut above the ordinary with respect to a given pursuit doesn't mean a whole lot. People who can run really fast are a cut above the ordinary with respect to the rest of us, but so what? We're also to think of others as good as ourselves, or better than ourselves. And I think a lot of intellectuals need to think seriously about that.

Confucius defined himself as "eager to learn." After a long life of pursuing truth philosophically, do you still hunger and thirst for new understanding?

I guess I do. I don't feel much different along those lines from the way I felt many, many years ago. Although I guess these desires do burn a little lower, as you get old, than they do when you're, say, in college. But they're still there in substantially the same way. I'm still deeply in love with philosophy, and find it fascinating. I'm still very curious about lots of facets of Christian faith, and lots of things about God that I don't know and won't find out, I guess, until the next life. I don't know if that's my own personal idiosyncrasy, or part of the human condition, but what he says certainly rings a bell with me.

Can you give an example of something you're curious about now, that you're looking into?

I'm curious right now about the following: It seems to me there is powerful evidence for evolution, for the evolutionary history of humankind. It looks to me that there's good evidence for thinking that we human beings have descended from simian ancestors. And I'm really curious how to fit that together with the proper way to understand the first chapters of Genesis. People for centuries wondered exactly how to understand them, and for centuries have taken some parts of them to be metaphorical or symbolic. Augustine thought that the days might be very long periods, not just twenty-four-hour periods. You've got all these elements: There's the talking snake. There's the original human pair, Adam and Eve. There is God's prohibition. There is their going contrary to that prohibition and falling into sin. How much of that does the Christian take literally? How much does the Lord intend us to take literally? And once you've got that figured out, how does that fit in, if at all, with respect to current evolutionary theory? And if it doesn't fit in at all, what is the right procedure? What's the next step, so to speak?

So I'm inclined to think that Christian faith does require that there be an original human pair, and that there be something like a fall from an innocent state, if only because in the New Testament Paul brackets Christ the second man with Adam the first man, and so on. And I might see how one could put that together, if at all, with current theories as to how humankind has developed.

But then you've got predation and cruelty from hundreds of millions of years ago, which seem to make it more problematic and difficult to figure out.

It does. So one question is whether death, including predation and so on, comes into the world via sin. Another question is whether it comes into the world via human sin. And I guess I'm inclined to do what Dan Dennett says I'm trying to do, namely, refer to Satan and his cohorts as an account of natural evil. As C. S. Lewis, too, suggested, well maybe God has allowed Satan and his cohorts a special hand with respect to the evolution of life on our planet, and it takes the form that it does take partly because of Satan and his cohorts. In which case it would be due to their sins, but not to the sin of human beings.

Ralph Winter, who is one of the subjects of this book, had some thoughts along those lines. To me it seemed a hard saying.

I suppose you could take the line that William Dembski does and says, "Well, God foresaw that human beings would fall, and therefore he brought about all the chaos and cruelty and death in the animal world" [paraphrased]. But I'm not convinced of that. Just as God allows us to cause suffering and so on, he did the same with respect to Satan and his cohorts. So with respect to our evolutionary history … You asked me something I would like to know about, and don't. Well, that's one of them, for sure.

BIBLIOGRAPHY

Banerjea, Krishna Mohan. *The Relation between Christianity and Hinduism*. Calcutta: Oxford Mission Press, 1881. Reprinted in T. V. Philip, *Krishna Mohan Banerjea: Christian Apologist*. Madras: Christian Literature Society, 1982.

Bauerschmidt, Frederick Christian. *Holy Teaching: Introducing the Summa Theologiae of St. Thomas Aquinas*. Grand Rapids: Brazos, 2005.

Boyd, Robin. *An Introduction to Indian Christian Theology*. Delhi: ISPCK, 1991.

Brand, Paul, and Philip Yancey. *Pain: The Gift Nobody Wants*. New York: HarperCollins, 1993.

Burge, Tyler. "Individualism and the Mental." In *Midwest Studies in Philosophy*, vol. 4, edited by Peter A. French, Theodore E. Uehling, and Howard K. Wettstein, 73–121. Minneapolis: University of Minnesota Press, 1979.

Chapman, Allan. *Oxford Magazine* (Noughth Week, Hilary Term, 2011): 17.

Dutta, Krishna, and Andrew Robinson, ed. *Selected Letters of Rabindranath Tagore*. Cambridge: Cambridge University Press, 1997.

Froese, Paul. *The Plot to Kill God: Findings from the Soviet Experiment in Secularization*. Berkeley: University of California Press, 2008.

Gonzalez, Guillermo, and Jay W. Richards. *The Privileged Planet: How Our Place in the Cosmos is Designed for Discovery*. Washington, D.C.: Regenery Publishing, 2004.

Hopkins, Gerard Manley. "Spring." In *Hopkins: Poems and Prose*, edited by Peter Washington, 25. New York: Knopf, 1995.

Jenkins, Philip. *The New Faces of Christianity: Believing the Bible in the Global South*. New York: Oxford University Press, 2006. Quoted in Joel Carpenter, "Back to the Bible," *Books and Culture* 13, no. 3 (2007): 23.

Jones, E. Stanley. *Eastern Tidings* 22, no.1 (January 1, 1927): 1.

Kugel, James L. *The Great Poems of the Bible: A Reader's Companion with New Translations*. New York: Free Press, 1999.

Lamoureaux, Denis. "Darwinian Theological Insights: Toward an Intellectually Fulfilled Theism." Lecture, annual meeting of the American Scientific Affiliation, Washington, DC, August 1, 2010.

Lewis, C. S. *Mere Christianity*. New York: Macmillan, 1958.

———. *Miracles*. New York: Simon & Schuster, 1996. Reprint, New York: HarperCollins, 2001.

———. "Williams and the Arthuriad." Chap. 4 in *Arthurian Torso*, edited by Charles Williams and C. S. Lewis. London: Oxford University Press, 1948.

Lowther, Roger. "Beauty through Japanese Eyes: *The Tale of Genji* as a Window to Japan." *Japan Harvest* (Winter 2011): 28–31.

Marshall, David. *Jesus and the Religions of Man*. Seattle: Kuai Mu, 2000.

———. *Why the Jesus Seminar Can't Find Jesus and Grandma Marshall Could*. Seattle: Kuai Mu, 2005.

———. *The Truth about Jesus and the "Lost Gospels."* Eugene, OR: Harvest House, 2007.

Martin, Raymond. *The Elusive Messiah: A Philosophical Overview of the Quest for the Historical Jesus*. Boulder: Westview Press, 2000.

Nouwen, Henri. *Adam: God's Beloved*. Maryknoll, NY: Orbis, 1997.

O'Collins, Gerald. "The Holy Trinity: The State of the Questions." In *The Trinity: An Interdisciplinary Symposium on the Trinity*, edited by Stephen T. Davis, Daniel Kendall, and Gerald O'Collins, 1–25. Oxford: Oxford University Press, 1999.

Pramoj, Kukrit. "The Hell which Heaven Forgot." *Practical Anthropology* 13 (May–June 1966): 129–39.

Putnam, Hilary. "The Meaning of 'Meaning.'" In *Language, Mind, and Knowledge*, Minnesota Studies in the Philosophy of Science, vol. 7, edited by Keith Gunderson, 131–193. Minneapolis: University of Minnesota Press, 1975.

Rauser, Randal. *Finding God in the Shack: Conversations on an Unforgettable Weekend*. Colorado Springs: Paternoster, 2009.

Richardson, Don. *Peace Child*. Ventura: Regal Books, 1974.

———. *Eternity in their Hearts*. Ventura: Regal Books, 1981.

———. *Theology in Search of Foundations*. Oxford: Oxford University Press, 2009.

Sen, Keshub Chunder. "Who Is Christ?" In *Keshub Chunder Sen*, edited by D. C. Scott, 215–16. Madras: Christian Literature Society, 1979.

Singh, Sundar. *The Search after Reality*. Reprinted in T. D. Francis, *The Christian Witness of Sadhu Sundar Singh: A Collection of His Writings*. Madras: Christian Literature Society, 1993.

———. *With and Without Christ*. London: Harper & Brothers, 1929. Reprinted in T. D. Francis, *The Christian Witness of Sadhu Sundar Singh: A Collection of His Writings*. Madras: Christian Literature Society, 1993.

Torrance, Thomas F. *Space, Time and Incarnation*. New York: Oxford University Press, 1969.

———. *Preaching Christ Today: The Gospel and Scientific Thinking*. Grand Rapids: Eerdmans, 1994.

Willis, Garry. *Lincoln at Gettysburg: The Words that Remade America*. New York: Touchstone, 1992.

———. *What Jesus Meant*. New York: Penguin, 2006.

Wilson, Dorothy Clarke. *Ten Fingers for God*. Grand Rapids: Zondervan, 1989.

Wink, Walter. *Engaging the Powers: Discernment and Resistance in A World of Domination*. Minneapolis: Fortress, 1992.

Winslow, J. C. *Narayan Vaman Tilak: The Christian Poet of Maharashtra*. Calcutta: Association Press, 1930.

Winter, Ralph D. "Autobiography." Speech, Lake Avenue Church, Bakers Square breakfast group, Pasadena, October 7, 2003.

———. "The Embarrassingly Delayed Education of Ralph D. Winter."

———. Introduction to *Mission Frontiers 1979–1981*. Reprint, 2004. http://www.ralphwinter.org/A/view.htm?id=4&part=1&section=1.

———. "Ten Frontiers of Perspective." Seminar, August 20, 1999. Revised January 21, 2003.

Winter, Roberta H. *Once More around Jericho: The Story of the U.S. Center for World Mission*. Pasadena: William Carey Library, 1979.

———. *I Will Do a New Thing: The U.S. Center for World Mission and Beyond.* Pasadena: William Carey Library, 1987. Reprinted and revised in 2011. Page references are to the 1987 edition.

———. "Winter Initiatives." Unpublished document, Pasadena, September 31, 2000.

Yancey, Philip. *Where Is God When It Hurts?* Grand Rapids: Zondervan, 1977, 1990.

———. *In His Image.* Grand Rapids: Zondervan, 1984.

———. *The Gift of Pain: Why We Hurt and What We Can Do About It.* Grand Rapids: Zondervan, 1993, 1997.

———, and Paul Brand. *Fearfully and Wonderfully Made.* Grand Rapids: Zondervan, 1980.

INDEX